THE ART OF TRAVEL

THE ART
OF TRAVEL

Essays on Travel Writing

Edited by
PHILIP DODD

LONDON AND NEW YORK

First Published 1982 in Great Britain by
FRANK CASS AND COMPANY LIMITED

Published 2016 by Routledge
2 Park Square, Milton Park, Abingdon, Oxfordshire OX14 4RN
711 Third Avenue, New York, NY 10017

First issued in paperback 2016

Routledge is an imprint of the Taylor and Francis Group, an informa business

British Library Cataloguing in Publication Data

The Art of travel.
  1. Travel in literature
  I. Dodd, Philip
  809'.9332   PN56.T7

ISBN 13: 978-1-138-96386-3 (pbk)
ISBN 13: 978-0-7146-3205-6 (hbk)

This group of studies first appeared in a Special Issue on
'The Art of Travel: Essays on Travel Writing' of *Prose Studies,*
Vol. 5, No. 1, published by The publisher

Typeset by John Smith, London

Contents

Notes on Contributors

Philip Dodd   Lecturer in English, University of Leicester. He is the editor of *Prose Studies* and of *Walter Pater: An Imaginative Sense of Fact* and the author of a number of essays on nineteenth- and twentieth-century literature.

Joel J. Gold   Professor of English, University of Kansas. His edition of *A Voyage to Abyssinia* will be published shortly in the Yale Edition of *The Works of Samuel Johnson*. He is also editing the letters of John Wilkes.

Jenny Mezciems   Lecturer in English, University of Warwick. Dr Mezciems, assistant editor of the *Modern Language Review* and the *Yearbook of English Studies*, has published articles on Swift and on some Renaissance writers of satire and utopian fiction. She is currently writing a book on *Gulliver's Travels*.

Peter Miles   Lecturer in English, Saint David's University College, Lampeter. He is reviews editor of *The Powys Review*, author of a number of articles on the novel from the eighteenth to the twentieth century, and has recently co-edited Wilkie Collins' *The Woman in White*.

Margery Sabin   Professor of English, Wellesley College, Massachusetts. Professor Sabin is the author of *English Romanticism and the French Tradition*, and is currently working on a study of English language traditions in the modern novel.

F. S. Schwarzbach   Assistant Professor of English, Washington University in St Louis. Professor Schwarzbach's publications include *Dickens and the City* and essays and articles on Victorian literature and art. He is writing a book about the impact of urbanization upon English literature in the nineteenth century.

Joanne Shattock   Bibliographer in the Victorian Studies Centre, University of Leicester. Dr Shattock is the co-editor of *The Victorian Periodical Press: Samplings and Soundings*, and the author of a number of essays on nineteenth-century literature.

Martin Stannard   Lecturer in English, University of Leicester. Dr Stannard is the editor of the forthcoming volume on Evelyn Waugh in the Critical Heritage series, and the author of essays and reviews on Waugh.

John Thieme   Senior Lecturer in English, Polytechnic of North London. Dr Thieme, who has published numerous articles, including essays on West Indian and Commonwealth literature, has recently completed a full-length study of V. S. Naipaul's fiction.

Preface

The Art of Travel is the first collection of critical essays to be devoted to British travel writing. It attempts to give a sense of the wealth of such writing, to map some of its forms and conventions and, implicitly, to claim a place for travel writing in any revised definition of literature. For this collection, travel includes sea voyages, European tours, commissioned enquiries into social conditions, and urban writing; travel writing ranges from works such as *Sea and Sardinia* by D.H. Lawrence whose status as a novelist guarantees his travel books some attention, through the essays and books of Victorian middle-class travellers into working-class London, to the work of V.S. Naipaul, a contemporary writer, who has increasingly preferred the travel book to the novel. Since travel writing shares borders with a number of other forms, including autobiography, biography and history, it seems appropriate to open the volume with an essay which explicitly recognises the interaction between travel books and other kinds of writing. The succeeding essays have been chosen to show the range of interests travel writing can generate and sustain.

The prominence given to twentieth-century travel books represents an attempt to extend interest in modern travel writing and to accommodate discussion of books of which no serious accounts exist. One aspect of the collection the editor does regret: the absence of women travellers. A contributor who had offered an essay had to withdraw at the last moment and there was insufficient time to commission a replacement.

The editor would like to thank Ronald Corthell, Claude Luttrell and R.K. Biswas for their help with the preparation of the volume.

PHILIP DODD

" 'Tis not to divert the Reader": Moral and Literary Determinants in some Early Travel Narratives

It is an ancient Mariner,
And he stoppeth one of three.
"By thy long grey beard and glittering eye,
Now wherefore stopp'st thou me?"

I

A major fascination of early travel literature, especially that concerning voyages to the west, lay in its new scope for the imagination. It was the appeal not of fiction but of new facts: of facts, moreover, which promised an opening up and a reordering of the known world. New regions could be exploited most easily (but not only) in the mind, in a variety of ways and with interests that ranged from the religious and moral to the scientific and also to the simply greedy. The last might be the commonest, but it could parade respectably under the banner of religious or national zeal, duty to God or one's king and country. The literary genre that grew with the activities of Renaissance travellers, in particular, had however to establish an identity by reference to somewhat uncomfortable criteria. In travel literature the borderline that traditionally separated poetry from prose, the romantic from the practical, shifted because fact itself could offer romance just at a time when the physical world was gaining importance to man through his ability to measure and control it. Scientific reality had gradually to free itself from dependence on the realities of religious faith and artistic imagination, while at the same time leaning for support on the same established systems with which it was in uneasy competition.

A text that illustrates some of the problems is Bacon's *New Atlantis* (published, unfinished, in 1626). It is not really a travel narrative but the projection in fantasy of a society that honours and is transformed by the scientific academy at its centre. The first significant feature is its placing not in the future or in extra-terrestrial regions (as would be the case with later technological or socio-political fantasies), or in the distant and mythical past (like the original Atlantis of Plato), but within an unknown but discoverable area of the real world, so that the fantasy could just possibly be fact, presented by travellers who might just possibly be real. The second important feature is that science in this fantasy in no way disturbs ancient social foundations, which are on a seemingly Hebraic and certainly religious model, while the inhabitants grasp classical learning and Christian beliefs, when these are made available, with the same easy reverence that they display for science. What Bacon advocated seriously in *The Advancement of Learning* (the establishment of the future Royal Society and a new status for science) is as serious and almost more persuasive in a fiction that uses romance and tradition to introduce something new and make it sound feasible. He writes of what could become fact; he "proves" it by presenting it as already implemented, and we accept his decorating a hypothesis with art.[1]

Bacon's text provides a point of reference for one concern of this essay: an interdependence between fact and fiction in travel narratives mostly of the Renaissance period, and the ground of their attraction for readers. My other concern is with the authority of the traveller as narrator, in a period that began to offer new dominance not only to the physical world but to the experience of the individual exploring it, recording his findings, and presenting his interpretations for use by others – readers and patrons. In communicating his experiences the traveller became a literary man, or at least a man important in literature. Whether his aim was to convey an accurate and useful account of lands his king or church might claim, and for the discovery of which he might be rewarded, or whether he astutely recognized the romantic appeal of such material (his own or another's) artfully arranged to court a growing market among ordinary readers, he was among those with something to sell, needing to develop skills of narrative in informing, persuading, or merely delighting. Although the traveller's authority was of course questioned, as was the value of his information, his attraction was that of a new kind of individual, offering unique experiences the truth of which could not readily be checked by others (or not before a king had gambled a pension or an expeditionary force) and which were not subject to traditional or doctrinal world pictures. While in literature the apparent advantage of his situation could be exploited by plagiarists and inventors of fiction disguised as fact, for reputation or gain, moralists and satirists could criticize sternly in fictions of their own the integrity and the appeal of the persuasive adventurer and the effect on the old world of opportunities in the new one. An earlier ancient mariner than Coleridge's might hold the attention of at least one in three, but in the Renaissance he had to establish himself not as a romancer but as a source of new truths with wide application for the material world. His pose becomes a feature of the genre in which his writing develops; it is that of the ordinary man of common sense whose personal observations may be trusted by virtue of his lack of specialist skills (especially literary ones) and his possession of ordinary faculties responsibly exercised in isolation from society. The responsibility is affirmed in the gratuitous assurance that so commonly prefaces both spurious and genuine travel narratives: that the writer's aim, in William Dampier's words, is not merely "to divert the Reader".[2]

An accompanying claim, even more universally requisite in both factual and fictional travel narratives, is to the writer's truthfulness. The defensive tone of such statements regularly reveals a consciousness in the travel writer that he may not be taken seriously. One of his problems, at the very time of widened horizons and opportunities in the Renaissance, was that travel narrative traditionally belonged to fantasy. The new material, however factual, was strange and therefore romantically exciting; readers themselves would give the narrative the status of literature (indeed, such status would be courted by a writer often vain as well as greedy) and accommodate it within an existing literary tradition. But in this tradition travellers from Odysseus onwards were conventionally liars or poetic inventions, and their accounts real only as myth is real; while exploring unknown tracts of the physical world, Renaissance men were also making discoveries in the world of classical literature, some of which partially undermined the newness, as well as the value, of all things modern. The earnest modern traveller has his credentials undercut by Lucian, for example, whose second-century travel fantasy *The True History* was among works picked up and recommended with delight by humanist scholars (Erasmus and Thomas More collaborated in translating some of his dialogues). Lucian's stolidly unsurprised voyager is important to the history of travel literature because, though himself a fictitious purveyor of outrageous fantasy, his function is a moral one, of ridiculing the credulity of the common reader, of questioning the authority of the written word, and of showing that deception, at a level of art beyond that of the plain-speaking liar, may nevertheless be used to undeceive.

Lucian may thus provide a starting-point for an examination of travel narratives chosen less to chart any chronological progress from a literature of fiction to one of factual reality than to represent points on a scale which defeats time and shows some of the difficulties underlying any assumption that truth is fact and fiction is untruth. My terminus will be the arrival home of Swift's Gulliver, who is a fictional traveller in Lucian's mould and who thus makes the voyage truly circular. Between these two, one encounters travellers who may seem more committed to factual reality but whose would-be scientific aims are in the end more dubious. One might take as a working rule a simple polarizing distinction on which to decide whether a travel narrative is intended to be taken as fiction or fact. The former turns the strange into the familiar (new worlds prove identical with the old one), while narratives with pretensions to fact are committed to the discovery of lands and societies as different as possible from our own. The first is the model for satire, with its conservative insistence that man cannot escape his own nature by surrounding himself with exotic scenery. The second belongs temperamentally to the man of science and progress and also of romance, who seeks power in change and in the enlargement of his scope, though he may delude himself as well as others, intentionally or not.

Lucian's narrator introduces himself, as do most travellers, in a consciously literary preface (Dampier, that plain real English seaman of the 1690s, did the same, which suggests that some conventions do not change and that recognition of the literary potential of travel material remains constant). Offering a travel tale as ideal intellectual diversion, he outlines the conventional features of a work he is sure will interest and entertain with "the remarkable nature of its subject matter," "the beauty of its style," and "the plausibility of its various flights of fancy." He promises witty parody of solemn liars and shrewd plagiarists who have imitated the "obviously quite untrue" histories of Ctesias and Iambulus with "so-called histories of their travels describing all the huge monsters, and savage tribes, and extraordinary ways of life that they had come across in foreign parts": so much for the New World and exotic discoveries of the sixteenth century! Citing Odysseus as the archetypal liar, Lucian goes on to expose a serious moral crux: the reader's culpability, in accepting the authority of a narrator for the sake of his unique experiences, is a matter of choosing laughable criteria which make credibility the measure of truth. Admitting a common but usually unacknowledged motive ("I too am vain enough to wish to leave some record of myself to posterity, and as no interesting experiences have ever come my way in real life, I have nothing true to write about"), he delivers a final sting to unillusioned superiority and sets his reader to lap up the most candid falsehoods of all time (249-50).[3]

Lucian is a coolly rational debunker of philosophical or religious mysteries and their power in a superstitious age, and his monstrous lies entertain with the moral purpose of releasing the faculty of common sense into a world mesmerized by fallible authorities. It is significant therefore that such humanist Renaissance educators as Erasmus and More should seize on Lucian with joy, translating and imitating his various *jeux d'esprit* in a context of Christian belief which similarly required urgent discrimination in matters of faith and superstition, spiritual and temporal authority, new facts and old dogma. More's *Utopia* is itself in one sense a travel narrative; his "hero," Raphael Hythlodaeus, is allowed claims on contemporary reality by being associated with Vespucci, as one of the party left behind in the New World (at his own request) and still unwilling to resettle in Europe. That Raphael's excitement does not centre on extravagant riches or power, but holds up instead a simple and sober closed society in contrast to greedy European expansionism, makes a whole series of witty points in relation to the opportunities of travel and the serious usefulness of most travel narratives. More's New World proves less glamorous than Europe, and its manners descend from an ancient model in Plato's *Republic*. Supported by testimonials and recommendations from real friends who vouch for its truthfulness; provided with a fictitious narrator whose credentials include scholarly wisdom, worldly experience, and a name that means something like "bringer of salvation through nonsense"; ornamented with joking clues that claims to veracity are guarantees of deliberate deception, the fiction is vindicated by its moralistic purpose. The joke turns into a cautious warning about the limits of human potential among both travellers and readers, abroad or at home. At the time More was writing

Utopia, his brother-in-law, John Rastell, must have been preparing his own expedition, which foundered no further away than the Irish coast in 1517, and so More's interest in the subject was probably more than academic. One can at least be sure, however, that More had nothing of worldly value to gain from his writing – beyond the respect of friends and scholars.[4] His aim in presenting a fiction as though it were fact is to impose a dimension of moral responsibility on the excited imagination.

II

If travel might be assumed to be a means of escape or of advantage, fantasy excursions do not so far seem to offer either, though More's modern fiction does seek salvation in terms of a world beyond Utopia and beyond Plato's philosophy. Otherwise the traveller carries his corruption with him, as More had opportunity to learn and as we may do on turning now to real travellers and to different species of fiction, including lies plain and fancy. The narratives of Vespucci and of Columbus, and the impact of their discoveries, would have been known to More, and a matter of particular interest to several of the circles in which he moved (some of whose ambitions at home are criticized more seriously in Book I of *Utopia* than any aspects of gain by exploration). In so far as these accounts of real journeys, or journeys important for their basis in factual information, were a new development, they may be set against the previously influential and widely popular narratives of Sir John Mandeville or Marco Polo, both of whom described an old world mostly inaccessible to western Europe. The enterprise of Marco Polo is closer to the spirit that fired Columbus and other adventurers whose aims were as much mercantile as scientific, but the element of romance in the telling provides example of another kind of opportunism: Marco's collaborator, Rustichello of Pisa, seized on what to him was material for art, and it is as a story of the wonderful rather than an account of the potentially useful that Marco's experiences reach the reader, padded with set-pieces and extra material from other sources in romance. Marco was evidently both businesslike and curious, if sometimes boastful, but it is a transformation into the literature of romantic convention that brings his story to the attention of "Emperors and Kings, dukes and marquesses, counts, knights and burgesses" who will value the inclusion of "some things ... that he did not see, but only heard tell of by men worthy of credit."[5]

Mandeville's *Travels* were not truthful or useful in the sense of being accurate reports of real personal experience, but the falsehood they present may seem justifiable in terms of conventions which again go back to an earlier period and which present a different concept of reality. The blend of fact and fantasy in this case involves a real geography (though of mythical status, in that the centre of Mandeville's world is the Holy Land and his directions are addressed to pilgrims), a real narrator (though one whose motives may be more worldly than admitted, who may never have travelled in spite of appearances, and whose identity has always been controversial), and real information (though culled, without acknowledgement, from others). Mandeville is an example of the lying narrator whose declared intention and manner of address serve an honourable purpose, and whose fantasies seem chiefly a feature of rhetoric. The work is of relevance to the present discussion because it was popular enough at the time of more modern Renaissance travel to be translated and printed widely throughout Europe at the turn of the fifteenth century. By this date such a narrative would have a special kind of obsolescence, in that legend could no longer be an adequate guide to travellers. The criteria which turn Mandeville's travels into a fiction would probably have surprised him: the truths he abuses had less value in his own day.

But Mandeville's "facts" are sacred *as facts*, to be handled reverently and yet to be conveyed with some consciousness of literary style by translators in their turn. The Bodleian text (MS Rawl. D.99) justifies the procedure: "And thus in proce I shal bigynne this werke, because that often in romaunce and ryme is defaust, and nouʒt accordement founden to the matir."[6] The formal "Guide to the Holy Land," with routes and incidental attractions detailed in a manner not unfamiliar in our own time, mostly dispenses with pretence at personal experience, and the narrative consists largely of digressive fables which, like the more practical information, usually bear such credentials as "they say," "men go," "some say." Nevertheless, the narrator's personal presence is emphasized very particularly from time to time, and he makes distinctions between places he says he has seen and places he has regretfully missed. The impression is, however, that it is not his own integrity but the very existence of places long known that might be questioned if he did not vouchsafe witness. Particularly interesting is the insistence on personal presence in an episode which anticipates those later satirical narratives in fiction which criticize Europe from outside:

> Now will I tell you what the Sultan did tell me upon a day in his chamber. He gert all men void his chamber … for he would speak with me in privity between us two. And, when all were gone forth, he asked me how Christian men governed them in oure countries. And I said, 'Lord, well, thanked be God.' And he answered and said, 'Sickerly, nay. It is not so.' [he here embarks on a long sermon in shrewd remonstrance against Christian hypocrisy] When I had heard the Sultan speak these words and many more which I will not tell at this time, I asked him with great reverence, how he came to thus mickle knowing of the state of Christianity. (I, 96-9)

It transpires that the Sultan and his court have visited Europe, have learned its languages, practices, and beliefs, and are qualified to comment on them in the tradition of the informed fictional alien. The episode stands out, for its device of the confidentially reported confidence, its matter, and its level of unexpected sophistication; but whatever the provenance of the passage, its fabrications plainly serve a specific occasion. There are fabulous marvels in Mandeville's narration, but where on one occasion he lingers to doubt the evidence of his own senses he seems to be making a gesture towards recognizing his own and a general human fallibility which leaves room for things comprehended only by God, to be wondered at rather than explained: "whether it were as it seemed, or it was but fantasy, I wot not" (I, 197-8). Mandeville's truthfulness includes an admission of his own inability always to distinguish between fantasy and fact, and he sometimes seeks other evidence than personal experience. Disarmingly, in his conclusion, Mandeville recommends his book as having been vetted by the Pope (whom he places anachronistically in Rome instead of Avignon for the important audience), and bases the approval of this supreme authority on the Pope's assurance that "he had a book of Latin that contained all that and mickle more" (I, 221-2).

The discovery and exploration of new continents and islands from the Renaissance onwards, with the dependence of narrative accounts on new facts for validity (how to get there, what is to be found, and who has first claim), threaten paradoxically to reduce and impoverish reality. The narratives of Columbus and Vespucci at the beginning of the period serve a worldly reality in which kings as patrons are anxious enough to believe. They make no claims beyond the recording of fact and of efficient enterprise, though they contain elements of romance that have been taken up and transformed in certain fictions. The reports of Columbus, such as they are, survive only in versions heavily edited by others (Bartolomé de Las Casas, for example), and may never have been composed by Columbus in the first place; it has been argued that he was barely literate and needed to present himself through an agent. His several *Letters* and *Journal*, especially those describing the earlier voyages, are factual records which convey in economical plain prose the required information. They contain, in a naive form, distortions which are as much a matter of self-deception as of a desire to deceive, but a rhetoric so dependent on statistics, and which has no stylistic eloquence, can all the same reveal as much as it conceals and prove to be a kind of fiction after all. Interestingly, at a time when one man could take charge of impressions to be officially conveyed home to a speculative investor, the distortions are not in the facts but in their presentation. Columbus could presumably have made the new realms sound a good deal more exciting as possessions for Castile, but his exaggerations are not extreme. He is inclined towards evasive limitation of detail rather than enthusiastic expansion, so that his own frustrations are transferred to reader or patron with the emphasis on promise, not fulfilment. There is, however, a remarkable lack of concern with that potential for the religious conversion of native populations which fills the zealous narratives of the Jesuits later, although the spreading of Christianity was ostensibly the declared motive for European expansion and of specific appeal to Isabella (Las Casas did his best to make it sound the overriding concern).

Columbus does soften a little before the beauties of luxuriant vegetation and of naked girls, but reiterated again and again is the elusive presence of gold. Española is "a land to be desired," "richly endowed," but above all he stakes his prince's claim on "the situation most convenient and in the best position for the mines of gold and for all intercourse as well with the mainland here as with that there, belonging to the Grand Khan [his west being determinedly amalgamated with east, of course, and about to yield not only actual resources but mythical ones], where there will be great trade and gain" (I, 12).[7] Mostly it is a promise that "here we are in the neighbourhood of many mines of gold"; or "in one of their islands ... to which we did not go, there is much gold"; or of changing course "because there was news of gold in that direction" (I, 66, 38, 62). There are, later, embarrassing excuses for having insufficient evidence to bring home of all this plenty, but it is interesting to note how long the word of the man on the spot prevents his master from getting nervous. Other disappointments suggest different expectations both of places and of accounts of places. Columbus is almost apologetic that he has found no monsters, as though his brief were to measure and quantify the materials of legend, without which reality is somehow shortchanged, but he can offer cannibals without emotion, making them appear pretty much like the rest of us (I, 14, 26-32).

But there are further failures which the modern editor of Columbus suggests in his introduction are more personal disappointments. If the voyager worked hard at aggrandizing his prince, he kept to himself some private ambitions, and these I propose now to relate to a more significant image that emerges from the narrative to assume a romantic, potentially heroic, literary stature. It is that of the traveller figure throughout fictional tradition: as a liar, on the one hand, but also as the powerfully mysterious alien who attracts readers by recounting experiences none can share, and whose authority is that of an individual in possession of a reality unique to himself and in his gift to others. In this context it is particularly ironic that Columbus was finally a frustrated and perhaps paranoid man, who ended his career in trouble as he began it in obscurity, whereas Vespucci, whose name is perpetuated in that of America, has since attracted attention mainly on the subject of questions as to how much of a charlatan he was and what support for the accusation can be found in his narratives.

Columbus was evidently something of a visionary, inspired by the sense of being chosen for a divine mission, mysterious about his background, obsessively if secretly ambitious not just for the kind of fame that Vespucci took from him but perhaps for personal rule over realms of his own discovery that would surpass the realities of the new west and incorporate indeed the legendary riches of the east or of the lost Atlantis. Cecil Jane found clues in Columbus' repeated tendency to sail unexpectedly southwards and in this passage which, he implied, expresses more than the puzzlement over a confusion of west with east: "I sent two men inland to learn if there were a king or great cities. They travelled three days' journey and found an infinity of small hamlets and people without number, but nothing of importance. For this reason they returned" (I, 4). Columbus spent a number of impatient years courting the interest of several European monarchs in what must have seemed a wildly impractical scheme for which he had little technical qualification. From a pen whose lack of fluency in an acquired language may be aggravated further by editors' pruning to serve their own purposes as well as his, one would not suspect how much the figure of the man was that of heroic dreamer turned commercial traveller, nor guess what personal qualities might persuade where social and intellectual ones were lacking.

There are, however, descriptions of Columbus which strongly suggest a very particular *type*. Fernandez de Oviedo, deliberately building up an image, describes him as a stranger whose origins are hard to place, "a man of decent life and parentage, handsome and well-built, and of more than average height and strength. His eyes were lively and his features well proportioned. His hair was chestnut brown and his complexion rather ruddy and blotchy; he was well spoken, cautious and extremely intelligent. He had good Latin and great cosmographical knowledge; he was charming when he wished to be and very testy when annoyed." But at court, "as his cloak was poor and ragged, he was considered a dreamer and everything he said was taken to be fantastic. Being an unknown foreigner he found none to back him."[8] He argued his overwhelming desire to serve the crown (or any crown, one might protest, that would have him), and claimed to have left wife and family for the king's service.[9] A reader may legitimately suspect Oviedo of fictionalizing Columbus here, or even wonder if Columbus himself cultivated an image other than real. His form acquires features common to contemporary fictional travellers, in *Utopia* (1516) and in the early works of Rabelais (1532-4). Thomas More explicitly associates his traveller-narrator with Vespucci – but since More is making a play with deception, and since deception enters the rivalry between Columbus and Vespucci, it would have been an apt joke to put Raphael Hythlodaeus in the ship of a real man whose narratives may be false! Raphael Hythlodaeus significantly refuses to put himself at the service of any court, or to resettle himself in Europe, preferring his freedom to wander. He has also, interestingly, not only a charm of presence hard to resist but a testiness which obliges More to humour his opinions. Texts of both Columbus and Vespucci were available well before More began writing *Utopia* on the continent, and *Utopia* would be widely known by the time Oviedo's histories appeared in 1526 and 1547. If there are debts, of fiction to fact and of fact back to fiction, in the creation of an image, it is hard to establish creative precedence. The recognition of a recurring image of "the traveller" seems a matter of conventional portrayal rather than of direct influences or borrowings.

Rabelais' fictions of giants might seem out of place here, though they are contemporary with Oviedo and refer openly to Utopia. But when Pantagruel first meets Panurge, an incorrigible and usually self-misdirecting traveller, he describes him as "un homme beau de stature et elegant en tous lineamens du corps, mais pitoyablement navré en divers lieux," who nevertheless "n'est pauvre que par fortune, car ... Nature l'a produict de riche et noble lignée, mais les aventures des gens curieulx le ont reduict en telle penurie et indigence."[10] More's Raphael Hythlodaeus is "a stranger, a man of advanced years, with sunburnt countenance and long beard and cloak hanging carelessly from his shoulder, [whose] appearance and dress [resemble] those of a ship's captain." His love of travel is used to associate him with Ulysses and with Plato (as well as Vespucci), he is a fine scholar in Latin and Greek, and (in contrast to More's own life of heavy commitment) he has left his family for the sake of travel.[11] To take the image of the traveller back to Plato, and give him the aspect of the philosopher as well as of the dreamer; to be reminded that he advises kings on the strength of his experience instead of ruling his own empire (*pace* Robinson Crusoe); and to recognize over again the striking form of the stranger grown shabby among alien societies, deprived of responsibilities in his own (or choosing to evade them), is to see him claiming an extraordinary degree of individual authority that makes him a perpetual archetype of fascinating untrustworthiness. He is a figure from whom Columbus and later travellers in real life might indeed dissociate themselves with some difficulty, supposing they wanted to. As long as new emphases and experiences are presented through old forms, of narrative and narrator, they continue to be related to old values in spite of themselves, and to be constrained by the very vehicles through which they seek acceptance.

III

If the Renaissance was a period for thrusting individuals, it was also a time of fierce competition between nations, and the series of heroic buccaneer pirates (who might as easily be courtiers as obscure criminals) could exploit the ambitions of both self and society. A globe which remained oddly unified, inside a hazy mythic outline as long as its shape remained uncertain, became subject, once circumnavigated, to fragmentation among rival claimants. The great collectors and editors of voyage literature (Hakluyt, Purchas, John Churchill; Montalboddo; the editors of the Jesuit letters) were repackaging geography into history, and history into fiction in so far as reality was rearranged to suit a series of conflicting interests. Religious zeal required savages to be vicious, not only for the conquering Spaniards, whose stakes were marked out with crosses (apparently in more senses than one), but for the Lutheran Hans Staden, whose more domestic descriptions (like his expectations among cannibal hosts) were mostly culinary.[12] Las Casas, particularly in his *Brevissima relación de la destruición de las Indias* (1552), was as vehemently propagandist in favour of the Indians, against his own countrymen, on Christian humanitarian grounds. One might say that a development begins in which attention shifts more purposefully towards the figure of the reader as focus of attention, as the literature itself becomes a recognizable medium for conversion, not of the savage but of the literate European. In travel narratives that claim to be factual the romantic traveller-image diminishes rather, until with the second wave, in the second new age (of science) his pose becomes that of the humble Baconian collector of specimens adding to the store of human knowledge on which he is not required to pass judgement or suggest any particular arrangement. His is a different kind of encyclopaedism from that of the large voyage-collector, but in both cases the tone and framework in which narratives are presented require some kind of prefatory address, identifying now not the princely private patron but the common middle-class bookbuyer whose taste for romance must be respectfully wrapped in didactic plain brown paper.

Purchas' seventeenth-century collection is on the comprehensive model, meanwhile, and retrogressive in its rhetoric of exhortation. Enticement is in "the profit to be reaped by this worke" – not only for "the veritie and varietie ... of things ... remotest and rarest," but for the "true greatness" and the "store of gold in Pegu and Sumatra" which navigation will bring to kings fostering "the good of Christendome" (I, xxxix, vii, 53). The narrator's editorial boast here is that he has *not* travelled, and his posture, like his language, is ostentatiously poetic: "Least Travellers may be greatest Writers. Even I which ... never travelled 200 miles ... herein like a ... Candlestick holding many Candles, without which it selfe is unseene in the darke ... and as the Compasse is of little compasse and motion, yet teacheth to compasse the World" (I, 201). There are further magisterial gestures from the editor orchestrating the reader's response: marginal comments direct our reading of Nunno di Gusman's narrative ("Preaching by the sword a worthie, holy, meritorious, satisfactory worke," I, 56), and Spanish texts are grouped for greater provocation to the English; giving Las Casas the last condemnatory word on his countrymen, Purchas allows it to be just, "howsoever his zeale flings forth fiery tearmes, and paints out their Acts in the blackest Inke, and most Hyperbolical Phrases" (XVIII, 67-8).

Whether the new impetus to the travel genre that came towards the end of the seventeenth century is primarily a matter of changing political or scientific or philosophical situations, it does seem to have been a kind of second Renaissance, and the archetypal traveller-figure that I described earlier is even in fiction a shadow of his former self (perhaps more accurately the substance of his former shadow). He matures (or degenerates) into the sober and unpretentious sailor, whether he is real (like Lionel Wafer and William Dampier), or "realistic" (like Crusoe and Gulliver), or a total fake, like William Symson (Sir Thomas Herbert, as a very literary poseur, is an exception). It becomes important that his narrative should be disarmingly naive, without claims to literary or scholarly or even gentlemanly competence, without, in effect, any possible superiority over the reader except that of different opportunity, and certainly without moralistic pretensions. Editors, publishers, or booksellers may intervene between writer and reader, dusting down the traveller, making him fit for company (as in Gulliver's case), or he may present himself with apologies which refurbish an old prescriptive convention.[13] Partly this makes remote places feel more accessible to the common man; partly it is a transference of authority by means of which a new reality becomes the property of any man's sensations and powers of expression and measurement.

It was presumably as easy to adapt narratives to suit a new popular model of the traveller, or to borrow material to fit, as to follow any other. Just as Swift's Gulliver has an imaginary author (and Gulliver's "cousins" are William Dampier and an imaginary Richard Sympson), so William Symson's *A New Voyage to the East Indies* (1715) has one, who is "an English Captain ... of more Curiosity than the common Sort of Commanders" – note the newly "scientific" motive, in line with Robinson Crusoe and Gulliver later, and with Lucian's far-sighted mocking prototype.[14] It is the reader's curiosity that is here exploited: the writer has "labour'd to gather some particular Remarks of his own ... but the Places he touch'd at, having been so often resorted to, and describ'd ... it was a matter of much Difficulty, in a trading Voyage, to observe enough to oblige the Publick." Avoiding "the Romantick Strains of Travellers," Symson takes trouble to purchase suitable tales where his own experience falls short, and adds "some useful Instructions" for good measure. Swift probably borrowed from this work a passage on the handwriting of the Lilliputians,[15] but also reminiscent of it is Gulliver's concern for his reader in another place:

> I thought this Account of the *Struldbruggs* might be some Enter-tainment to the Reader, because it seems to be a little out of the common Way; at least, I do not remember to have met the like in any Book of Travels that hath come to my Hands: And if I am deceived, my Excuse must be, that it is necessary for Travellers, who describe the same Country, very often to agree in dwelling on the same Particulars, without deserving the Censure of having borrowed or transcribed from those who wrote before them. (215)[16]

There is just the possibility here that Swift, in borrowing the claim to novelty, and the caveat, is also borrowing the very story Gulliver so self-congratulatingly refers to.[17]

But if Swift mocks such deceptions with his own, he is mocking their saleability – and that is the fault of the reader: knaves need fools for customers, and Swift's manner is that of Lucian. The reader who dismisses classical and romantic literary heritages along with other authorities, and comes to reality as though it were pristine fresh for him to make his own sense of, deserves to be exploited. More insulting, because more pretentiously deceiving, is the narrative of Sir Thomas Herbert, which is listed among that library of travel books which Swift read so avidly with fascination as well as scorn. *Some Yeares Travels into Africa and Asia ...* (in a number of editions; I have examined that of 1665) is what one can only call a cavalier work. Swift wrote in his own copy (of 1634): "If this Book were stript of its Impertinence, Conceitedness and tedious Digressions, it would be almost worth reading, and would then be two thirds smaller than it is." As gentleman, or as writer, with or without the experience of travel, Herbert would furnish Swift with a perfect example of that decadence in the English nobility which Gulliver notes in Glubbdubdrib. Calling up the spirits of the dead to ascertain whether history has been fair with them, "it gave [him] melancholy Reflections to observe how much the Race of human kind was degenerate among us, within these Hundred Years past," in contrast to "*English* Yeomen of the old Stamp ... once so famous for the Simplicity of their Manners, Dyet and Dress" (201). Swift's criticism of Herbert is dated "1720," a year when he was supposedly preparing his own *Travels*; in taking for his imaginary traveller a modern figure to suit the world of the modern reader, he would find no aristocratic ally against the upstart authority of the Gulliverian Englishman. Herbert's narrative is full of predictable entertainments from an old world, however. Monsters and cannibals abound, and his style and self-image may be briefly exemplified from the dedicatory letter: "Having past the Pikes, I take new courage to come on again. One blow more and I have done. Ten to one it lights on my own pate. But if my head stand free, my hand shall not be guilty of more Intrusion: No more pressure to the press. The Crowd is too strong already: and I will get out by Head and Shoulders rather than faile."

In a way, the insulting indifference to any kind of reality, old or new, literary or scientific, factual or fictional, which Herbert represents, seems deserved. The Royal Society, rather than the Ulyssean wanderer or the avaricious monarch, was the traveller's new image-maker. Robert Boyle, in his *General Heads for the Natural History of a Country ... Drawn out for the Use of Travellers and Navigators* (1692) despatches the English voyager equipped (as Gulliver was with watch, spectacles, compass – pointedly unsuitable tools for moral reflection) with various ingenious mechanical devices and the instructions to weigh and measure and record everything he experiences: not to reflect upon its value, but to register it statistically. He will carry buckets to catch up sea water (following a carefully prescribed method), and is "to be provided with a Nice Pair of Scales, and exact Weights, for measuring the Weights of the several Waters that occur" (14). Swift created triumphant satire out of just such observations on Gulliver's part, while Boyle solemnly asks amateur scientific investigators (and, no doubt, expects truthful reporters) "to enquire whether the Relations of a whole City's being turned into Stone be true, and if not what gave the first rise to it" (64); "to enquire whether the Appearance of Legs and Arms of Men, related to stand out of the Ground, to a great Number, at five Miles from *Cairo*, on *Good Friday*, do still continue, and how that Imposture is performed" (72). Given the timeless propensity of travellers, like other men, to desire to give satisfaction in hope of reward, Boyle might be lucky if, having put his voyager right back into the world of Mandeville, he were to find in him Mandeville's own caution: "whether it were as it seemed, or it was but fantasy, I wot not." In a world where human confidence need leave no mysteries unmeasured it seems unlikely. As P.G. Adams says (viii), "because the eighteenth century was so avid in its search for data about man and his physical surroundings, it was inclined to be gullible and fall victim to facts that were not facts and to travel books that were partly, even completely, false."

There were of course some attractive and ordinary real travellers who, if it cannot be proved that they never plagiarized, at least have no literary mannerisms or false humilities. If Swift (who was a voracious reader of travel literature) could justly despise Sir Thomas Herbert, he would find Lionel Wafer and William Dampier less culpable on grounds of style and (ostensible) purpose. Their narratives are entertaining and informative, modest in address, sane and balanced in tone. They come into the category of useful documents in a plain style that suits the material, the occasion, and the status of the writer: "Proper Words in proper Places, makes the true Definition of a stile," said Swift, and even a learned man should so respect his audience as to deliver nothing "which he may not express in a Manner to be understood by the meanest among them."[18] To Swift, however, a decline in literary standards began with the Puritan revolution, which he blamed for the "Infusion of Enthusiastick Jargon [that] prevailed in every Writing," only to be followed by "that Licentiousness which entered with the *Restoration* [he does not mean mere bawdy]; and from infecting our Religion and Morals, fell to corrupt our Langage" (*Works*, IV, 10) – he might have been describing the style of Sir Thomas Herbert.

A change in styles of prefatory apology reveal that the readership made new demands, which some authors professed in fun to satisfy, as they offered fantasy to a world with modern values. Thus already in 1658 James Harrington prefaced his *Commonwealth of Oceana* with an "Epistle to the Reader," lamenting that his work "is but a rough draft ... my Papers ... have been dispersed into three Presses ... by which means the weaknesse of my performance hath been ... strangely mangled." William Symson gestures towards his market by striking out "innumerable Passages relating to the Winds and Tides," together with other "minute Descriptions ... in the Style of Sailors," because he "was resolved to fit the Work as much as possible to the general Capacity of Readers" (9-10). Dampier's preface to *A New Voyage round the World* (1697) is also sensitive to the reader's "general Capacity" and tolerance: "As to my Stile, it cannot be expected, that a Seaman should affect Politeness. ... [but] I am perswaded, that if what I say be intelligible, it matters not greatly in what words it is express'd." He has also "not been curious as to the spelling of the Names of Places, Plants, Fruits, Animals, &c," and begs the reader to entertain what he finds with "Judgment and Candour" (4, 5). In Wafer's preface to his first edition (1699) he tells us: "My principal Design was to give what Description I could of the ISTHMUS OF DARIEN," leaving out much of his own story and yet having to apologize that "I cannot pretend to so great an Exactness, but that I may have fail'd in some Circumstances." He has been especially careful "to say nothing but what, according to the best of my knowledge, is the very Truth," and he urges the dissatisfied reader to consult other authorities where doubts arise (lxviii). Thus a plain motive and a plain style support each other and defer to the reader's final judgement.

IV

It would seem that as the modern traveller in real life finds his feet, or his sea-legs, he gains independence from earlier tradition in a literature that gives dignity to the word and the experience of the common man, who aims to address the common reader on equal terms. Yet he does look back, for the physical facts and the information he offers do remain strange, in spite of all, and though the conventions of romance are strenuously avoided the material of romance is still there, whatever writer and reader may pretend. What begins to happen to romance in travel is that it now follows the criteria of scientific reality, so that spurious narratives ape the new manner of real ones, and fiction pretends to be fact in a new way. The standard is a narrative of observation without surprise or judgement: it becomes scientific, unemotional, and amoral.

The trouble is that Wafer and Dampier, as well as being observant reporters, were also buccaneers or pirates (the distinction was a fine one) who had to present their activities in a guise acceptable to society at home. Wafer's A New Voyage and Description of the Isthmus of America was published in 1699, recording adventures in 1680-1. As a surgeon (like Gulliver) he had some education, but his success and appeal come at least partly from his Crusoesque resourcefulness: he was able to live with the native Indians, "to sail with buccaneers, to deal with highly placed politicians, to experience great physical hardships, endure hostility, forget grievances, and to accept better fortune, with a serene face."[19] He supported Dampier, as he states unequivocally, in troubles with fellow officers and with the authorities. They sailed together, and Dampier evidently had a difficult and volatile personality. A large part of the exploits of these and other marauding Englishmen consisted of raiding and looting, with the Spanish as their chief prey. Their narratives describe unemotionally the various tricks and deceptions which brought them prizes as well as punishments. Behind the cool modern scientific prose are to be glimpsed adventurous fortune-hunters of an anachronistically heroic kind – who faced public censure and secret encouragement, promises and treachery, from those with power or money to wield.

What we might call fictions (in the sense of false appearances) were needed to cover the real private and public motives of Wafer or Dampier. Dampier's dedicatory address to the President of the Royal Society stresses scientific inquiry: in these travels "there may be some things ... New even to you; and ... not altogether unuseful to the Publick." The

appeal is to a "Zeal for the advancement of Knowledge, and the Interest
of your Country," with the conventional promise not to be literary:

> I have not so much of the vanity of a Traveller, as to be fond of
> telling stories ... nor can I think this plain piece of mine, deserves a
> place among your more Curious collections ... Yet dare I avow,
> according to my narrow sphere and poor abilities, a hearty Zeal for
> the promoting of useful knowledge, and of any thing that may never
> so remotely tend to my Countries advantage: And I must own an
> Ambition of transmitting to the Publick ... these Essays ... being
> desirous to bring in my Gleanings ... to that general Magazine, of
> the knowledge of Foreign Parts (1).

As the more general "Preface" constates, " 'tis not to divert the Reader
... but for method's sake, and for the Reader's satisfaction" that there is
any "Account of the Concomitant Circumstances" (3).

A more ominous turn is taken by Wafer for the second edition of his
book in 1704: here his "Design" is not description but "to represent
to the World how far it would be the Interest of England to make
an Establishment upon that Continent; the Product of whose Bowels
enriches the other Three Parts of the World," and "plainly [to] demon-
strate the thing might be very easily effected," so that "there will remain
but little to be said against so Glorious an Undertaking" (lxix). This new
edition includes profitable accounts of gold mines, and a zeal for the
dispossession of the Spaniards which rather alters the face of the modest
traveller and suggests a far from disinterested attitude on the part of
author and potential reader alike. It is no wonder that Swift, wary
of imperialistic justifications and recognizing the savagery with which
civilized nations negotiated with Christians and primitive pagans alike,
should have furnished his rational Utopia with Houyhnhnms instead of
gold mines and made his navigator a Yahoo.

It begins to appear that the modern common man as traveller, as
unjudging observer of material phenomena, as writer without literary
pretensions and with no other standards than those of the market, needed
saving from himself. His salvation was, as we might expect, in fiction:
specifically in what has appropriately been called the first "novel." Defoe
in 1719 did his best for Robinson Crusoe, who is so ordinary that his
perversity is a rebellion against that comfortable "middle station of life"
into which inertia and enterprise alike, a good father, and finally God
himself, conspire to drive him. The reader enjoys the unnecessariness of
Crusoe's journeys, and the reassuring domesticity to which all strangeness reverts. Defoe hardly needs to pretend that his narrative is "a just
History of Fact"; it is better than that, an "Improvement of it" in a
sense he did not mean. It is the life of modern man, with most of his
faults exposed and then moralized into a superbly self-forgiven image,
in a fiction that is at last made-to-measure by and for himself. To see
Crusoe's travels as allegorical, in the sense of there being a symbolic
spiritual pattern behind the worldly progress through disaster to success,

is perhaps most useful as offering, not comparison, but contrast to such models as Bunyan's *Pilgrim's Progress*. For surely Defoe's traveller reverses the force of allegory in applying the pattern to the physical world and making that the ultimate reality.[20]

Crusoe is only one among Defoe's gallery of rogues, and not the only one whose redemption entails travel abroad, but as the most popular he is also the closest to Swift's Gulliver, who followed him in 1726. Swift, too, offers redemption to his modern traveller, by the quite opposite method of stressing his isolation – not as a man making his own world (island, empire, fortune, salvation) but as one utterly dependent on his author's borrowings and associative references to that long literary tradition of forms and figures and value-systems which Crusoe may imagine he can do without. Appropriately, Swift "borrows" some features from Crusoe, as well as from contemporary real travellers and from older ones in fact and fiction, though behind Gulliver's back, so to speak, since Gulliver like Crusoe is not a great reader in spite of his shipboard library (and there is no recorded admission that Swift ever read Defoe).

Gulliver's borrowings are thus of two kinds. Those from literary tradition are indirect, unspoken, and so doubly inaccessible to the modern reader whose world-view does not require him to measure Gulliver against Odysseus or Hythlodaeus. The direct borrowings are from modern travellers, real and spurious, and achieve a nice point about the way narratives that claim originality and need to be "new" are themselves derivative in matter and mannerisms. Gulliver's editorial manner does nothing to prepare us for fantasy; the shock effect depends on the accuracy of Swift's assumption that we will relate to Gulliver's standards, his credentials, his conventional ordinariness. The 1735 "Letter to Symson" reinforces the role of the "publisher" as dedicatee and authority on market research. Editor and printer undermine Gulliver's text with errors of fact and the need "to hire some young Gentleman ... to ... correct the Style, as my Cousin *Dampier* did by my Advice" (5). The traveller seems to have followed Boyle's instructions in the unsurprised statistical measuring of alien societies, relating physical appearances to his own proportions and making even moral degeneracy a matter of size or shape. His admissions of perversity at setting out (over and over again) echo Crusoe, as do his unexceptional background and the touches of moralistic enthusiasm, which in his case is not redemptive.

Gulliver's postscript (Bk. IV, ch. 12) matches the prefaces of real travellers, and is the more effective from a pen that is finally so alienated: "Thus, gentle Reader, I have given thee a faithful History of my Travels ... wherein I have not been so studious of Ornament as of Truth. ... I rather chose to relate plain Matter of Fact in the simplest Manner and Style; because my principal Design was to inform, and not to amuse thee." He has the rhetoric to castigate those travellers who, "to make their Works pass the better upon the Publick, impose the grossest Falsities on the unwary Reader" and is indignant "to see the Credulity of Mankind so impudently abused." For his own motives, "what Objections can be made against a Writer who relates only plain Facts that happened in such distant Countries, where we have not the least Interest with respect either to Trade or Negotiations? ... I write without any View towards Profit or Praise. I never suffer a Word to pass that may look like Reflection" (291-3). Such complacencies are cold comfort to the reader who cannot extract from beneath familiar declarations any information which he might put to familiarly corrupt use. The vicarious experiences turn against us, as individuals, as a society, as a species. The more "out of the common Way" Gulliver's discoveries are, the more they assert home truths from which there is no worldly advantage to be gained.

In bringing the traveller full circle back into fantasy and to the morality which, in Lucian's spirit, can be expressed only through absurdity, Swift denies the progress I have charted by examining a few representative figures. His book belongs to the category of conservatism that I described initially as refusing European civilized man any illusions or ambitions or escapes into any new world, including one of his own making. Swift writes in that humanist tradition which, looking back through the Renaissance to the classical world, sees little virtue in originality. He uses the genre of travel literature for another campaign in the perennial battle between Ancients and Moderns, so that "modern" is a pejorative term and "the novel" – in so far as Swift might sense what Defoe had achieved in Crusoe's first narrative – is a form to be resisted. The theme of travel furnished Swift with an opportunity to restate the pessimistic view that man cannot change by cutting himself off from traditional values or by measuring everything in terms of his experience of the physical world. The zeal for exploration and colonial projects for "the public good," which Gulliver wields in obligatory fashion in his final chapter, turns against deceiver and deceived alike. It is the printer (and the buying public) whom he accuses at last of imagining that his travel narrative could reform the world. His own last words are: "I have now done with all such visionary Schemes for ever."

JENNY MEZCIEMS
University of Warwick

NOTES

1. I have discussed some features of Bacon's fiction in the context of Utopian literature in "The Unity of Swift's *Voyage to Laputa*: Structure as Meaning in Utopian Fiction," *Modern Language Review*, 72 (1977), 1-21.
2. *A New Voyage Round the World* (1697), ed. Sir Albert Gray (London: Adam & Charles Black, 1937), "Preface."
3. *The True History*, in *Lucian: Satirical Sketches*, trans. Paul Turner (Harmondsworth: Penguin Books, 1961).
4. I have not seen a copy of Rastell's *A New Interlude and a Mery of the Nature of the IIII Elements* (ca. 1519), which is described as "a lecture in verse, disguised as a

play, on natural science." It was apparently a propagandist piece appealing for support in further ventures; see Boies Penrose, *Travel and Discovery in the Renaissance, 1420-1620* (Cambridge, Mass.: Harvard U.P., 1960), p. 313.

5. *The Travels of Marco Polo*, trans. Aldo Ricci from the text of L. F. Benedetto (London: Routledge & Kegan Paul, 1931), p. 1.

6. *Mandeville's Travels*, ed. Malcolm Letts, 2 vols. (London: The Hakluyt Society, 1953), II, 419; I, 3 note. Quotations are from this edition.

7. Quotations are from *Select Documents Illustrating the Four Voyages of Columbus*, trans. and ed. Cecil Jane, 2 vols. (London: The Hakluyt Society, 1930, 1933), and information from the introduction to Volume I.

8. The quotations are from an extract of Oviedo's *General and Natural History of the Indies* (1547), Book II, chs. 2 and 4, in *The Four Voyages of Christopher Columbus*, trans. and ed. J.M. Cohen (Harmondsworth: Penguin Books, 1969), pp. 27-8, 34.

9. See *Select Documents*, II, xviii, xxiv.

10. *Pantagruel*, ch. 9, *Oeuvres complètes*, ed. Pierre Jourda, 2 vols. (Paris: Garnier, 1962), I, 263.

11. *Utopia*, in *Complete Works*, ed. Edward Surtz, S.J., and J.H. Hexter (New Haven and London: Yale U.P., 1965), IV, 49, 51. These figures are discussed further by me in "Swift's Praise of Gulliver: Some Renaissance Background to the *Travels*", in *The Character of Swift's Satire: A Revised Focus*, ed. C.J. Rawson (Newark, Delaware: U. of Delaware Press, forthcoming), and, especially, "Utopia and 'the Thing which is not': More, Swift, and other Lying Idealists", *UTQ*, forthcoming.

12. See, for example, "The Relation of Nunno di Gusman" written to Charles V (1530), in Samuel Purchas, *Hakluytus Posthumus, or, Purchas his Pilgrimes*, 20 vols. (Glasgow: James MacLehose & Sons, 1905), XVIII, 52, 53, 55; and *Hans Staden: The True History of his Captivity* (1557), trans. and ed. Malcolm Letts (London: George Routledge & Sons, 1928).

13. For a brief discussion of such prefaces see Arthur Sherbo, "Swift and Travel Literature," *Modern Language Studies*, 9 (1979), 114-27 (117). The essay considers motives and claims to truthfulness in an examination of possible specific sources. See also Percy G. Adams, *Travelers and Travel Liars, 1660-1800* (Berkeley and Los Angeles: U. of California Press, 1962), p. 88.

14. "My reason for [setting sail]? Mere curiosity": *True History*, p. 250.

15. See R.W. Frantz, "Gulliver's 'Cousin Sympson'," *HLQ*, 1 (1938), 329-34 (331-2).

16. Quotations are from *Gulliver's Travels*, Volume XI (revised ed. 1959) in the *Prose Works*, ed. Herbert Davis and others, 16 vols. (Oxford: Basil Blackwell, 1939-74).

17. So thought W.A. Eddy, *Gulliver's Travels: A Critical Study* (Princeton, N.J.: Princeton U.P., 1923), pp. 68-71. The story in question is *Wasaubiyauwe* (1774), too late for Gulliver but supposedly based on oral versions which could have travelled to Europe with Dutch sailors. Apart from making death seem desirable, Tithonus-style, the fable, of ever-youthful inhabitants, seems to bear little resemblance to the Struldbrugg episode, though other parts of the story have Gulliverian echoes.

18. "A Letter to a Young Gentleman, Lately enter'd into Holy Orders" (1720), *Works*, IX, 65, 66.

19. Introduction, p. xiii, to the edition by L.E. Elliott Joyce (Oxford: The Hakluyt Society, 1934).

20. For a brief gathering of recent views from Ian Watt, E.M.W. Tillyard, G.A. Starr, Barbara Hardy, and J. Paul Hunter, see the introduction to J. Donald Crowley's edition (London and Oxford: Oxford U.P., 1976); pp. xi-xii.

The Voyages of Jerónimo Lobo, Joachim Le Grand, and Samuel Johnson

Most eighteenth-century travel books combined narrative with facts in a first-person account that tried to avoid – at least in the early part of the century – too much that was personal or egotistical. One recent study of such books, Charles L. Batten Jr's *Pleasurable Instruction*, emphasizes the "generic blending of factual information and literary art," and argues persuasively that travel books provided "the kind of mimetic entertainment more often associated with narrative literature than with merely philosophical studies" and "joined pleasure with instruction in what became, perhaps, one of the most characteristic forms of the century."[1] What has not been examined, as far as I know, is how a single book of travel can go through a series of versions produced by shifts in the period of publication, in the political or religious climate, in the nationality of translators and publishers, and in the conventions and appeals of different literary forms. Such a book grew out of the travels and missionary work of a seventeenth-century Portuguese Jesuit priest, Jerónimo Lobo, who lived and worked in Abyssinia, or Ethiopia, between 1625 and 1635. Perhaps the best-known version of his text is the translation or "epitome" from the French by Samuel Johnson, which appeared in 1735.

Even before the Portuguese reached Abyssinia early in the sixteenth century, Europeans had long been familiar with rumours of an isolated Christian kingdom somewhere in Asia or Africa ruled by Prester John. The reality was somewhat different. Converted to Christianity in the fourth century, the Abyssinians later rejected the doctrine of the Council of Chalcedon and its definition of the dual nature of Christ. About the middle of the seventh century, increasing numbers of external enemies and the spread of Islam in surrounding nations served to isolate the Abyssinians in their mountain fastnesses. "Encompassed on all sides, the Aethiopians," in Gibbon's familiar words, "slept near a thousand years, forgetful of the world, by whom they were forgotten."[2] This seclusion helped to produce a monophysite Christianity indigenous to Abyssinia, a religion that led the Jesuits, Lobo among them, to make great efforts to convert these "hérétiques" and "schismatiques," heretics and schismatics who, it ought to be added, thought *they* were the Christians.

Some biographical and historical information will set the context.[3] Jerónimo Lobo was born in Lisbon in 1595. After studying at Coimbra, he was educated for the priesthood and determined to be a missionary. By

April of 1621, ordained a deacon and a priest, he had left Lisbon and was on his way to the Indies. But the voyage was so filled with misfortunes, dangers, sickness, and periods of exhaustion that it had to be abandoned, and the ill-fated travellers finally made it back to Lisbon in October 1621. Although he was confined to his bed for three months to recover from the effects of that failed attempt, Lobo was ready by the following March to try a second voyage. He embarked in March 1622 and finally towards the end of that year reached the Indian city of Goa, command-post for the missions of India and Africa. For more than a year he remained at Goa studying theology; then, joining the new Patriarch on his way from Portugal, Lobo reached the African continent and began the dangerous and arduous journey inland from the Red Sea coast. By the third week in June 1625, some four years after Jerónimo Lobo had left Lisbon on his first unsuccessful voyage, he finally arrived at the Jesuit House in Abyssinia.

The next few years were taken up with the work of the mission, the teaching, the attempts at conversion, and the rebaptisms that engendered so much ill-will toward the Jesuits. In 1626 he undertook a task that he describes at length, the search for the relics of Cristovão da Gama, son of the explorer Vasco da Gama, murdered almost a century earlier. The recovery of these relics took a month. Two years later he was bitten by a cobra and was seriously ill for some time. In the following year, 1629, he journeyed to examine the sources of the Nile. Over the next few years the missionaries continued their work with only occasional protests from the native clergy and from the people themselves. As Lobo's account makes clear, the accession to the throne of Abyssinia in 1632 of an emperor antagonistic to the missionaries marked the beginning of the end. New problems and new dangers arose. By the end of April 1633 the Patriarch and his company had fled from an interior province and taken shelter with Lobo at the Jesuit House in Fremona. It was only a matter of time before all the missionaries were banished from the territories of Abyssinia. Aided initially by friends among the local chiefs, they were subsequently betrayed and delivered to the Turks at Massawa and Suakin. Lobo and most of his companions were finally released from imprisonment after pledging a substantial ransom payment for the Patriarch and another priest. The long, hard journey eastwards to Goa and from there westwards to Portugal, begun in February 1635, was interrupted by shipwreck, capture by Dutch pirates, and near starvation on a desert island. Lobo finally reached Lisbon in December 1636.

Although Lobo did return to India, the adventures I have been recounting here are the relevant ones for an examination of the various versions of his "Itinerário." Between March 1639 and March 1640 Lobo was in Lisbon writing of his travels in a manuscript which had not been published when he died in 1678. Various shorter Lobo manuscripts were the source over the years for abridgements, adaptations, and translations. Balthasar Telles included in his *Historia geral de Ethiopia a Alta* (1660), itself an abridgement of a manuscript history by Manuel de Almeida, important information gleaned from Lobo. In addition, at the urging of Robert Southwell of the Royal Society, Lobo wrote short essays on five topics: the river Nile, the unicorn, the title Prester John, the reason for the name Red Sea, and the palm tree. Translated into English for the Society by Sir Peter Wyche, these were published in a slim duodecimo volume of 105 pages – about 14,000 words – in 1669, as *A Short Relation of the River Nile, Of its sourse and Current; Of its Overflowing the Campagnia of Aegypt, till it runs into the Mediterranean: And of other Curiosities: Written by an Eye-witnesse, who lived many years in the chief Kingdoms of the Abyssine Empire.* Although Lobo's name is not mentioned on the title page or in the text, the author does refer to his crossing the Nile and having the location named after him: the passage of Father Jerome. The essays avoid controversial topics, refer hardly at all to religious matters, and make a show of presenting first-hand information about history, natural history, and geography.

An intriguing marginal note in this adumbrated version of the Lobo material emphasizes the author's reliability, a point made vigorously later by Johnson in the preface to his translation of the *Voyage*, and also underscores his role as an eye witness. There is a description of a tower in the Nile at Cairo on which graduated markings indicated how many degrees the river had risen; each night the figures were proclaimed publicly. At this point a note calls attention to a unique reliance on hearsay:

> *The Author, a faithfull Eye-witnesse of all he relates, and so of undoubted Credit, took this onely thing upon report that the Nile washeth the walls of Gran-Cairo, and that on the inside of this Tower in the walls, should be kept the Register of the innundation of the Nile, which is on a Marble Pillar, placed in the middle of the River, near a long Island called Rhodes opposite the Gran Cairo; upon this Island and over the Pillar is built a Mosque, with such an Arch towards the River, to give the water passage. This place and Pillar is so superstitiously secured from the sight of Christians, that I found the attempt vain and dangerous; onely saw in January the bottome of the Pillar in the water: The other Circumstances of the number of Degrees and the Proclamations, are truly related.[4]

My purpose is not to praise Lobo's veracity: Johnson does that while James Bruce, as we shall see, denigrates it. What I wish to do is to indicate the ways by which Lobo's account is being transformed by this division into shorter essays. The essays themselves are similar enough to extended sections of the *Itinerário* and the *Relation historique* to suggest that Lobo merely provided such appropriate sections to the Royal Society. Eschewing certain topics more relevant to his role as missionary, Lobo's essays lack the narrative flow of the voyage genre and seem, rather, factual accounts of topics of interest to intellectually curious readers. In order to establish the credibility of this informant, a note like the one quoted above is quite effective.

The emphasis on that very full title page on the long-standing questions about the sources of the Nile and the reasons for its overflowing, the promise of "other Curiosities," and the attraction of the narrator who has "been there" all provide insights into what readers were looking for, and what the appeal of the work might have been in this abbreviated form. In the next few years Wyche's English version was translated into French, German, Italian, and Dutch, often with his name on the title page. His reputation as an authority on Abyssinia was growing.

It is quite likely therefore that the French Oratorian, Joachim Le Grand, understood the value of the Portuguese manuscript he was shown during his tenure in Portugal as secretary to the French ambassador during the 1690s. But other translations and other duties took up Le Grand's time before he returned to the extensive Lobo manuscript, a version of the *Itinerário*, some time in the 1720s. It was Le Grand's translation, the *Relation historique d'Abissinie* (Paris, 1728), that Johnson read at Oxford.

Living in Birmingham in 1733, Johnson recalled the book as one that might be suitable for a translation and abridgement. Boswell's account of Johnson's engaging "to supply the press with copy" and then succumbing to "his constitutional indolence" comes from Johnson's friend Edmund Hector, who represented to Johnson the sad plight of the poor printer and his family. "Johnson upon this," writes Boswell, "exerted the powers of his mind, though his body was relaxed. He lay in bed with the book, which was a quarto, before him, and dictated while Hector wrote. Mr. Hector carried the sheets to the press, and corrected almost all the proof-sheets, very few of which were even seen by Johnson."[5] The translation appeared in 1735 under the title of *A Voyage to Abyssinia*.

So much for the immediate historical and biographical contexts. In the remainder of this essay I intend to examine the changes that occurred to this book as it went from the Portuguese to the French to the English texts.[6] Although I shall touch on some of the changes brought about by the nature of translation or by the influences of altered political and religious climates, I want to focus on differences of form.

The manuscript which Joachim Le Grand translated into French has disappeared. And until the middle of the twentieth century the long manuscript on which Lobo had been working after his return from Abyssinia was missing, presumed lost in the Lisbon earthquake of 1755, the event one scholar aptly labels "that impregnable refuge of inefficient librarians."[7]

In 1947, in a public library in northern Portugal, Father Manuel Gonçalves da Costa discovered the *Itinerário*, a manuscript almost twice as long as Le Grand's French version.[8] Although almost all of the passages in Le Grand's first 136 pages have their counterparts in the *Itinerário*, we should always keep in mind that we are making certain assumptions about a shorter manuscript source which has not yet been found.

Father da Costa published Lobo's *Itinerário E Outros Escritos Inéditos* in 1971. In manuscript form the *Itinerário* takes up 174 folios, written on both sides. Lobo apparently employed two amanuenses, one of whom transcribed the first 104 folios, the second the remainder. Perhaps most pertinent for the argument I am attempting to establish is the fact that that manuscript was not divided into chapters: it had only three divisions or headings. At the beginning appears the heading: "Relação do tempo que ha say de Portugal e as navegações e caminhos que fis, sucessos que tive, terras que vi e as cousas particulares que nellas notei."[9] There is another division on folio 9: "Como parti a segunda vez pera a India com o Conde da Vidigeira, Vice-Rey a segunda ves."[10] The only other heading occurs on folio 65: "Do Imperio Abexino, seus principios e progresso, dos emperedores que teve, a relegião que profesou e quando entrou a fee Catolica nestes reinos, por quem, o tempo que perseverou e quando se perdeo com mais outras coriozidades pertencentes à materia de que trato."[11] Only three different headings in a book of almost 350 pages. Obviously Lobo is writing a kind of journal, labelled at the beginning as the account of his travels, interrupted at the ninth folio by his realization that he had made a false start on meeting the promise of the first heading. The second heading – how I left a second time – marks a new beginning. The only other section heading – on the Abyssinian Empire – would have suggested itself to Lobo as a logical announcement of a movement from autobiographical narrative to generalized description of the empire. When, some ten folios further, Lobo returns to a more personal narrative, there is no new heading, but his gradual and intermittent slipping into this mode meant that there was no specific point at which the shift ought to have been marked.

The final pages of the *Itinerário* – about 55 folios – containing Lobo's long and eventful voyage back to Portugal, do not appear in Le Grand's book, nor, obviously, in Johnson's. The *Itinerário* can be described as an autobiographical account of the various voyages, adventures, and tribulations of Jerónimo Lobo. These personal experiences are interspersed with descriptions of the countries, institutions, and natural phenomena of the lands he traverses. Indeed, sections on the history of Abyssinia or on conjectures about what makes the Red Sea red also include what might be called "action" segments. The result is a free-flowing narrative interrupted by a storyteller who has come to an interesting aside or a point that ought to be explored before the action picks up again.

Let us consider now what happened when Joachim Le Grand translated a version of this manuscript approximately fifty years after the death of the traveller, the earliest purveyor of the text. The first 93 folios of Le Grand's manuscript translation, in the Bibliothèque Nationale, present Lobo's account of his travels.[12] Heavily rewritten and interlineated, passages are re-arranged and revised to reduce their length and tighten the style. A fair copy of this section, in another hand, contains a few changes by Le Grand. The author appears also to have transcribed source materials for some of the sections added to the Lobo material. Examination of the "Table Sommaire" (Fig. 1) reveals Le Grand's

TABLE SOMMAIRE.

DISSERTATIONS.

Figure 1. "Table Sommaire" (reduced in size) from *Relation historique d'Abissinie* (1728). Reproduced by permission of the University of Illinois Library. (Pages 25-7)

TABLE SOMMAIRE.

Cette lettre fait voir que le Roi d'Ethiopie n'a eu
nulle part à la mort du fieur du Roule, & détruit
ce que dit là-deffus le Memoire rapporté pag. 436.
Autre preuve par la lettre fuivante.

Lettre

T A B L E.

A P P R O B A T I O N.

J'Ai lû par l'ordre de Monfeigneur le Garde des Sceaux un Ma-
nufcrit qui a pour Titre : *Relation Hiftorique de l'Hiftoire de l'A-
biffinie , traduite du Portugais fur les Manufcrits du R. P. Jerôme Lobo
Jefuite , continuée & augmentée de plufieurs Differtations.* Cet ouvrage
m'a paru très-digne de la curiofité du Public & le plus inftruðtif qui
ait été publié jufques à prefent fur l'Abiffinie. Les Differtations
qui l'accompagnent font remplies de fçavantes recherches & qui
éclairciffent beaucoup de difficultés touchant ce vafte Pays fi peu
connu. L'Auteur de ces mêmes Differtations y traite à fond de la
Religion & de la croyance des Abiffins ; & perfonne ne nous en a
mieux inftruit que lui , ni n'a rendu plus de juftice à cette Nation.
Enfin tout l'Ouvrage eft fuivi de Relations nouvelles & de Pieces
importantes touchant cet Empire ; ce qui ne peut manquer de faire
beaucoup de plaifir aux Leðteurs. C'eft le témoignage que nous
croyons devoir rendre de cet Ouvrage après l'avoir lû avec autant
d'attention que de fatisfaðtion. Fait à Paris le 29. Mars 1727. J. DE
TARGNY, *Doðteur en Théologie & la Faculté de Paris, Abbé de S. Lo ,
& Garde de la Bibliotheque du Roi.*

P R I V I L E G E   D V   R O I.

LOUIS par la grace de Dieu Roi de France & de Navarre : A nos amez & feaux Con-
feillers les Gens tenant nos Cours de Parlement, Maiftre des Requeftes ordinaires de
noftre Hoftel , grand Confeil , Prevoft de Paris , Baillifs , Senechaux , leurs Licutenans

Relation historique d'Abissinie to be a very different book from
Lobo's *Itinerário*. Where the Portuguese wrote a relatively straightforward account of his travels with occasional historical or geographical
sections, Le Grand includes most of that material, dividing it into the first
voyage "manqué," the second voyage, the account of the Abyssinian
Empire, and a description of the Nile, and adds a "Suite de la Relation
d'Abissinie." At this point Le Grand appends sixteen documented,
scholarly dissertations of his own on topics such as Ludolf's History of
Abyssinia, the Eastern Side of Africa, Prester John, the Red Sea and the
Navigation of Solomon's Fleets, the Queen of Sheba, Circumcision, the
Errors of the Abyssins, the Eucharist and Penance, and so forth. The
longest dissertation is about twenty pages, the shortest about six, and the
average about ten. Approximately 180 pages of Le Grand's text are taken
up with these learned and occasionally contentious essays. About another
140 pages present various accounts, memoirs, and letters touching on
Abyssinian matters before and after Lobo's experiences. There are translated letters from Arabic into French, memoirs concerning a counterfeit
ambassador supposedly sent from Ethiopia to the Court of France at the
turn of the eighteenth century, a letter from the Emperor of Ethiopia to
Pope Clement XI, another from a Patriarch of Alexandria to the Pope,
brief letters from Sultan Segued on his conversion to Roman Catholicism
and from his brother Rassela Christos. In fact, the actual material translated from Jerónimo Lobo constitutes only the first 136 pages of a 514
page book, about a quarter of the total.

What happens when the "voyage" material is set into such a framework, of course, is that it becomes much less significant, reduced to *one* of
the components in a "relation historique," to be supplemented by all the
other apparatus – dissertations, memoirs, letters, etc. on topics opened up
by Lobo's experiences. The shape of the whole book has changed. It is no
longer Lobo's *Itinerário*, no longer his autobiographical account of the
mission and the country. The book was published with the usual required
approvals for printing and appeared in 1728 with a relatively uncluttered,
attractive title page (Fig. 2). Although other states of the title page have
the wording *Voyage historique*, a number of pieces of evidence analyzed
some years ago by Donald M. Lockhart[13] make it clear that the original
title was *Relation historique* : the official "Approbation" (Fig. 1) included
in the front matter of the published work was for a book entitled *Relation
historique*; the running title is *Relation historique*; and the feminine
endings of "traduite," "continuée," and "augmentée," appropriate with
Relation on the title page, are foolishly retained with the masculine
Voyage. My guess is that the title was changed to help the book sell better,
and that Johnson was probably working with a French text with the
Voyage title page.

Let us consider what happens when Le Grand's Lobo is taken over
by the young Samuel Johnson. "In this Translation (if it may be so
call'd)," he announces in the Preface, "great Liberties have been taken,
which, whether justifiable or not, shall be fairly confess'd, and let the

RELATION

HISTORIQUE

D'ABISSINIE,

DU R. P. JEROME LOBO

DE LA COMPAGNIE DE JESUS.

Traduite du Portugais, continuée & augmentée
de plufieurs Differtations, Lettres & Memoires.

Par M. *LE GRAND*, *Prieur de Neuville-les-Dames
& de Preveffin.*

A PARIS,

Chez la Veuve D'ANTOINE-URBAIN COUSTELIER,
& JACQUES GUERIN Libraires, Quay des Auguftins.

MDCCXXVIII.

AVEC APPROBATION ET PRIVILEGE DU ROI.

Figure 2. Title page of *Relation historique* (reduced in size). Reproduced by permission of the University of Illinois Library.

Judicious part of Mankind pardon or condemn them. In the first part," he continues,

> the greatest Freedom has been used, in reducing the Narration into a narrow Compass, so that it is by no Means a Translation but an Epitome. ...
>
> In the Account of Abyssinia and the Continuation, the Authors have been follow'd with more exactness, and as few Passages appeared either insignificant or tedious, few have been either shortened or omitted.
>
> The Dissertations are the only part in which an exact Translation has been attempted, and even in those, Abstracts are sometimes given instead of literal Quotations ... and sometimes other parts have been contracted.
>
> Several Memorials and Letters, which are printed at the end of the Dissertations to secure the credit of the foregoing Narrative, are entirely left out.[14]

Although it is not my intention here to focus on the differences in the two translations, collation of the 1728 French text and the 1735 English one has revealed a surprising variety of techniques and alterations lumped under "great Liberties."[15] Virtually every page of the English version, *including* the dissertations, illustrates the extent of Johnson's activity: he translated in places, epitomized in others, omitted some sections, expanded others, added asperity to the tone, or softened the wording, rearranged elements for greater clarity, balanced phrases and clauses for smoother syntax, inserted transitions for easier reading, and interspersed editorial comments to point the moral. Obviously all of these editorial practices alter Le Grand *and* Lobo.

What is impossible to determine is whose decisions produced the shape of the book. Who decided – Johnson or the publisher Thomas Warren – to omit those "several Memorials and Letters"? And note that Johnson's "several" would not lead an English reader to realize that more than 150 *pages* of the French text have been omitted – pages which, I have been arguing, helped to produce the special scholarly character of Le Grand's book.

Moreover, the title page of this shorter English version (Fig. 3) – 396 octavo pages to the 514 quarto pages of Le Grand – should be compared to the French title page (Fig. 2). In place of the stately layout with ornament and plenty of white space of the French, Johnson's publisher has provided a catalogue of highlights on the title page. Considering that the materials from Jerónimo Lobo himself occupy little more than a third of Johnson's book, they are remarkably prominent in the detailed offerings of the title page. Readers are promised accounts of the dangers Lobo underwent, the description of the coasts of the Red Sea, the history, laws, and customs of the Abyssins, the story of the admission of the Jesuits and the expulsion, a description of the Nile and the causes of its inundations. Such an emphasis suggests something about the audience at

A VOYAGE

TO

ABYSSINIA.

BY

Father *Jerome Lobo*,

A PORTUGUESE JESUIT.

CONTAINING,

A Narrative of the Dangers he underwent in his firſt Attempt to paſs from the *Indies* into *Abyſſinia*; with a Deſcription of. the Coaſts of the *Red-Sea.*

An Account of the Hiſtory, Laws, Cuſtoms, Religion, Habits, and Buildings of the *Abyſſins*; with the Rivers, Air, Soil, Birds, Beaſts, Fruits and other natural Produ&tions of that remote and unfre-quented Country.

A Relation of the Admiſ-ſion of the Jeſuits into *Abyſſinia* in 1625, and their Expulſion from thence in 1634.

An exa&t Deſcription of the *Nile*, its Head, its Branch-es, the Courſe of its Wa-ters, and the Cauſe of its Inundations.

With a Continuation of the Hiſtory of *Abyſſinia* down to the Beginning of the Eighteenth Century, and Fifteen Diſſertations on various Subje&ts relating to the Hiſtory, Antiquities, Government, Religion, Manners, and natural Hiſtory of *Abyſſinia*, and other Countries mention'd by Father *JEROME LOBO.*

By MR. LE GRAND,

From the *FRENCH.*

LONDON:

Printed for A. BETTESWORTH, and C. HITCH at the *Red-Lyon* in *Paternoſter-Row.*

MDCCXXXV.

Figure 3. Title page (originally printed in red and black) of Johnson's translation. Repro-duced by permission of the Kenneth Spencer Research Library, University of Kansas.

which Warren was aiming. Like so many of the travel books of the period, this one was promising adventure, far-off exotic lands, and information or instruction. More specifically, Warren was selling religious controversy, a *Jesuit's* account of his mission, as well as some scholarly dissertations on important matters of church and state. One final point before we move from the title page to the Preface of Johnson's translation: for the neutral phrasing of "R.P. Jerome Lobo de la Compagnie de Jesus" of the French translation, Johnson's publisher has identified Father Lobo as "A Portuguese Jesuit," a label with a somewhat greater emotional impact for eighteenth-century English men and women.

The issue of a Portuguese Jesuit mission comes to the surface early in Johnson's Preface, where Lobo is specifically praised while the missionaries come under Johnson's lash. In Lobo's account of his mission, writes Johnson,

> where his Veracity is most to be suspected, He neither exaggerates overmuch the Merits of the Jesuits, if we consider the partial Regard paid by the Portuguese to their Countrymen, by the Jesuits to their Society, and by the Papists to their Church, nor aggravates the Vices of the Abyssins, but if the Reader will not be satisfied with a Popish Account of a Popish Mission, he may have recourse to the History of the Church of Abyssinia, written by Dr. Geddes, in which he will find the Actions and Sufferings of the Missionaries placed in a different Light, though the same in which Mr. Le Grand, with all his Zeal for the Roman Church, appears to have seen them.[16]

The language – "Papist," "Popish Account of a Popish Mission" – obviously creates a tone not present in Le Grand. In addition, although referring his readers to such a vehemently anti-Catholic account as Michael Geddes's *The Church-History of Ethiopia* (1696) does not indicate that Johnson endorsed Geddes's strong views, it does suggest that an alternative to the Catholic viewpoint might be appropriate. And a book that *might* require such a counterbalance is a very different work from the *Itinerário* or the *Relation historique*.

Moreover, the Preface, like Johnson's translation itself, seems to set up a kind of dialectic between the actors in the original story and the English translator. In the text, for example, Johnson almost always weakens the Jesuits' case against the Abyssinian Christians by substituting milder and occasionally startling terms for words like "hérétique" and "schismatique." These alterations occur frequently enough to indicate "a determined effort to avoid the harsher terminology, to point out that 'heretic' meant only one opposed to the Church of Rome."[17] Johnson's attitudes do not allow him to translate "hérétiques" as "heretics," and his language in turn affects the way readers respond to the material. Despite his warning in the Preface that "great Liberties" have been taken, we are not quite prepared for the transformation he achieves when he translates "les hérétiques" as "these People that adhered to the Religion of their Ancestors."[18] A different response is required of a reader of the English translation with its critical, even antagonistic, Preface than of the French translation which is pretty much all of a piece – the apparatus generally supportive of the actors in the drama. The point might be seen more clearly if we consider the inevitable impact of the most vehemently anti-Jesuit and anti-Catholic paragraph in Johnson's Preface:

> Let us suppose an Inhabitant of some remote and superiour Region, yet unskill'd in the Ways of Men, having read and considered the Precepts of the Gospel, and the Example of our Saviour, to come down in search of the True Church: If he would not enquire after it among the Cruel, the Insolent, and the Oppressive; among those who are continually grasping at Dominion over souls as well as Bodies; among those who are employed in procuring to themselves impunity for the most enormous Villanies, and studying methods of destroying their Fellow-creatures, not for their Crimes but their Errors; if he would not expect to meet Benevolence engaged in Massacres, or to find Mercy in a Court of Inquisition, he would not look for the True Church in the Church of Rome.[19]

Obviously, such a paragraph influences the way a reader approaches the book and, among Protestant readers of eighteenth-century England, may be presumed to support widespread prejudices.

At the same time we are made suspicious of the Jesuits and perhaps even of Lobo's discussion of religious matters, we are also made to appreciate the traveller as a careful and truthful narrator of what he has seen. Johnson's well-known praise of Lobo serves to focus attention on the veracity and judiciousness of the eyewitness – a shaping of the reader's perceptions similar to the effects of the marginal note in Sir Peter Wyche's translation. "The Portuguese Traveller," Johnson tells us,

> contrary to the general Vein of his Countrymen, has amused his Reader with no Romantick Absurdities or Incredible Fictions, whatever he relates, whether true or not, is at least probable, and he who tells nothing exceeding the bounds of probability, has a right to demand, that they should believe him, who cannot contradict him.
>
> He appears by his modest and unaffected Narration to have described Things as he saw them, to have copied Nature from the Life, and to have consulted his Senses not his Imagination; He meets with no Basilisks that destroy with their Eyes, his Crocodiles devour their Prey without Tears, and his Cataracts fall from the Rock without Deafening the Neighbouring Inhabitants.[20]

Although, as we shall see, a later traveller to Ethiopia, James Bruce, did not share Johnson's admiration for Lobo and thought he could indeed contradict the Portuguese traveller, these paragraphs from Johnson's Preface do provide a kind of testimonial that directs the reader's response to the narration.

That narration enters much more quickly into the action itself than did

Lobo's *Itinerário* with its slower building towards the successful entry into Abyssinia. Johnson deleted most of Lobo's story of his first aborted voyage (included by Le Grand) and shortened the section on the second voyage, thus advancing the action to the borders of Abyssinia much more quickly than either Lobo's original or Le Grand's translation did. In the opening pages of Lobo's narrative the English text provides a series of footnotes to identify places like Ormus, Mozambique, and Cochim. The identifications can be found in Laurence Eachard's *Gazetteer*, numerous editions of which were printed during this period. The practice stops, however, after sixteen pages and eleven footnotes. Considering the amount of work that would have been involved – Lobo visited or mentioned a vast number of out-of-the-way locations – it is not surprising that the practice was broken off so quickly. One note, identifying Caxume as "the Capital of the kingdom of Tigremahon in Abyssinia,"[21] is clearly in error. Le Grand (16) and the *Itinerário* (219) print *Caxem*, annotated by the contemporary editor of Lobo as Qishn, a city on the coast of Yemen. The mangled geography created by the mistaken identification led James Bruce into a sneering page-and-a-half about the ignorance revealed or, worse, the attempt to deceive. "How is it possible," he concludes, "a ship from the coast of Malabar should get 200 miles from any sea, among the mountains of Tigre? I hope the publisher will compare this with any map he pleases, and correct it in his *errata*, otherwise his narrative is unintelligible, unless all this was intended to be placed to the account of miracles – Peter walked upon the water, and Lobo the Jesuit sailed upon dry land."[22] Here, and elsewhere, the attempt to make Lobo's journeys more intelligible to a contemporary British reader by annotating exotic place-names, transforming it from straight-forward travel narrative to travel narrative *cum* geographical footnotes, has led to criticism, not only of Johnson and his publisher, but more importantly of Lobo. A second faulty identification taken from the *Gazetteer* leads Bruce to comment that "Dr Johnson, or his publisher, involves his reader in another strange perplexity."[23] Where the Portu-guese and the French had read "Dancali," a coastal area, Johnson's text has "Dancala," and the footnote unfortunately goes on to compound the difficulties: "a City of Africk in the upper Æthiopia, upon the River Nile in the Tract of Nubia, of which it is the Capital."[24] Now, Lobo the traveller is subjected to the scorn of James Bruce, who had visited the country and who knew very well how impossible the geography of *A Voyage to Abyssinia* had become: "It is very difficult to understand how people, in a ship from India, could enter Abyssinia by the way of Dancala, if that city is upon the Nile; because no where, that I know, is that river in Abyssinia within 300 miles of any sea; and still more so, how could it be in Nubia, and yet in Upper Ethiopia."[25]

The emphasis on Lobo's accuracy and his status as reliable eyewitness, so prominent in both the Wyche translation of the brief essays and Johnson's translation from the French, seems almost to have triggered

Bruce's scorn. He is even more vehement on the point of the non-existent man-eaters of Patta ("Paté"):

> Lobo has said, (30, 31) 'that a Portuguese galliot was ordered to set him ashore at Pate, whose inhabitants were man-eaters.' This is a very whimsical choice of a place to land strangers in, among man-eaters. I cannot conceive what advantage could be proposed by landing men going to Abyssinia so far to the southward, among a people such as this, who certainly, by their very manners, must be at war, and unconnected with all their neighbours. And many ages have passed without this reproach having fallen upon the inhabitants of the east coast of the peninsula of Africa from any authentic testimony; and I am confident, after the few specimens just given of the topographical knowledge of this author, his present testimony will not weigh much, from whatever hand this performance may have come.[26]

On the face of it, such a demonstration of Lobo's unreliability as a traveller and narrator seems crushing: Lobo appears to be amusing his readers with "Romantick Absurdities" and "Incredible Fictions." The approach would seem to be that of *Travels into Several Remote Nations of the World* rather than that of *A Journey to the Western Islands of Scotland*.

But once again Lobo is innocent of Bruce's charge. First of all, Bruce's "quotation" about the Portuguese galliot having been " 'ordered to set him ashore at Pate, whose inhabitants were man-eaters' " is a manufactured one: it does not occur in Johnson's translation. Bruce has deleted fifteen lines of Johnson's text between the setting "ashore at Pate" and the phrase, "were man-eaters." The missing material describes the people whom they will meet on their way into Abyssinia, not the inhabitants of Patta. The English translation reveals that these people "were Savage, that they had indeed began to Treat with the *Portuguese*, but it was only from Fear, that otherwise they were a Barbarous Nation, who finding themselves too much crouded in their own Country, had extended themselves to the Sea shore, that they ravaged the Country, and laid every thing waste, where they came, that they were Man-eaters, and were on that Account dreadful in all those Parts."[27]

However, even granting the licence Bruce is taking with the account, we are still faced with cannibals in *a region* where, as Bruce demonstrates, they were not known to exist. "One would almost be tempted," he concludes, "to believe that Jerome Lobo was a man-eater himself, and had taught this custom to these savages. They had it not before his coming; they have never had it since; and it must have been with some sinister intention like this, that a stranger would voluntarily seek a nation of man-eaters."[28] If one compares Johnson's translation to Le Grand's French, one finds a straightforward and accurate rendering of the passage about these people who "s'étoient étendus jusqu'à la mer, pillant & ravageant tout, & mangeant les hommes."[29] The evidence does seem to be all on Bruce's side. One further step backwards, however, in the translating chain provides an answer that clears Jerónimo Lobo of all of Bruce's charges. Although it cannot be proved that the passage in Le Grand was translated from the only version of the *Itinerário* we now have, it seems very likely that Lobo's account of the fierce Gallas is the same as it would have been in the copy Le Grand had. The French translator appears to have misunderstood Lobo's metaphorical account of these savages who erupted from their country, conquering new lands, "e vierão destruindo e comendo quanto encontravão até chegarem ao mar."[30] They did not *eat* everyone they met: they destroyed (devoured) everything in their path (whatever they met) to the sea. Obviously Lobo's text has been transformed, egregiously in this instance, by the pitfalls of translation.

Where a structural change can be seen most clearly, is in the chapter divisions of the 1735 English edition. A pattern for eighteenth-century travel-adventure books has been imposed upon Le Grand's Lobo. Le Grand had generally followed Lobo's major divisions – four in the 136 pages of Le Grand that represent Lobo's travels; someone, and I doubt very much that it was Johnson, imposed chapter divisions and composed chapter headings for the English epitome. Lobo's *Itinerário*, transformed once into the scholarly tome of Joachim Le Grand, has been transformed once more by the Birmingham publisher for a British reading public accustomed to a certain format. Because Johnson omits the first abandoned attempt, *A Voyage to Abyssinia* opens with Chapter I: "The Author arrives after some Difficulties at Goa. Is chosen for the Mission of Æthiopia. The fate of those Jesuits who went by Zeila. The Author arrives at the Coast of Melinda."[31]

The first three chapters are about seven pages long in the octavo format, about 2100 words. Chapter IV is about five pages and 1500 words. Most chapters in the sections preceding the dissertations are in this range. Although we should be cautious about reading too much out of this schema, we might recall the similar formats in other books of travels as well as in many of the novels of the period. Figure 4 reveals the kinds of chapter headings in Johnson's book to show what happened to Lobo's *Voyage* when it was fitted out with new clothes in Birmingham in the 1730s. The reader may consider the amount and variety of informative and exciting material that is being promised. What has happened to that spare account of Jerónimo Lobo's travels in Abyssinia? Or even to Joachim Le Grand's version of those travels? It has become a different kind of book altogether. Like the adventures of Don Quixote or Joseph Andrews, the adventures of Jerónimo Lobo are presented with short enticements: an account of the coco-tree, the author wounded, a broil with the Moors, the plain of salt. And if the *Voyage* now looks like so many other popular travel accounts or books of adventure, so much the better.

There is another way of making the point. If we were to insert at an appropriate place in the chapter headings for the *Voyage* (Fig. 4) one of the headings from *Gulliver's Travels*, it might be difficult to

( )

THE
CONTENTS.

A
VOYAGE
TO
ABYSSINIA.

CHAP. I.

THE *Author arrives after some Difficulties at* Goa. *Is chosen for the Mission of Æthiopia. The fate of those Jesuits who went by* Zeila. *The Author arrives at the Coast of* Melinda.   page 1.
                                    CHAP.

Figure 4. Partial "Contents" of *A Voyage to Abyssinia* (1735). Reproduced by permission of the Kenneth Spencer Research Library, University of Kansas. (Pages 37-40)

The C O N T E N T S.

A

The CONTENTS.

CHAP. VIII.

A
DESCRIPTION
OF
ABYSSINIA.

CHAP. I.

CHAP. II.

CHAP. III.

CHAP. IV.

CHAP.

The CONTENTS.

being

identify the interloper. Introduce, for example, between Chapters IV, V, or VI, one from Gulliver's second voyage: "The Country described. A Proposal for correcting modern Maps. The King's Palace, and some Account of the Metropolis. The Author's way of travelling. The chief Temple described."[32] How many of us would spot the replica? The argument comes down to this: we have little difficulty with the position that Swift achieved some of his purposes by setting up *Travels into Several Remote Nations of the World* to imitate those popular books of travels; his success in this regard is what would allow us to incorporate his chapter heading as one of the headings in *A Voyage to Abyssinia*. But the point can be turned around: both Swift's *and* Johnson's books have been decked out with certain trappings of a form they mimic – for different reasons, of course. The English version of *A Voyage to Abyssinia* has changed its colours, has been transformed not only by the interests and abilities of its translator, but also by the exigencies of the marketplace. The variations from Lobo through Le Grand and Johnson reveal an active and steady process. In the specific case I have been examining, a variety of forces – individual temperaments and situations, translating skills and inclinations, political and religious climates, changing tastes and changing attitudes in reading publics, publishers' appraisals of the market for a given work and their willingness to alter the shape of a book to reach that market – have produced these variations. Indeed, *A Voyage to Abyssinia* as I have edited it for the Yale Edition of *The Works of Samuel Johnson* will be simply one more version of Lobo. With a long, detailed introduction that covers the historical, political, and religious background, textual notes that indicate changes, explanatory notes that call attention to relevant phrasing in Le Grand's *Relation historique* and Lobo's *Itinerário*, along with most of the expected apparatus of a modern scholarly edition, the Yale *Voyage* is only the latest demonstration of this kind of transformation.[33]

JOEL J. GOLD
University of Kansas

NOTES

1. Charles L. Batten, Jr, *Pleasurable Instruction: Form and Convention in Eighteenth-Century Travel Literature* (Berkeley: U. of California Press, 1978), pp. 5-6 and 8.
2. Edward Gibbon, *The History of the Decline and Fall of the Roman Empire* (London: Methuen & Co., 1909), V, 176.
3. Most of the information that follows is drawn from the long and detailed Introduction by Father M. Gonçalves da Costa in his edition of Lobo's *Itinerário E Outros Escritos Inéditos* (Barcelos: Companhia Editora do Minho, 1971) as well as from Lobo's writings themselves.
4. *A Short Relation of the River Nile* (London, 1669), pp. 24-5. In his recent essay, "Jerónimo Lobo: His Travels and His Book," *Bulletin of the John Rylands University Library of Manchester*, 64 (1981), 10-26, C.F. Beckingham discusses the *Short*

Relation and his own detective work in establishing it as Lobo's (pp. 12-14).
5. James Boswell, *Boswell's Life of Johnson*, ed. George Birkbeck Hill, rev. and enlarged by L.F. Powell (Oxford: Clarendon P., 1934-50), I, 86-7.
6. In addition to Johnson's English translation of Le Grand, there was a German translation of it towards the end of the century: Theophil Friedrich Ehrmann, *P. Hieronymus Lobo's, eines portugiesischen Jesuiten, Reise nach Habessinien, und zu den Quellen des Nils*, 2 vols. (Zurich, 1793-4).
7. C.F. Beckingham, "The 'Itinerario' of Jeronimo Lobo," *Journal of Semitic Studies*, 10 (1965), 262.
8. Gonçalves da Costa argues that this manuscript (MS 813 in the Public Library in Braga) was the one Lobo was writing in 1639-40 (*Itinerário*, p. 97ff.).
9. *Itinerário*, p. 139. [An account of the time when I took leave of Portugal and the voyages and journeys which I made, the experiences which befell me, the lands I saw, and the particular items I beheld there.] My colleague, Professor Jon S. Vincent, has smoothed over the roughest spots in my translations.
10. *Itinerário*, p. 171. [How I departed a second time for India with the Count of Vidigeira, Viceroy for the second time.]
11. *Itinerário*, p. 346. [Of the Abyssinian Empire, its origins and its development, of the emperors who held sway, the religion it professed and when the Catholic faith entered these realms, by whom it was introduced, the time it lasted and when it was lost, along with other curiosities relating to the material which I treat.]
12. BN MS fr. 9094-9095.
13. Donald M. Lockhart, "Father Jeronymo Lobo's Writings Concerning Ethiopia" (Diss., Harvard Univ., 1958).
14. *A Voyage to Abyssinia* (London, 1735), pp. xi-xii.
15. See Joel J. Gold, "Johnson's Translation of Lobo," *PMLA*, 80 (1965), 51-61.
16. *A Voyage to Abyssinia*, pp. viii-ix.
17. Gold, *"Johnson's Translation of Lobo,"* p. 60.
18. *Relation historique d'Abissinie*, p. 114; *A Voyage to Abyssinia*, p. 110.
19. *A Voyage to Abyssinia*, pp. ix-x; I have changed the wording from the obviously incorrect "not expect to meet Benevolence, engage in Massacres, or to." The second edition (1789) and the forthcoming Yale Edition of the *Voyage* print the reading I employ here.
20. *A Voyage to Abyssinia*, pp. vii-viii.
21. *A Voyage to Abyssinia*, p. 6.
22. James Bruce, *Travels to Discover the Source of the Nile, in the Years 1768, 1769, 1770, 1771, 1772, & 1773*, 2nd ed. (Edinburgh, 1804), IV, 326. In an Appendix, another writer aims his barbs at Johnson as well as at Lobo: "The work of Le Grande has been translated into English by Dr Johnson, who prefixed to it a pompous preface, which shews, at the same time, his want of discernment respecting the merits of books of travels, his ignorance of oriental literature, and, to use his own expression, an unhappy instance of his having been at times *deflected* from the truth in his critical judgment" (V, 462). In criticizing James Bruce ("a quarrelsome man") and his treatment of Lobo, C.F. Beckingham, "Jerónimo Lobo: His Travels and His Book," pp. 18-20, also comments on this confusion of Caxume and Qishn.
23. Bruce, *Travels,* 2nd ed., IV, 326.
24. *A Voyage to Abyssinia*, p. 4.
25. Bruce, *Travels*, 2nd ed., IV, 326.
26. Bruce, *Travels*, 2nd ed., IV, 327.
27. *A Voyage to Abyssinia*, p. 7.
28. Bruce, *Travels*, 2nd ed., IV, 328.
29. *Relation historique d'Abissinie*, p. 19.
30. *Itinerário E Outros Escritos Inéditos*, p. 225.
31. *A Voyage to Abyssinia*, p. 1.
32. Jonathan Swift, *Travels into Several Remote Nations of the World* (London, 1726), I, 215.
33. This investigation was supported by University of Kansas General Research allocation # 3655-20-0038.

A Semi-Mental Journey: Structure and Illusion in Smollett's Travels

From mid-1763 to mid-1765 the novelist and historian Tobias Smollett was abroad. His travels took him down through France to Nice, where he made his headquarters, and included an extended excursion into Italy. In 1766 there was published in London the two volumes of Smollett's *Travels through France and Italy*, a work cast in the form of forty-one travel-letters.[1] The status of those travel-letters, however, in terms of their relationship to letters which it is known Smollett himself wrote from the Continent to his friends – and those now lost that he may be supposed to have written – has long been a matter of debate in Smollett studies, and, in larger terms, raises intriguing questions about the perception of travel-writing by author and reader.

Thomas Seccombe's pioneering studies of the *Travels* provide the debate with a point of departure. Seccombe has no doubt that the task facing Smollett in preparing the *Travels* for the press consisted of modifying the body of correspondence which the novelist had written home, but is equally confident that under the pressure of all the tasks awaiting him on his return Smollett was unable to fulfil this plan, and that in consequence the "Letters appeared pretty much as he wrote them."[2] Smollett himself spoke of having "thrown into a Series of Letters" the observations he had made in France and Italy, a turn of phrase which through its association with pottery or carpentry (to "throw" on a wheel or a lathe) may be understood as suggesting not so much a cavalier process of preparation as a craftsmanlike shaping of his material.[3] Since Seccombe, discussion of the *Travels*, after a concern with Smollett's sources in existing travel-guides, has indeed placed most emphasis on exploring the satiric-fictive shaping of the work, and has tended to leave behind as literalist fallacy readings of the work as raw autobiographical account – in the form of letters actually sent – of Smollett's journeyings. Instrumental in this process has been the recognition of the presence of a persona, a figure who simultaneously is and is not Tobias Smollett, a shaped projection of the author moulded within certain literary conventions and to certain literary ends.[4] Thus the perception of the *Travels* as text has become far more complex: the work can no longer be viewed simply as historical record, nor even simply as the unmodified opinions and reflections of the historical figure Tobias Smollett – for the distinctive concerns of the persona intervene between that figure and the text. Nobody now, as Lewis Melville did, could without any apparent qualm deploy extended quotation from the *Travels* by way of presenting Smollett's biography: at the very least an acknowledgment of the imaginative status of the letters in the *Travels* as against that of the order of letters collected by Knapp in his standard edition of Smollett's letters would be expected.[5] And yet the *Travels* refuses to be liberated entirely into the realm of fiction: the persona is a projection of the author and not an entirely separate character. Most strikingly, the experiences of the persona, in terms of events undergone in place and time – if not necessarily in terms of the organized response to those events – seem to be largely limited to those of the author. Smollett and the Traveller (as I shall refer to the supposed writer of the letters of the *Travels*) may not be one, but they are Siamese twins, for the most part making the same journeys, seeing the same sights, meeting the same people. The kinds of inquiries which Felsenstein so successfully pursued in his annotation of the *Travels*, into the identity of the ships the Traveller sails in, the people he meets, the routes he takes, the houses he stays in, are only possible on the basis of the work's maintenance of this symbiosis of author and persona, of contingent and literary self. If, inevitably, some people and places have to remain listed as "unidentified," this, one senses, implies only that the revelation of their identity is more problematic than in most instances, rather than that they have no basis in historical fact.

But can we not then expect that a similar relationship to that between the persona and the author subsists between the pattern of letter-writing which evolves from the pen of the persona, and such a pattern as we may infer was mapped out by the historical Tobias Smollett? Learning from the *Travels* that the persona is accompanied by his wife, his servant, and two girls, one of whom is named Miss C——, and that he meets such people as the consul at Villefranche and Mr A——r, we have no reason not to believe that Smollett travelled with Anne Lassells, Alexander Tolloush, Anne Curry, and that he met John Buckland and Henry Archer. When there are allusions to individuals not encountered on the journey, such as "Dr. Sm——ie" and "our friend Hamilton," we have no reason not to assume that these are allusions to people of Smollett's acquaintance, Dr Smellie and Archibald Hamilton.[6] But what then of the Traveller's correspondents? Are they alone to have no coherence of conception or factual basis in our minds? Why should we not proceed on the expectation that as the outlines of the Traveller's journeys and circumstances mirror those of the author, so the pattern of his letter-writing to some degree mirrors that of his author, in such respects as choice of correspondent, continuity of subject-matter and so on? Are we to allow the Traveller to share Smollett's illnesses and his wife, but not his correspondents? This is not to fall into the literalist fallacy – for it is still not to suggest that the letters of the *Travels* were actually *sent* – but rather to suggest that they have distinct "imagined recipients" either at the level of the offered illusion or at the level of Smollett's working towards the text: when Smollett has his traveller write "Dear Sir" or "Dear Doctor," it seems unlikely that the author has no clearer conception of the imagined recipient of the letter than what those rather anonymous appellations confer. Rather it seems likely that their identities lie among

Smollett's friends, and it is possible that a fuller sense than we have yet recognized of their individuality, and even of their identity, lies buried in the *Travels*. Past reluctance to pursue this line of thought, however, would seem to have been as much due to a number of apparent paradoxes that open up before the investigator as to reaction against Seccombe's literalist oversimplifications.[7] Suggestions have certainly been advanced about the identity of the recipients of particular letters, but these have tended to be made in isolated forays rather than followed through within the framework of a consistent view of the imaginative status of the correspondence as a whole.[8] Moreover, while one commentator may be drawn to identify a named person as receiving a particular letter, another is happy to work with the literary concept of the "mock-correspondent."[9] The problem of illusion in the *Travels* – the extent to which the work presents itself as a self-contained fiction and the extent to which it implies a mirroring of a historical correspondence – may be considerably clarified through a closer attention to the structure of the correspondence and the variety of correspondents the Traveller addresses.[10]

The attempt to see separate lines of continuity being woven through the work, by tabulating the recipients of the Traveller's letters in an effort to arrive at the basis of the distinctions that the Traveller makes between his correspondents, is hampered by immediate difficulties. In particular, many commentators have regarded the Traveller's comment in Letter VIII as effectively putting discussion of the matter at all out of court:

> The truth is, I considered all the letters I have hitherto written on the subject of my travels, as written to your society in general, though they have been addressed to one individual of it; and if they contain any thing that can either amuse or inform, I desire that henceforth all I send may be freely perused by all the members. (VIII, 63)

The mention of the "members" of the recipient's "society" may simply mean the recipient's friends, relations and colleagues – the people he moves among – or it may mean a slightly more formal kind of society: Felsenstein annotates the remark "remember me to our friends at A——'s" (V, 41; XIV, 134) as "possibly the Anderston Club in Glasgow" (389), while in his own letters Smollett makes mention of his "Chelsea Club" and his "Brotherhood at the Swan," the latter possibly implying Smollett's membership of a Masonic Lodge.[11] Whatever is meant – and the idea of a club of some kind being in receipt of the Traveller's letters does enhance the effect of the quasi-scientific methodicality of many of the Traveller's letters – one quite reasonably concludes that what must follow in the writings of the Traveller is just that much less of a responsiveness (expressed through style, choice of subject-matter and social and cultural allusion) to the individuality of the recipient of any particular letter. The temptation, in fact, is to accept the passage quoted as an iron-clad authorial instruction for the reading of the *Travels* as text, and to downgrade the significance of the Traveller's being in correspon-

dence with more than one individual. The remark cannot be disregarded,
but it should also be recognized as a reflection of Smollett's attitude
towards his own letters from France rather than as a textual signal relating
narrowly to the *Travels* as text, as a personal letter of 1764 from Nice to
Dr William Hunter attests: "As I take it for granted you have seen my
Letter to Dr. Macaulay, I need not repeat what I have said to him with
respect to my Situation."[12] The idea in the *Travels* suggests more of a
declared programme than here in Smollett's correspondence, but the
frames of mind of author and persona are obviously closely akin. Moreover, there is certainly no evidence that Smollett stripped all habitual
distinctions from his own personal letters from the Continent: nor on the
strength of the passage from the *Travels* need it be assumed that the
Traveller does.

   The Traveller's correspondence contains a number of obvious inconsistencies in the handling of dates in relation to places visited, and these
have been frequently rehearsed.[13] Should, however, such inconsistencies
be regarded as evidence of a basic lack of organization, or as failings
within a scheme which in other respects aims at a measure of consistency?
There are features of the work that suggest that Smollett embodied a
more sophisticated organization of the correspondence in the *Travels*
than such inconsistencies and the apparent implication of Letter VIII
at first suggest, but these have received little if any attention. One
such feature concerns the dating and sequence of the letters. If Smollett
were not distinguishing between correspondents, the safest and simplest
way of proceeding would be to have the Traveller write his letters at
regularly distanced intervals, and to present them in a straightforward
chronological sequence. This, however, does not always happen. On
three occasions two letters are dated the same day: Letters VI and VII
(12 October, 1763); Letters XXI and XXII (10 November, 1764), and
Letters XXXIV and XXXVII (2 April, 1765). In addition there are
five distinct disruptions to the chronological sequence: Letter XV,
dated 3 January, 1764, does not appear between XII and XIII (dated 6
December, 1763 and 15 January, 1764) but between letters in fact dated
20 January and 2 May; Letter XXV, dated 1 January, 1765, does not
appear between XXIII and XXIV (dated 19 November, 1764 and 4
January, 1765) but between the letter dated 4 January and one dated 15
January. Three further letters are out of sequence in their dating (XXXV,
XXXVI and XXXVIII), the order running:

XXXII	Nice, 10 March, 1765
XXXIII	Nice, 30 March, 1765
XXXIV	Nice, 2 April, 1765
XXXV	Nice, 20 March, 1765
XXXVI	Nice, 23 March, 1765
XXXVII	Nice, 2 April, 1765
XXXVIII	Turin, 18 March, 1765
XXXIX	Aix en Provence, 10 May, 1765.

Editorial error on Smollett's part or compositorial error on that of the printer cannot be entirely ruled out as explanations of these anomalies, but until some such arguments are adduced, it seems reasonable to look for some constructive strategy in this ordering – or some residual reflection of the contingencies of an historical correspondence.

The letters also contain explicit cross-references and implicit internal allusions, and the apparently inconsistent nature of some of these has been seen as a symptom of a basic lack of organization in the work. Felsenstein, for example, examining modes of address in the openings of the letters, notes:

> In Letter XXII, addressed 'Dear Sir', he mentions two streams 'which I have described in a former letter', actually Letter XVI, specifically addressed 'Dear Doctor'. Again, in Letter XXV ('Dear Sir'), he refers his reader back to a 'former letter' (XXI, addressed 'Dear Doctor') in which he explains the *droits du port* at Nice and Monaco. (xxxvi, n. 4)

Were this to be accepted as an inconsistency, one should perhaps still look to set the occurrence of compatible cross-references against that of such faults. As it happens, there are grounds for at least querying the assumption that letters opening "Dear Doctor" and "Dear Sir" are always and necessarily written to "different correspondents."[14] This issue will be taken up below.

Bearing these problems in mind, how far can we move towards the tabulation of individual letters against particular recipients? In the first place, we are not asked to assume that the forty-one letters in the work represent all the letters that the Traveller sends. We know he writes others: there are, for example, the letters written in connection with the detention of his books by the customs, to which he refers (II, 12), sundry other letters in connection with his travelling arrangements, a letter written to Mr B—— at Geneva in May 1765 (XVIII, 157), and the implying of a previous letter to his correspondent of the moment in which he first mentioned the possibility of sending "the packet" (IV, 21). The letters we have, it seems, represent a selection from a larger pool of letters "sent" by the Traveller – although chosen in such a way as to maintain narrative continuity. However, only three of the letters are headed with any indication of the precise identity of the recipient: Letter VII is addressed to Mrs M——; Letter VIII is addressed to Mr M——; and Letter XXXVIII is addressed to "Dr. S—— at *Nice*." The collocation of Letters VII and VIII, the Traveller's remark to Mr M—— "I was favoured with yours at Paris" (VIII, 63) and the dating from Paris of the previous letter to Mrs M——, together lead readily to the conclusion that Mr and Mrs M—— are husband and wife, and that their letters reached the Traveller at the same time, by the same route – probably under the same cover. Letter XV is the only other letter addressed to a female correspondent, opening with the word "Madam,"

and the obvious association with Letter VII is borne out by the fulfilment
of a promise:

> I have a great many things to say of their military character,
> and their punctilios of honour, which last are equally absurd and
> pernicious; but as this letter has run to an unconscionable length,
> I shall defer them till another opportunity. (VII, 62)

> In your favour which I received by Mr. M——l, you remind me of
> my promise, to communicate the remarks I have still to make on the
> French nation. (XV, 135)

The remarks that follow are indeed on the topic of duelling ("their
military character, and their punctilios of honour"), and so there is no
problem in concluding that Letter XV, like Letter VII, is addressed to
Mrs M—— (see Figure, a).[15] It is tantalizing that Smollett should here
show a distinct willingness to maintain continuity, and indeed to do so by
leaping over the seven letters between VII and XV: he reserves a topic of
correspondence promised to an individual until he writes to that correspondent again – despite the comment in Letter VIII about writing to the
correspondent's society in general.

There is also little problem in assigning Letters I-VI: the Traveller tells
us in VIII that "all the letters I have hitherto written … have been
addressed to one individual." Letters I-VI open "Dear Sir" or "Sir";
Letter VII is explicitly addressed to Mrs M—— and so must be excluded
from the generalization, leaving I-VI being addressed to the same
individual (see Figure, b).[16] That recipient is clearly of some importance
amongst the Traveller's circle of friends, since from late June 1763 to
early October 1763 the Traveller appears to write of his travels only to
him.[17] He can self-evidently be distinguished from Mr M——, and I shall
refer to him as Mr Alpha.

Proceeding further necessitates coping with the problem of cross-
references between any of the six letters opening "Dear Doctor" and the
remaining letters that bear no indication of the addressee beyond opening
"Sir" or "Dear Sir." The problem, however, may well be no problem at
all: Letter XXXVIII, addressed to "Dr. S—— at *Nice*," in fact opens not
"Dear Doctor" but "Dear Sir," suggesting that some flexibility in the use
of forms of address is in evidence. In practice, commentators have also
regularly proposed medical men as the recipients of letters opening
"Dear Sir."[18] Smollett's habits in his own letters are extremely revealing
in this respect. While on the Continent, Smollett probably wrote to at
least six doctor-friends: Dr George Macaulay, Dr John Moore, Dr John
Armstrong, Dr William Hunter, Dr Alexander Reid and Dr Thomas
Harvie. At least one non-medical man, Charles Bell, also received a letter
– and probably there were a great many more correspondents during this
period, some of the profession, and some not.[19] But the bulk of the
surviving evidence suggests that doctors formed a considerable, if not the
largest, proportion of Smollett's correspondents. (Seccombe assumed

FIGURE

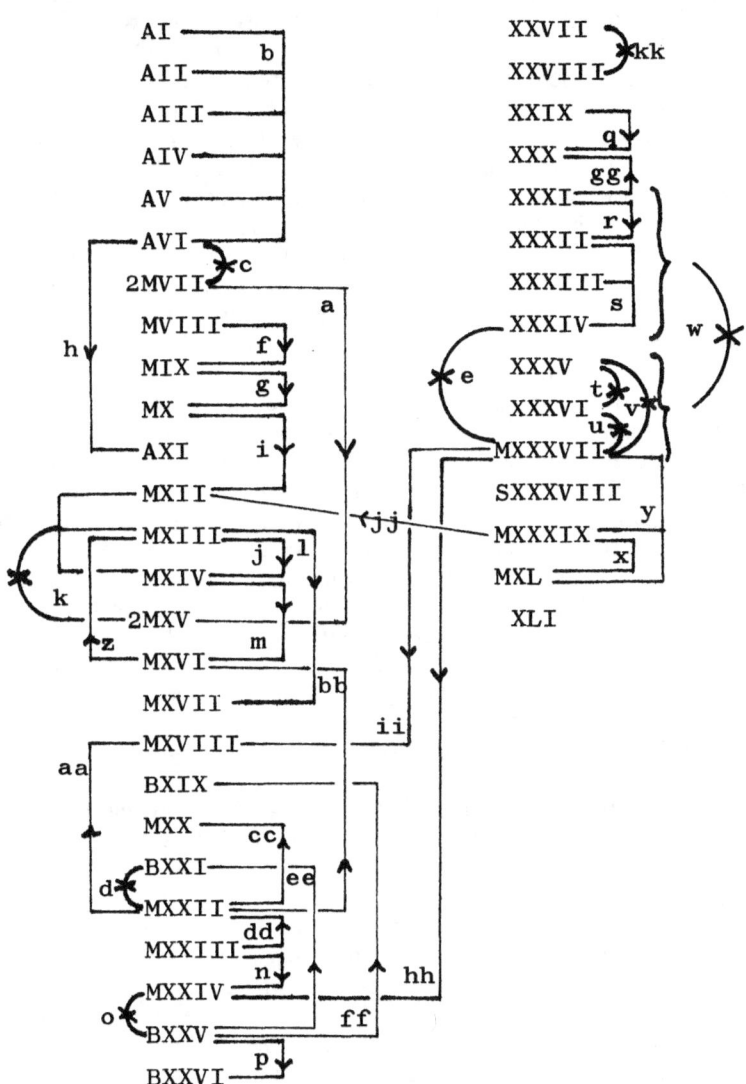

KEY TO FIGURE

A = Mr Alpha   M = Mr M——   S = Dr S——
B = Mr Beta   2M = Mrs M——

Straight lines with arrows indicate presence and direction of cross-reference.
Curved lines with crosses indicate separate recipients.
Notation a-z, aa-kk keys into discussion in text.

that the amount of time devoted to the Traveller's health was due to that fact.)[20] In consequence, the six letters in the *Travels* opening "Dear Doctor" (plus Letter XXXVIII) seem a curiously small proportion to be addressed to doctors. Could some of the letters opening "Sir" or "Dear Sir" also have doctors as their imagined recipients? Medical topics, despite the famous instance of Letter XI, are certainly not restricted to the letters opening "Dear Doctor." Of the fifteen surviving letters that Smollett wrote to Dr John Moore, he never once used the term "doctor" in opening, closing, or addressing those letters. Nor does he use the term in his one surviving letter to Reid. In the six letters written to William Hunter between 1762 and 1767 which survive, Smollett always refers, however, to Hunter as "Dear Doctor," though five out of the six times he opens the letter "Dear Sir" and reserves the term "Dear Doctor" for closing the letter. In the nine surviving letters to Dr Macaulay, only twice does Smollett fail to refer to Macaulay as "Dear Doctor," and on six occasions, as is the practice in the *Travels*, he uses the term to open the letter.[21] Clearly, Smollett had well-defined personal habits in addressing correspondents: some doctors he seems likely to have addressed as "Sir" (Moore and Reid), some he does indeed seem inclined to address as "Doctor" (Macaulay), and some he tends to address by both terms, often in the same letter, though giving prominence to "Sir" (William Hunter). It thus seems more than likely that doctors lurk as the imagined recipients of letters in the *Travels* opening "Dear Sir" or "Sir"; in consequence, a cross-reference between one letter opening "Dear Sir" and another opening "Dear Doctor" need not be regarded as in the least inconsistent. If this position is accepted, ways of reading the *Travels* are opened up considerably. The alternatives look most unlikely. Are we to assume that the Traveller writes only to one doctor and to one non-medical man (if that) apart from Mr M——?

Let us now return to the question of dating. We know that Letters VI and VII are addressed to correspondents of different sex: the letters to them are both dated 12 October, 1763, and we may well take this as a signal corroborating that the letters go to separate correspondents (see Figure, c). That being so, we may suggest that Letters XXI and XXII are similarly addressed to separate correspondents (see Figure, d), being both dated 10 November 1764, and similarly Letters XXIV and XXXVII, being both dated 2 April 1765 (see Figure, e). The Traveller not being in the dilemma of Pamela or Clarissa, letters to the same correspondent on the same day seems a most unlikely proposition, and to assume these relationships (or rather this lack of them) does not involve bringing in considerations about forms of address.

We can now turn to the matter of explicit cross-references, instances for the most part where the Traveller refers to his "next," "last," "former," or "subsequent" letter, or to continuing a subject at another opportunity. Interpreting what may be regarded as implicit internal allusion is far more problematic – and often ambiguous – and so has not been brought into play in what follows. Letter I merely promises a

continuation of the correspondence with Mr Alpha: "may serve to introduce observations of more consequence" (I, 8). Letter III ends "In my
next, I shall endeavour to satisfy you in the other articles you desire to
know" (III, 20), and this is fulfilled by Letter IV when the Traveller
announces "Meanwhile I must fulfil my promise in communicating the
observations I have had occasion to make upon this town and country"
(IV, 21). Letter IV closes with "I shall defer, till another occasion, what I
have further to say on the people of this place" (IV, 29), and that
occasion seems to occur in Letter V, with the link "But to return to the
people of Boulogne" (V, 31) and the subsequent analysis and discussion
of the classes of people in the town. All this goes to corroborate the
Traveller's assertion to Mr M—— about the recipient of Letters I-VI.
Letter VI ends with "The next letter you have from me will probably be
dated at Nismes, or Montpellier" (VI, 51). In fact, the next letters we see
the Traveller writing are from Paris and Lyons: here again, as with Letter
VII, is a willingness on Smollett's part to construct a thread of correspondence with one individual which loops over intervening letters: the
reference to "you" is a personal one to Mr Alpha, and not a general one
to his society. Letter IX is indeed from Montpellier (Letters VII and VIII
being explicitly assigned to Mrs and Mr M——), but there are reasons for
believing it is not the promised letter to Mr Alpha. Letter VIII ends:

> the enormous expence of living in this manner has determined me to
> set out in a day or two for Montpellier, although that place is a good
> way out of the road to Nice. My reasons for taking that route I shall
> communicate in my next. (VIII, 71)

Letter IX includes a forthright fulfilment: "My reasons for going to
Montpellier, which is out of the strait road to Nice, were these" (IX, 73).
Letter IX may thus also be seen as being addressed to Mr M—— (see
Figure, f). The same is true of Letter X, for whoever receives IX also
receives X. Letter IX ends with a promise to describe the Pont du Gard
and the antiquities of Nîmes, and this is indeed the subject into which the
Traveller plunges in Letter X (see Figure, g). Here the continuity is
interrupted: Letter X closes with "the next time you hear of me will be
from Nice" (X, 88), but Letter XI is again from Montpellier and so cannot
be addressed to the same recipient as Letter X. Letter XI, however,
is also the last letter from Montpellier, and the Traveller has promised
a letter to Mr Alpha from Nîmes or Montpellier way back in Letter VI.
In consequence, although Letter XI opens "Dear Doctor" and is wholly
concerned with medical matters, it may well be seen as a letter to Mr
Alpha (or perhaps we should call him Dr Alpha?). If we needed further
evidence that X and XI are written to separate correspondents, then
certainly their datings, 10 November and 12 November, seem too close
together (see Figure, h). Letter XI ends with a tentative promise which is
not taken up in XII, and indeed does not seem to be taken up in the
Travels again: "the physicians in this country ... often confound the
symptoms of [scurvy], with those of the venereal distemper. Perhaps I

may be more particular on this subject in a subsequent letter" (XI, 104). Letter XII is addressed from Nice, and with no evidence to suggest a wholly new correspondent, it may be seen as fulfilling the promise in X and constituting the resumption of correspondence with Mr M—— (see Figure, i). The distinct impression of Letters XII, XIII and XIV is that they form a group united by continuity of subject-matter; Letter XIII may be seen as linking with XIV in promising another letter from Nice "in good time" (see Figure, j), but most significant seems the evidence of the dating and placing of Letter XV. As we have seen, this letter is addressed to Mrs M——, and by its dating it should fall after Letter XII. The holding-back of Letter XV from its chronological place – on account of its demonstrably different correspondent and distinctiveness of topic – consolidates one's sense of the unity of Letters XII-XIV: there exists a continuity in that group which Smollett does not want to break (see Figure, k).

Letter XIII links forward with XVII by means of a comment in the middle of the letter. The Traveller is giving an account of the local administration of Nice, the city's senate, consuls, intendant, commandant and garrison, but promises "of all these particulars, I shall speak more fully on another occasion" (XIII, 121). In Letter XVII he does indeed do so:

> In the sixteenth century there was a college erected at Nice, by Emanuel Philibert, duke of Savoy, for granting degrees to students of law; and in the year one thousand six hundred and fourteen, Charles Emanuel I. instituted the senate of Nice; consisting of a president, and a certain number of senators, who are distinguished by their purple robes, and other ensigns of authority. (XVII, 151-2)

The account continues at some length, establishing the connection of the letters (see Figure, I). Felsenstein (417) further notes that Letter XIV points forward to Letter XVI and this relationship may also be accommodated (see Figure, m).

Letters XXIII and XXIV link together simply and closely (see Figure, n):

> What further I have to say of this climate and country, you shall have in my next; and then you will be released from a subject, which I am afraid has been but too circumstantially handled. (XXIII, 193)

> The constitution of this climate may be pretty well ascertained from the inclosed register of the weather, which I kept with all possible care and attention. (XXIV, 194)

The "release" of the correspondent may be a release from the topic of Nice, but it may also imply a temporary or lasting halt to this particular chain of correspondence. The reader is certainly released in one sense, for volume I ends with Letter XXIV – but more importantly, volume II begins with an instance of a-chronological sequence. Though, like XXIII and XXIV, Letter XXV begins with a mode of address involving the word "Sir," we must conclude that a different correspondent is being implied: apart from the subject-matter being totally distinct (the beginning of the account of the Italian journey), essentially it is absurd to imagine this letter being written and sent between Letters XXIII and XXIV (as the dating would require) to the very same correspondent and thus squeezing in between two letters on the topic of Nice, not to mention violating the relationship between XXIII and XXIV described above. Letter XXV is thus sent to a different correspondent from the one who receives Letters XXIII and XXIV (see Figure, o). In addition, the promise at the end of XXV to continue the description of Genoa is taken up in XXVI, and so at least the first two letters of the second volume can be seen as going to this new correspondent, whom I shall refer to as Mr Beta (see Figure, p). XXIX and XXX link together happily enough through the Traveller promising further remarks on Rome in his "next" (see Figure, q), as do XXXI and XXXII in the same way (see Figure, r).

At this point in the analysis we enter the most complex time-warp presented by the *Travels*: after Letter XXXIV, dated 2 April, we have letters dated 20 March (XXXV), 23 March (XXXVI) and 2 April again (XXXVII). The back-tracking suggests strongly that Letters XXXII-XXXIV are presented as a group: the author wishes to avoid breaking their continuity by introducing XXXV-XXXVII in their proper order (see Figure, s). Narrative continuity, however, is strictly maintained as the letters appear in the work: Letter XXXIV, dated 2 April, describes the Traveller's wet, dismal and disastrous journey to Florence; Letter XXXV, although dated nearly two weeks *previously*, carries on the story without a qualm: "The season being far advanced, and the weather growing boisterous, I made but a short stay at Florence" (XXXV, 304). Clearly Letters XXXIV and XXXV represent stages in the telling of the same story to two separate correspondents, one narration being well in advance of the other. Whether XXXV-XXXVII in turn constitute a group is complicated by the closeness of dating of XXXV and XXXVI (20 and 23 March), and the fact that XXXVI begins with an allusion to a question received from the correspondent, a query unlikely to have been received in a leisurely-paced, long-term correspondence in the interval since the Traveller's last letter on 20 March. Again, XXXVI does not tie up happily with XXXVII: it ends with a promise on "another occasion" to talk about the future of France and her relationship with Britain, and this is not fulfilled in XXXVII. There is then the possibility that Smollett is organizing the correspondence here to suggest that XXXV, XXXVI and XXXVII are all written to separate correspondents, none of whom is in turn the correspondent to whom Letters XXXI-XXXIV are written (see Figure, t-w).

In the light of Felsenstein's discussion (466-7), Letter XXXVIII has to be regarded as *sui generis*, probably an adaptation of a letter received by Smollett ("Dr. S—— at *Nice*"). It may thus be significant that no explicit cross-references appear to involve this letter.[22] It is the most a-chronologically placed letter, and Felsenstein's view of its dating as "suspicious" is well founded. The letter has a sort of promise at the end, or at least an awareness that an account of Turin is called for – but such is the strangeness of this letter that the promise is virtually retracted in the giving – and it is certainly not fulfilled.

Although XXXIX and XL respectively open "Dear Sir" and "Dear Doctor," they are clearly linked: the Traveller declares "In my next, I shall say something further of these waters" (XXXIX, 332), and in XL he does indeed do so (see Figure, x). Moreover, XXXIX and XL deal with those towns of which the Traveller had promised a description way back in Letter XXXVII (Antibes, Toulon, Marseilles, Aix, Avignon and Orange), and so the three letters may be linked (see Figure, y).

The few remaining discernible parts of the jig-saw take the form of explicit references to previous letters. Felsenstein (420) notes that Letter XVI links back with XIII (see Figure, z) in its discussion of a Roman bath. Letter XXII looks over its shoulder on no less than three occasions. The Traveller speaks of "the fishing, which I have already described" (XXII, 184) – an operation performed in XVIII (see Figure, aa); of two streams "which I have described in a former Letter" (XXII, 185) – the letter, as we have seen Felsenstein note, being XVI (see Figure, bb); and also remarks on *polenta* meal and his comments in a "former letter" (XXII, 186), taking us back to Letter XX (see Figure, cc). The recipient of Letters XVI, XVIII, XX and XXII can thus be isolated with some confidence. Letter XXIII simply throws us back to XXII: "In my last, I gave you a succinct account of the silk-worm" (XXIII, 190; see Figure, dd).

Felsenstein has noted (433) that Letter XXV refers back to XXI (see Figure, ee), and also (434) that it throws us back to Letter XIX ("those excellent apples called *pomi carli*, which I have mentioned in a former letter"). Letter XIX thus becomes the first letter in the work to be addressed to the correspondent Mr Beta (see Figure, ff).

As Letter XXIX links forward with XXX, so XXXI links back with XXX, Letter XXXI opening "In my last I gave you my opinion freely of the modern palaces of Italy" (XXXI, 263) – opinion proffered in Letter XXX (see Figure, gg). This link means that one can now posit a run of letters to the same correspondent from XXIX through XXXIV. The change to a different correspondent in Letter XXXV can be corroborated by the comment in that letter, "Thus have I given you a circumstantial detail of my Italian expedition" (XXXV, 308): now Letter XXXV is dated 20 March, and Letters XXXIII and XXXIV, though having dates later than 20 March, "continue" to give details of the Italian expedition. As at the beginning of volume II, we clearly have two overlapping chains of correspondence here, with letters being "selected" from each chain to sustain narrative continuity for the reader of the *Travels* as text.

Letter XXXVII makes two semi-explicit references back which I find strong enough to pursue, because they indicate a change of attitude from a previous position about which the correspondent has been informed in the past. It begins, "As I have *now* passed a second winter at Nice, I think myself qualified to make some *further remarks* on this climate" (XXXVII, 315; my italics): the use of the term "further remarks" suggests that the correspondent has already received one set of remarks, and that takes us back to the observations on climate in Letter XXIV (see Figure, hh). Similarly, the Traveller comments:

I *now* find, by experience, it is great folly to buy furniture, unless one is resolved to settle here for some years. The Nissards assured me, with great confidence, that I should always be able to sell it for a very little loss; whereas I find myself obliged to part with it for about one-third of what it cost. (XXXVII, 316-7; my italics)

This takes us back to Letter XVIII and the Traveller's first full exploration of his thinking on the subject of furniture (see Figure, ii).

Letter XXXIX has perhaps the most striking retrospective reference, because it throws the reader back the furthest, to Letter XII in fact, with the words "the mountain of Esterelles, which in one of my former letters I described" (XXXIX, 327; see Figure, jj).

Letter XXVIII also gives illumination by a reference back, though to a letter received from the correspondent rather than a previous letter of the Traveller's: "Your entertaining letter of the fifth of last month. ... You insist upon my being more particular in my remarks on what I saw at Florence, and I shall obey the injunction" (XXVIII, 233). Clearly, the Traveller has given the recipient of Letter XXVIII some comments on Florence already; the Traveller has been asked to be "more particular" in these. But Letter XXVII, dated 28 January, is involved in completing the account of Pisa, before then taking the correspondent on to Florence: if the Traveller is telling an orderly tale, this is the first time the recipient of XXVII has been introduced to the subject of Florence – and yet the Traveller has certainly sent the recipient of Letter XXVIII some comments on just that subject prior to 5 January. We can thus deduce that Letters XXVII and XXVIII are written to separate correspondents (see Figure, kk).

I have now dealt with all the cross-references which I have found to be explicit. Gaps in the total pattern still remain, although these could be plugged in a more or less impressionistic way. It is certainly not unreasonable to see continuity between Letters XXVI and XXVII in the arrival at and discussion of Pisa; nor is it unreasonable to see continuity between XL and XLI on the grounds of arrival at and subsequent discussion of Lyons. XXVIII and XXIX are neither explicitly linked or separated: the comment at the beginning of XXIX, "Having seen all the curiosities of Florence" (XXIX, 242), fits happily enough with XXVIII. But the danger of proceeding further, beyond the most evident implications of the dating-scheme and the most explicit cross-references, lies in the fact, as we have seen, that the achievement of the *Travels* in one respect consists in Smollett's providing a smooth narrative continuity on the surface for the reader of the *Travels* as text, while at the same time maintaining, in the correspondence to individual correspondents, a pattern in counterpoint. The moment one assumes that two adjacent letters are written to the same correspondent, merely on the ground of the flow of the topic from one letter to the next – and without some more explicit link – one is in danger of mistaking the surface narrative continuity of the work for the deep structure of relationships between letters as assembled in the Figure. After all, most of the contiguous letters in the *Travels* "fit" : that is one of the reasons why the perception and tracing of the deeper structures of relationship than those represented merely by the sequence of the letters has been delayed. Despite the temptation to force the argument on through less explicit links towards the goal of a pattern of assignment of all the letters to correspondents, it is better to rest with conclusions from those explicit links that have been presented : given the history of the discussion of the *Travels*, it is perhaps as important to establish the principle of the existence of such structures of relationship as I have been pursuing as to insist upon every detail of a particular, complete pattern of assignments.

Extrapolation from the explicit links, as well as the implications of dating which have been considered, results in a hypothetical assigning of thirty of the forty-one letters, including the run I-XXVI. Only one letter, Letter XLI, the last in the work, has eluded being placed in some relationship with its fellows. Letter XXXVIII presents a unique problem, and the failure to find an explicit link with another letter in this case must be regarded as a positive piece of evidence about its unique status. There may well have been pieces of the jig-saw that have fallen off my table – and others may find them – but at the very least the trend of the evidence is extremely suggestive. Over forty separate pieces of evidence combine to place all but one of the letters within a coherent pattern of correspondence with a number of individuals. In the event there has been no need to weigh evidence of consistency in organization against evidence of inconsistency: though the pattern is not complete as here presented, inconsistency in the form of a letter assigned to Mr M——, say, having a cross-reference linking it to a letter elsewhere assigned to Mr Alpha, or any other such combination, has yet to appear. Indeed, instead of inconsistency, some parts of the pattern as shown in the Figure reveal a high degree of corroboration. The results become the more striking when one compares them with those obtainable from a similar work such as Samuel Sharp's *Letters from Italy*. Sharp gives a circumstantial account of the authenticity of his letters, of having gathered them up for publication from the correspondents to whom they were sent.[23] But Sharp is unsystematic in his dating of the letters (which only begins to show signs of coherence in the last third of his work), and despite an occasional attempt to create an illusion of many being in receipt of his letters,[24] the dozen or so cross-references that do occur (most of them backwards, because he has omitted to mention something first time around) go to construct nothing in particular. "I write miscellaneously, as my thoughts occur," remarks Sharp at one point, and we have no reason to doubt him.[25] Plainly Baretti was right to speak with some contempt of Sharp's "imaginary correspondent."[26]

How do these findings affect one's view of the *Travels*? Those who would read the work as an exercise in artifice, in synthesis, in the fictive, may now find themselves dealing with a far more sophisticated text than previously believed. The iconic qualities of the text as autonomous entity allow one to view the explicit cross-references examined as effectively constituting necessary relationships between the letters, in spite of the illusion that the letters included have been "selected" from a larger pool which, if we could examine it, might provide equally qualified candidates to those isolated as participants in the process of cross-reference. However, inside the boundaries of the text, such candidates are as inscrutable as Lady Macbeth's children. The reader of the *Travels* as fiction may now find it lit by the presence of distinct imagined recipients of the letters, and a dynamic concern with the theme of friendship occupying the foreground. This concern expresses itself through the growth of the Traveller's correspondents in number from just Mr Alpha at the beginning to a plethora by the end, a movement which both reflects and is in part the cause of the Traveller's long transition from a situation of lonely isolation to renewed awareness of the multitude of his friends to whom he at last, in confidence and trust, returns. But the analysis has also increased the likelihood of a close relationship existing between the letters of the *Travels* and Smollett's own historical correspondence. Mr M——, Mr Alpha and Mr Beta all receive letters opening "Dear Doctor." To find at least three doctors as correspondents in the *Travels* is to move the whole work nearer to what we know and can reasonably infer of Smollett's own correspondence. We may begin to look at the *Travels* as an idealized version of Smollett's correspondence in which he very possibly preserves in his own mind the identity and individuality of the original correspondents: we know after all that Mr Alpha, in receipt of Letter XI, is not Dr William Hunter, since he is mentioned in the third person in that letter (XI, 89); and similarly that Mr Beta in receipt of Letter XXV is not Dr Armstrong (XXV, 202). Beyond this, the essential problem is one of deciding whether the disposition of the dating of the letters and the cross-references is the product of Smollett the writer organizing his text, or reflects an actual body of correspondence sent by Smollett (as certain features of Letter XXVIII suggest).[27] If the decision were to go to the latter, then we would be some way towards viewing the *Travels*, whatever else it is, as a distinct echo of a lost body of correspondence, and towards being able to relate the "imagined recipients" in the *Travels* to actual historical personages. This, however, is yet in the distance. Relationships between letters which can be conceived as necessary within the text may not be so once one steps outside of it: the lost pool of letters from which they are "selected" ceases to be a facet of the illusion and becomes actual, though lost. Though the very obscurity of the structure elicited makes it unlikely that it could be the result of fictional contrivance (could Smollett really have expected his readers to carry all those connections in their head?), at the same time such inconsistencies which cannot be argued away – for example the addressing of letters from Nice when the Traveller must be in Italy – suggest a failure of the fictive rather than any conceivable reflection of mistakes made in an actual correspondence and carried through into the *Travels*.[28] If we regret not being able, at this stage, to break through the barrier into Smollett's own correspondence with an invulnerable certainty, we can at least console ourselves with a refreshing sense of Smollett's imaginative organization of the *Travels* – an organization so elaborated that it leads us to the conclusion that it must *somehow* reflect the intricacies of an actual correspondence – and with a firmer sense of the probabilities of the relationship between the Traveller and his letters, and Tobias Smollett, pen in hand, writing to his old friends across the sea.

PETER MILES
Saint David's University College, Lampeter

NOTES

1. Tobias Smollett, *Travels through France and Italy*, ed. Frank Felsenstein (London: Oxford U.P., 1979). All page references in the text are to this edition; references in large Roman numerals are to the individual letters of the *Travels*.
2. Thomas Seccombe, "Introduction," in *Travels through France and Italy*, ed. Seccombe, The World's Classics, 90 (London: Oxford U.P., 1907), p.xiii. For an earlier article by Seccombe, see n.7 below.
3. *The Letters of Tobias Smollett*, ed. Lewis M. Knapp (London: Oxford U.P., 1970), pp.125-6. Hester Lynch Piozzi was another travel-writer who spoke of "throwing" her thoughts into letters: see George M. Kahrl, *Tobias Smollett, Traveler-Novelist* (Chicago: U. of Chicago Press, 1945), p.104.
4. John F. Sena has proposed this persona as the splenetic or melancholy man; Robert Spector has stressed his public spirit and patriotism, and Scott B. Rice has seen the persona as that of the Juvenalian satirist coloured by the accentuated roles and preoccupations of the physician and valetudinarian. See: Sena, "Smollett's Persona and the Melancholic Traveler," *Eighteenth-Century Studies*, 1 (1968), 353-69; Spector, "Smollett's Traveler," in *Tobias Smollett: Bicentennial Essays Presented to Lewis M. Knapp*, ed. G.S. Rousseau and P.G. Boucé (New York: Oxford U.P., 1971), pp.231-46; Rice, "The Satiric Persona of Smollett's *Travels*," *Studies in Scottish Literature*, 10 (1972), 33-47; Rice, "Smollett's Seventh Travel Letter and the Design of Formal Verse Satire," *Studies in English Literature* (Rice University), 16 (1976), 491-503.
5. Lewis Melville, *The Life and Letters of Tobias Smollett* (London: Faber and Gwyer, 1926), pp.191-213. Melville here deals with the period of Smollett's travels, mixing actual letters by Smollett with extracts from the *Travels*.
6. For detail of these identifications, see Felsenstein, pp.374; 378; 401-2; 403; 471; 389-90.
7. Robert Anderson, who knew one of Smollett's correspondents, Dr John Armstrong, shrewdly remarked that the *Travels* was written "in the form of letters to his friends in England": "Life of Smollett," in *The Miscellaneous Works of Tobias Smollett, M.D.*, ed. Anderson, 6th ed. (Edinburgh, 1820), I, 84. Seccombe denied any fictive element to the *Travels*: "This was not, as in the case of 'Humphrey Clinker' [sic], a mere literary form. The letters were actually written (at the places and dates prefixed to each epistle) and sent to personal friends for their private edification and amusement. ... most of his

epistles were evidently written to his well-known friends in the medical profession, such as Drs Armstrong, Macaulay, William Hunter and John Moore" : "Smelfungus Goes South," *Cornhill Magazine*, 11 (1901), 195. Kahrl, p. 105, declares that Smollett's personal letters were not the basis of the travel-letters, and that the more specific addressing of some of the letters to individuals of Smollett's acquaintance was designed to single out in the published work "letters whose contents might be of special interest to the recipients." Martz, in rejecting Seccombe's view, sees "two separate and artificial series of letters on Nice and Italy," as well as finding "authentic evidence of actual correspondence" : Louis L. Martz, *The Later Career of Tobias Smollett*, Yale Studies in English, Vol. 97 (London and New Haven: Yale U.P., 1942), pp. 68-73. Felsenstein, p. xl, speculates that drafts of "many of the Letters were originally dispatched to his friends in England as newsletters" and that they "are synthetic only in that Smollett has written them not simply for his personal friends, but with the view to publish."

8. Felsenstein, p. 393, for example, takes issue with Kahrl and proposes Mrs George Macaulay rather than Mrs John Moore as the recipient of Letter VII; he also argues persuasively, pp. 466-7, that Letter XXXVIII is a version of a letter received rather than sent by Smollett, and argues that the novelist did not himself visit Turin in March 1765.

9. Rice, "Smollett's Seventh Travel-Letter," 496-7.

10. Most attention directed towards the epistolary form of the *Travels* has focused on the relationship of Smollett's work to the convention of the use of familiar letters in travel-writing: see, for example, Kahrl, pp. 101-8.

11. *Letters*, pp. 33; 118n.

12. *Letters*, p. 121.

13. These include the fact that the Traveller refers in a letter from Nice to an incident seen in Florence before he has in fact visited the latter city; also, that Letters XIX-XXII are all dated from Nice in October and November 1764, when the Traveller describes himself as having been in Italy. See Martz, pp. 69-70; Kahrl, pp. 104-5; and Felsenstein, p. xxxvi. Sena, 365, repeats Kahrl's error that the Traveller refers to a "murder" he has seen rather than a "murderer." Kahrl's view that the dating of Letter XXXV (about Italy) four months after the writer's return from that country constitutes an inconsistency is hardly valid.

14. Felsenstein, p. xxxvi.

15. Felsenstein, p. 418, accepts the linking together of these letters.

16. Melville, p. 196, assumes that Letter I is written to Dr Armstrong; Seccombe, "Introduction," p. xxvi, assumes Letter V is written to Dr Moore. One of them, at least, must be wrong.

17. The tenses used in the opening of Letter VII to Mrs M—— might lead one to think that a correspondence between the Traveller and Mrs M—— has already been under way: "I shall be much pleased if the remarks I have made on the characters of the French people, can afford you the satisfaction you require" (VII, 52). The Traveller, however, is probably referring to the discursive observations which he has already written, and upon which he is now drawing in writing to Mrs M——: the "remarks" are thus those that follow in the letter. Smollett probably worked in the same way as the Traveller, writing his observations on the spot, drawing on them in writing to his friends, and then, at some point, writing the travel-letters from the same observations, but with an awareness of his own actual correspondence and correspondents informing that process.

18. See, for example, n. 16 above; Kahrl, p. 105, also offers Dr Moore as the recipient of Letter VIII ("Dear Sir") and Felsenstein, p. 393, offers Dr Macaulay as the recipient of Letter VI (also "Dear Sir").

19. Three letters to Hunter and one to Reid survive from Smollett's stay on the Continent (*Letters*, pp. 115-24). A letter in farewell to Hunter includes a promise to write to Macaulay from Boulogne (*Letters*, p. 121). A reference in the *Travels* seems to imply receipt of a letter from Armstrong (XXV, p. 202). A letter to Moore survives announcing Smollett's return (*Letters*, p. 124), while Knapp records the evidence for

letters to Harvie and Bell (*Letters*, p.86n). Smollett received a letter from Samuel Derrick, another travel-writer, while at Nice in 1764; Tobias Smollett, *The Expedition of Humphry Clinker*, ed. Lewis M. Knapp (London: Oxford U.P., 1966), p.356.

20. Seccombe, "Smelfungus Goes South," 195.
21. Where necessary, I have accepted Knapp's assignment of letters to correspondents in the *Letters*.
22. See n.8 above.
23. Samuel Sharp, *Letters from Italy ... In the Years 1765, and 1766* (London, 1766; 2nd ed., 1767), sig. A2.
24. "After an absence of some months I am persuaded you will be pleased to hear from your old friend and acquaintance; and therefore, I shall not surfeit you with nauseous apologies for the trouble I give you. I take it for granted Mr M—— has communicated some part of my correspondence, as he tells me you shuddered at our passage over the *Alps*"; Sharp, p.67.
25. Sharp, p.145.
26. Joseph Baretti, *An Account of the Manners and Customs of Italy* (London, 1768), p.18.
27. The opening of Letter XXVIII may be read as referring very specifically to Smollett's involvement (or lack of it) in Bute's political schemings at home and the silk-weavers' riots of early 1765 (alleged by opponents to have been instigated by Bute). The specificity of reference to be understood makes this one of the rare moments in the *Travels* where Smollett appears in his own person rather than under the guise of the Traveller. For an account of Smollett's changing attitude towards Bute through the 1760s see my "Bibliography and Insanity: Smollett and the Mad-Business," *The Library*, 5th Ser., 31 (Sept., 1976), 205-22.
28. The surviving letters to Dr Hunter contain some material that is echoed in the *Travels*: Martz, p.68, sees it appearing in Letters XI, XII, XIII and XXI. If this fact discomposed earlier commentators, since two of the travel-letters open "Dear Sir" and two open "Dear Doctor," my hypothesis provides no clear solution, finding *three* different correspondents in receipt of the relevant letters in the *Travels*. However, the hypothesis also demands that the Traveller should write of the same episodes to different correspondents on separate occasions: if this procedure mimics Smollett's practice, the fact that the letters to Hunter which we do have fail to fall as a group into those assigned to Mr Alpha, Mr Beta, or Mr M—— neither confirms nor undermines the possibility of a close relationship between the correspondence in the *Travels* and Smollett's own.

"Terra Incognita" – An Image of the City in English Literature, 1820-1855*

The first half of the nineteenth century saw the transformation of England from an agrarian to an industrial, and from a rural to an urban society. During these fifty years, London's numbers grew from just over a million to nearly three million; in the 1820s alone, half a dozen large English cities increased their population by fifty per cent. This rapid and unprecedented change involved massive social dislocation: since cities were so unhealthy that the increase in the indigenous population was minimal, their growth was mainly the result of the migration of millions of persons from country to town. But also there was dislocation in another sense as society tried to understand the institutions, relations and places of the new England. The city was the *locus principus* of these changes, the centre of economic activity and of social development and also where the future shape of England was being determined and made manifest. If one were to come to understand the forces remaking England, one first must understand the city.

This was no small enterprise. For, as we shall see, the new cities and London were becoming environments literally and conceptually alien to the articulate and governing classes. Paradoxically, the more it was recognized that knowledge about the city was necessary, the more that knowledge seemed impossible to obtain. Nevertheless, attempts were made, and the city transformed into an object of study. This essay will investigate the ways in which writers and social critics in the early Victorian period went about doing this, by focussing upon an image of the city that appears frequently in their writings – the city as unknown land, "*terra incognita*." Indeed, this became the dominant image of the city, one which continued in common use well after the middle of the century, and even into the next. By investigating this image we can move towards a deeper understanding of the Victorian experience of urbanization and its role in the contemporary literary imagination.

The point at which I will begin, however, is at the close of the eighteenth century, just before the image gained common currency, with a consideration of a pertinent remark about London made by Dr Johnson. This will make it easier to gauge how great a change did occur in the way people thought about, looked at, and wrote of the city in the years immediately afterwards.

*I would like to thank the American Council of Learned Societies for generous support which allowed me to complete the research for this essay.

I

Towards the end of his life, on 12 April 1783, Dr Johnson held forth with
Boswell and another friend about the great metropolis. Boswell later
wrote this account of the conversation:

> He talked today a good deal of the wonderful extent and variety
> of London, and observed, that men of curious enquiry might see in it
> such modes of life as very few could even imagine. He in particular
> recommended to us to *explore Wapping*, which we resolved to do.[1]
> [Boswell's italics]

This remark, simple enough as it seems, might stand as a perfect example
of common eighteenth-century attitudes toward the city. For Johnson, as
for most of his contemporaries, it is axiomatic that the most natural and
proper object of man's study is man. It is equally obvious that in London –
unsurpassable in its "wonderful extent and variety" – the most diverse
human types are to be found. Clearly, then, students of human nature will
resort to the great city as a matter of course. That London contains "such
modes of life as very few could even imagine" is for Johnson and his two
auditors a highly interesting and wholly satisfactory state of affairs.
Wapping in particular, then a poor waterfront district inhabited chiefly
by dock hands, casual labourers, sailors of all nationalities and petty
criminals, would be well worth exploring.

Indeed, some years later, after Johnson died, Boswell and his friend
made the recommended journey. This is Boswell's report of it:

> We accordingly carried our scheme in execution, in October, 1792;
> but whether from that uniformity which has in modern times in a
> great degree spread throughout every part of the Metropolis, or
> want of sufficient exertion, we were disappointed.[2]

The city, Boswell notes, has become too monotonous, its various districts
too much alike – it is possible, of course, that he had become too lazy to
explore it properly. What is noteworthy is his disappointment at the lack
of variety in London life in the modern age. For Boswell, it has not
interest enough; it has grown dull.

How great a contrast is provided by the following account of another
journey of exploration in London, made some sixty years later. The
voyager was Charles John Chetwynd Talbot, Viscount Ingestre (later
19th Earl of Shrewsbury), who in his early twenties wrote an account of
his "discovery" of such modes of life in London as very few could even
imagine; but he did so in a very different spirit from that in which Johnson
made his recommendation, and in which Boswell took it up. What
Ingestre found were unimaginable modes of life – in fact, at first he could
hardly even believe the evidence of his eyes:

> I have seen so many different people, and their ways of living, in London, that I hardly know how to describe them to you, or where to begin. It was perfectly wonderful to me where the great mass of the people came from. ... Now for an attempt to describe to you what I have seen. ... The first place I went into was in Church-lane, a place so filthy that the stench is perfectly overpowering in the street itself; how much more so you can imagine on entering a small room, with about twenty-five or thirty people in it, most of them naked, and strangers to one another ... squalid, naked children, crying for food, and men reeling about drunk, and women in the same state of beastly intoxication. I literally saw, in many of these places, the vermin crawling about in myriads. ... [I]ndeed, they were really more like beasts than human creatures.[3]

Ingestre went on, describing in a similar manner more of what he had seen, all involving physical squalor and moral degradation. But he suspected that his readers would accuse him of exaggeration, when, in fact, probably he had not done full justice to these awful scenes. He advised anyone who doubted him to perform the same journey and gain ocular proof of his veracity.

The result of this journey through the city was obviously not disappointment, but horror and shock, and also in this case a thorough change of heart. Ingestre's explorations turned him into a social activist, and, already, as he wrote these remarks he was President of the new Society for Improving the Dwellings of the Working Class. His experience in London, unlike Boswell's, was at least not disappointingly dull.

It is worth emphasizing the pointed contrast between the attitudes towards the city and city life evident in Dr Johnson's remarks and in Ingestre's. Where Johnson had seen in the variety and extent of London cause for wonder, Ingestre saw cause for consternation, even terror. The diverse modes of life which Johnson had seen as a school for the study of human nature, Ingestre saw as horrifying examples of human extremity. To explore the city, for Johnson, had been to set out on a pleasant and instructive journey, not unlike a humble domestic version of the Continental Grand Tour; for Ingestre, to journey into the mazes and labyrinths of London was to enter a dark, uncharted region of danger and depravity. Ingestre had encountered the *terra incognita* of the modern city.

London, to be sure, like any great city, always had been a place of great contrasts. But the contrasts once were visible and expected: now they were hidden and unknown. A working man wrote:

> A casual observer, walking through the principal streets of London ... beholding everywhere the appearance of wealth in exhaustless abundance, might be led to imagine that all things were prosperous here. But let him go into the back streets and courts, and ascend, and descend to the homes of the operative, who supply the shops

with all those things which decorate their windows, and there he will find pictures as dark as the others are brilliant.[4]

It was as if everywhere in London the elegant and attractive surface one saw was but a thin, deceptive veneer that only barely hid the seething, malignant and perhaps uncontrollable growths beneath. In even the most attractive neighbourhoods such awful contrasts lurked just out of sight:

> The most aristocratic parishes ... have a background of wretchedness, and are too often so many screens for misery which would shock the mind and make men avert their gaze, could they indeed see them as they really are. ... Regent Street attracts the eye! Westminster, at once the seat of a palace and a plague spot; senators declaim, where sewers poison; theology holds her councils, where thieves learn their trade; and Europe's grandest hall is flanked by England's foulest grave-yard.[5]

Comparisons like this for centuries had been fodder for the homilist's platitudes: the contrasts between wealth and poverty and virtue and vice illustrated man's moral strengths and weaknesses, and the cautious student might profit from their study. Now, however, they revealed to the sensitive urban investigator the utter dislocation of the social structure in towns and cities, and symbolized the wide, perhaps unbridgeable gulf that separated the world of light from the *terra incognita*.

II

"Terra incognita" – the phrase and others like it occurred constantly in urban description throughout the first five decades of the nineteenth century. Dr Johnson's casual metaphor of exploration is revived in this image, but as an activity analogous to the exploration of the world's darkest, most dangerous regions – Africa, South America, the South Seas, or even the cold Arctic wastes. The image was familiar enough from travel literature, which was extremely popular throughout the eighteenth and nineteenth centuries. From the early seventeenth century, the phrase, or just the simple abbreviation *t.i.*, had been a standard mapmaker's tag, a shorthand abbreviation for those vast, uncharted regions as yet unpenetrated by voyages of exploration.[6]

Towards the end of the eighteenth century, the formation of the African Association (1788) and the increasingly insistent agitation against the slave trade focussed public attention more exclusively upon the exploration of the African interior: works like Mungo Park's *Travels in the Interior Districts of Africa* (1799), which went through eight editions by 1850, were immensely popular and generated considerable excitement about the exploration of these lands. What characterized all of these works was, in the first instance, what Park called the "passionate desire to examine into the productions of a country so little known."

The goal of discovery, then, was not only to find the place itself, but to examine the culture of its inhabitants. Park continues, in language which recalls Dr Johnson on London, that he was driven "to become experimentally acquainted with the modes of life, and character of the natives."[7] And what Park and the others did discover were strange modes of life indeed: native societies with alien, barbaric customs, prone to violence, savagery and moral depravity. It was as if the dark, mysterious and dangerous geography somehow produced the darker moral qualities in the inhabitants; in the words of one of Park's companions, there was a *"moral* geography" : "that physical geography gives rise to habits, which often determine national character, must be allowed by every person, who is a diligent observer of mankind."[8] The passion for physical discovery, and that for moral investigation, became as one. As a writer in the *Quarterly Review* wrote of a new work of African exploration in 1825:

> The importance of the information procured by our enterprizing travellers is not merely confined to geographical discovery, in which, however, a vast blank has been filled up, and a great jumble and dislocation of names on our maps rectified, – it is equally, perhaps more, important in the view which it gives us of the state of society and the moral condition of large masses of people, congregated in the central parts of Africa, and shut out, as it were, from the rest of the world, on one side by a frightful desert, and on the other by a range of lofty mountains, inhabited by uncivilized beings, of whom little or nothing is yet known.[9]

It was the imagery and language of geographical exploration, and the attendant atmosphere of mystery, wonder and fear, that writers about the city appropriated to suggest the mixture of feelings that the labyrinthine inner city districts inspired in those who penetrated them. And yet, paradoxically – though to be sure some writers were aware of the paradox – this was a journey not outwards to some distant foreign place, but inwards to explore the city that the adventurers and their readers inhabited and walked through, perhaps, every day of their lives. And, it is worth noting, the inward journey was, like the outward, moral as well as physical, involving the discovery not only of strange territories but also of their strange and frightening inhabitants.

One of the earliest uses of the phrase *terra incognita* for the city is in De Quincey's *Confessions of an English Opium-Eater*, published first in the *London Magazine*, in September and October, 1821, and it is worth devoting some attention to De Quincey's use of the image. The opening section of the *Confessions*, entitled "Preliminary Essay," is devoted mainly to an account of De Quincey's experiences in London at the age of seventeen during the winter of 1802-3, after he had run away from school and home the previous summer. Almost penniless, De Quincey spent many weeks in a state of near starvation, and slept either in the streets or in a rundown house occupied intermittently by a disreputable attorney. His only regular companions were a young servant girl in the lawyer's house and a fifteen year old prostitute named Ann, with whom he fell deeply (and apparently chastely) in love – neither of whom he saw again after that winter. Shortly afterwards, De Quincey was reconciled to his family and went off to Oxford. But in 1804, during a college vacation, he returned to London and there first took laudanum as a cure for toothache, upon the recommendation of a friend accidentally encountered in Oxford Street.

Once he had begun using opium, De Quincey writes, his dependence on the drug in the next few years was closely bound to his earlier experiences in the city. Usually he took it in London on Tuesday and Saturday nights to augment his enjoyment when he attended the opera, but also because Saturday nights were payday and the Sabbath eve, the most festive time for London's poor. In a trance he would wander the scenes of his own privations, but now in contrast he would be happy through vicarious participation in the joy and activity of ordinary working folk. Or, if times were hard, he would share their deprivations, and then console himself with opium. Some of these rambles, he concludes, went on for

> great distances: for an opium-eater is too happy to observe the motion of time. And sometimes in my attempts to steer homewards, upon nautical principles, by fixing my eye on the pole-star, and seeking amphibiously for a north-west passage, instead of circum-navigating all the capes and headlands I had doubled in my outward voyage, I came suddenly upon such knotty problems of alleys, such enigmatical entries, and such sphinx's riddles of streets without thoroughfares, as must, I conceive, baffle the audacity of porters, and confound the intellects of hackney-coachmen. I could almost have believed at times, that I must be the first discoverer of some of these *terrae incognitae*, and doubted, whether they had yet been laid down in the modern charts of London.

De Quincey's use of language often is extravagant, and he allows the metaphor of discovery and voyage to elaborate itself in what may appear to be a playful manner. But the end of the passage is more problematic:

> For all this, however, I paid a heavy price in distant years, when the human face tyrannized over my dreams, and the perplexities of my steps in London came back and haunted my sleep with the feeling of perplexities moral or intellectual, that brought confusion to the reason, or anguish and remorse to the conscience.[10]

What De Quincey had discovered in these unknown regions was in some sense an analogue of the complex emotional and psychological processes involved in his use of opium. Both the inner city and opium are unknown areas of experience to his middle-class readers, as at first they were to him. Both are associated for him with experiences of intense pleasure, on the one hand sharing the simple joys of the working poor on a Saturday evening, and on the other the exquisite delights of an opium trance.

Moreover, both involve intense pain, on the one hand the recollection of his early privations in London, and on the other the drug induced nightmares in which he wandered the labyrinthine byways and alleys of the city haunted by a "human face" (which he later revealed, in the 1856 revision of *Confessions*, was that of Ann, the child-woman of the London streets).[11]

Most importantly for De Quincey, both unknown regions involved experiences of terrifying human extremity: externally, amid the hidden squalor and degradation of London's poor in the labyrinthine back streets of the city; and internally, in the equally horrifying maze-like recesses of the human mind. It was as if the city streets were a physical manifestation of the psychological perplexities of his opium nightmares. For De Quincey, his discoveries in the uncharted, hidden depths of the mind were linked indissolubly to the uncharted *terra incognita* of London.

II

De Quincey's writing about London anticipates in striking ways the images and themes which became standard in urban description in the 1830s and 1840s. We can begin to appreciate this by reading several passages which employ the image of London as *terra incognita*: the first is from "Four Views of London," an essay describing a day's tour of strange city neighbourhoods, which appeared anonymously in *The New Monthly Magazine* in 1833; the second from a remarkable piece by Thackeray, "Half-a-Crown's worth of Cheap Knowledge," a content analysis of a dozen popular periodicals, published in *Fraser's Magazine* in 1838; and the last from a summary review of Dickens' first three books, published in the *Quarterly Review* in 1839.

> One-half of London, as I have said, is so much of a *terra incognita* to many who have lived all their days in the other half of it, that I felt curious to see these unfortunate beings in their own quarter, and took the first leisure day I had to wander amongst them. I had not been in that neighbourhood for thirty years, and was not surprised to find that everything seemed as new to me as if I had dropt into an alien city, and among men and things new and strange. It was the season of one of our holiday festivals, and afforded me an opportunity to trace them to their haunts for such poor amusements and enjoyments as they could find time to take and pence to purchase. Nothing could be more melancholy: the wretched tea-garden, (or rather a place so called, where, at two-pence a head, hot water and crockery are supplied to such parties as bring their own tea, sugar, &c.,) with its soot-black grass-plat and a swing for the children, the public-house and its covered skittle-ground, were the alpha and the omega of their amusements. ... One day, though a holiday, was not sufficient to make them forget all their privations and poverty.

See them, again, straggling from church or chapel on the Sunday; cleanly rags are their raiment, and squalor still saddens their faces, which even 'the light from heaven' cannot brighten into cheerfulness. Enter their homes, or content yourself with merely looking at them or into them: wretchedness is there, and is the hard landlord of their hearths. If there is one portion of this metropolis which more than another requires a thorough investigation into the comforts and wants of its working classes, it is Spitalfields.

*   *   *

We can judge ... here of the people in the great towns – a tremendous society moving around us, near and unknown to us – a vast mass of active, stirring life, in which the upper and middling classes, form an insignificant speck, and of which we (taking for granted that WE here applies to both writer and reader) are quite ignorant and uninformed. An English gentleman knows as much about the people of Lapland or California as he does of the aborigines of the Seven Dials or the natives of Wapping: or if he ever does venture to explore these unknown districts (as some daring spirits have) – to examine the customs, the amusements, and the social conditions of the inhabitants – he does so for an hour or two at midnight; taking the precaution of drunkenness before he makes the attempts, and moving stealthily among those dangerous and savage men, effectually disguised – *in liquor*. All the curiosities that such a traveller bring back from the *terra incognita* are, probably, a coat from which the pockets have been ingeniously separated, or a black eye, the parting gift of a native.

*   *   *

[The] nature and language ... of a vast number of her Majesty's lower orders ... excite a curiosity in the higher, their antipodes. Life in London, as revealed in the pages of Boz, opens a new world to the thousands bred and born in the same city, whose palaces overshadow their cellars – for one half of mankind lives without knowing how the other half dies; in fact, the regions about Saffron Hill are less known to our great world than the Oxford Tracts; the inhabitants are still less; they are as human, at least to all appearance, as are the Esquimaux or the Russians, and probably (though the Zoological Society will not vouch for it) endowed with souls.[12]

It is clear from these passages – typical of many describing the urban *terra incognita* – that the image was applied in a serious and deliberate manner. It was not used merely to suggest some rough equivalence between these journeys of exploration, or as a clever device to interest the reader: in all, there is the same striking quality of literalness in the comparisons between these urban slums and foreign lands.

Indeed, even before looking more closely at the use of the image one should note that there were similarities between the two groups of explorers, urban and foreign. The urban tended to be doctors and engineers; the geographical explorers military men; and among both groups there were some clerics. This is not strange, since the work of medical and religious men was by nature likely to bring them into contact with the poor, much as that of sailors and soldiers took them to foreign lands. But also these men were members of professions just emerging from a period of rather lax, semi-aristocratic dilettantism into one characterized by increased discipline and rigour. Within all these professions, there was a decreasing emphasis on birth and wealth as acceptable entrance qualifications, and stress instead upon intelligence and ability. Training procedures became more difficult and more lengthy, which encouraged the more serious-minded to enter them and winnowed out those without strong motivation. That motivation tended now to be altruistic and humanitarian, for rarely did practitioners receive great remuneration or public acclaim. On the contrary, their chosen careers involved considerable danger: like African explorers, urban explorers frequently risked their lives, if not from attack by hostile natives then from infectious fevers and other diseases. In their labours there is ample and impressive evidence of the Victorian devotion to duty, even to the point of self-sacrifice.[13]

The reports of the two types of explorers also present great similarities. One of the most notable features of the reports of visits to the inner city is the constant reminder that this is an account of an actual *journey*, a physical descent into uncharted regions. Writers usually assume the role of guide, figuratively taking the reader in hand and conveying him into this other world. Phrases like "the visitor will notice," "the explorer finds," "the reader sees," and so on, serve not only to heighten drama but maintain the fiction that the reader is in the midst of a genuine experience of the unknown. For example, Thomas Beames, in *The Rookeries of London*, adds immediacy to his account by addressing the reader in the second person:

> You cannot gain an idea of what *The Rookery* was without visiting these streets. ... You seem to leave the day, and life, and habits of your fellow-creatures behind you ... and you have scarce gone a hundred yards when you are in *The Rookery*. The change is marvellous.

The effect is sustained throughout the long passage: "you could scarcely have an idea ... and you begin to fancy ... you will tell us this must be exaggeration," and so on.[14]

There were also physical similarities between the jungles and wastes of distant lands and the urban slums. There is in descriptions of both an emphasis upon the darkness and closeness of the environment; the filth and the stench present in the crude habitations of the natives; the foulness of the air; and the awful quality of the water. But beyond these points of contact, there were even more frightening parallels in the discoveries of the moral and physical state of the inhabitants.

Over and over again, the material and moral condition of the urban masses was found to be no better – sometimes even worse – than that of savages. "It is a fact," stressed the *Parliamentary Gazetteer of England and Wales* in 1843, "that in St. Giles's, in the back streets of Drury-lane, around Westminster-abbey, in the parishes of Bethnal-green, Shoreditch, &c., ... and in the similar neighbourhoods of great towns, a state of social civilization exists, as low in degree as is found in the far-off regions of Africa!" Anticipating disbelief the author continues: "This is no rhetorical flourish."[15] As the reader will have noted from the passages above, likening city dwellers to African natives was quite common in these works, as were comparisons to North American Indians, South American Indians, South Seas islanders, Laplanders, Russians, Eskimos and Australian aborigines. But, in the opinion of one expert on Manchester's social conditions, the plight of its inhabitants was far worse than that of the savages, for they were forced to experience "all the privations and precariousness of existence incident to savage life, but without the advantages of that hardy and robust constitution which confers on savage tribes their power of endurance."[16]

Social conditions in the urban *terra incognita* were discovered to be similar to those of distant corners of the globe in another important particular, religion – or, to put it more accurately, in the lack of religion. One of the most important public groups supporting geographical exploration was the evangelical movement, whose members saw England as a standard-bearer in the struggle to bring Christianity to the heathen races. Urban explorers often had similar goals, and the groups sending missionaries to Africa shared membership lists and officers with those sending visitors into the slums. The work itself, in the cities or abroad, seemed somewhat interchangeable to clerics, as well: Pusey wrote to a fellow clergyman, "If I had no duties here, and had fluency, I would long ago have asked leave to preach in the alleys of London, where the Gospel is as unknown as in Thibet."[17]

Indeed, from the early 1800s it was common knowledge that the number of churches in large towns was too small to serve their growing populations. From the passage of the Church Building Act in 1818 there were continual efforts both public and private to remedy the situation, but population always seemed to grow faster than new construction. The religious census of 1851 only confirmed what long had been suspected, that England's cities were seething with non-conformists and atheists. In a speech in 1845, Lord Ashley summarized the inevitable conclusions of any inquiry into religion in the cities:

> [T]he population has widely outstripped the provision made for it, and thousands may be found in our highways and hedges, in our streets and alleys, in our courts and lanes, who are living in a state of practical heathenism – a heathenism as complete as if they were found in California or Timbuctoo.[18]

In fact, so irreligious were the urban poor that some thought comparisons of atheistical town dwellers to natives of foreign places more unfair to the savage than the Englishmen:

> The savage, roaming through his native wilderness, bows down with reverence before the objects he has been taught to worship. ... Thus far he is superior to that portion of the operative manufacturers which acknowledges no God.[19]

There were other motives than religious behind the effort to Christianize urban heathens, as there were behind missionary work overseas. It was obvious that religious instruction – especially of the young – could be an important instrument of social control. Supporters of a limited religious education, stressing the fundamental duties of a good Christian subject, argued that it would encourage sobriety and industriousness among the poorer classes, and so make them better, more productive workers. In addition, democratic and revolutionary principles were held to be incompatible with genuine religious belief, and to encourage the latter necessarily would diminish the former. In 1840, a reporter for the Manchester and Salford Town Missions explained:

> Your Missionary cannot refrain from drawing a parallel here, between the period of the first French revolution, and that of the introduction of Owenism into this country. At the former period, when the noxious principles of infidelity were wafted o'er the British Channel from France, a counter-acting influence was presented in England, by the good providence of God, in the institution of sabbath schools; at the latter, when the pestilential and soul-destroying principles of Owenism, were spreading from city to city, and from town to town, a fitting antidote was found in the establishment of those heaven-born institutions, City and Town Missions.[20]

Yet another promised benefit of religious schooling was a reduction in crime and civil disorder as the poor became less violent and more docile. The key concept here was "duty"; if, as one writer put it, rich and poor recognized their duties to each other,

> The rich will thereby discover that there is much good soil among the poorer classes, which only requires proper draining and cultivation to produce fruits of the greatest utility to society; the poorer will learn to look upon their wealthier neighbours as instruments in the hands of God, to lead them to industry, to happiness and peace.[21]

As in the colonies of the expanding Empire, duty had two meanings: for the colonial elite and the rich, to lead and govern; for the native and the poor, to follow and be led.

The realization that England's urban poor were in a state not far removed from that of savagery also inevitably affected the philosophy and attitudes of those who pondered the difficulty of governing them. As early as the 1790s, Pitt's government had regarded the manufacturing towns of the Midlands and North as virtually hostile enclaves of a foreign power, and during the French wars a massive effort was begun to build garrisons for troops to police them. In the 1830s, Edwin Chadwick went so far as to suggest that it was necessary to treat the urban masses as if they *were* inhabitants of a distant colony:

> A vast increase of population in some of the manufacturing districts is we submit to be regarded in respect of new arrangements in the same point of view as an actual increase of new territory. Much indeed of the Population in the manufacturing districts is not a native population brought up in the habits of obedience to the laws of that part of the empire in which they reside.[22]

For this reason, there were urgent appeals made to reshape local government into more modern, centralized, efficient and effective form, much as there were calls to reform colonial government along the same lines. The establishment of Peel's Metropolitan Police in 1828 was one such action.

Another common but more disturbing comparison of English city-dwellers to the natives of foreign lands was to the Irish – more disturbing because the Irish were emigrating to England *en masse* and becoming part of the indigenous population. In their unreformed native sloth and indecency, they were a demoralizing influence upon the English poor. In 1832 James Kay explained the likely social effects of continued Irish migration:

> Were such manners to prevail, the horrors of pauperism would accumulate. A debilitated race would be rapidly multiplied. Morality would afford no check to the increase of the population: crime and disease would be its only obstacles. .... A dense mass, impotent alike of great moral or physical efforts, would accumulate.... They would drag on an unhappy existence, vibrating between the pangs of hunger and the delirium of dissipation.[23]

This passage hints at another important feature of reports of urban exploration – the suggestion, often muted but sometimes explicit, that the natives of England's cities were not merely *like* another race but actually constituted another race.

It was in fact during the early decades of the nineteenth century becoming increasingly common to consider the existence of distinct human races as a proven scientific fact. Inevitably, however, the philosophy of race seemed to become racist philosophy, an effort to prove scientifically the superiority of white European peoples. The theoretical underpinnings of this belief developed from new research in the biological sciences, particularly in the classification of species, most of which was done in France from the 1780s through the 1840s. Buffon, the influential French naturalist, suggested that in certain environments (like the New World) animals and plants had degenerated from their original, higher forms. This could explain human variation, too: the original, pure white race had, in certain extreme climates like the tropics or the Asian tundra, deteriorated into the yellow and black races. Lamarck's theories about the inheritability of acquired characteristics served to buttress the argument. Baron Cuvier, another eminent French biologist, also maintained that the races were organized hierarchically – the white at the top, the yellow somewhat lower, and at the bottom, close to the animal primates, the black. Concurrently, the work of anthropologists, discovering "primitive" non-white peoples in areas of the globe just becoming known to Europeans, appeared to offer additional and irrefutable empirical evidence.

By the 1830s the theory of race was widely accepted in England and provided a ready-made vocabulary and conceptual framework for observations about the urban poor. For example, the Poor Law Report of 1834, one of the most widely circulated government blue books, instanced numerous cases which suggested that the English working classes had been transformed into a permanently demoralized and dangerous group. "The present race, which this illegal perversion of the poor Laws has created, are playing the game of cunning with the magistrates and overseers," wrote one magistrate: "give them ten years, and they will convert it into the dreadful game of force."[24] Other correspondents spoke of the inheritability of pauperism, noting as proof families in which three or more generations all had gone on the parish; others noted how a few paupers in a district would infect respectable people and demoralize an entire district, so that even the lower middle classes ended by demanding relief.

Peter Gaskell was well read in contemporary anthropology, and in his influential study, *The Manufacturing Population of England* (1833), attempted to make more scientific comparisons between urban factory workers and savage foreign tribes. The book is filled with casual remarks about similarities between factory operatives and primitive peoples, as when he observes that drunkenness among English workers is comparable to the North American Indians' love of alcohol, or that pregnant women who work in the mills continue their tasks almost to the hour of labour, quickly returning to work like Indian squaws after the birth. But Gaskell's arguments about the effects of factory work generally are more pointed. In chapter two, "Influence of Temperature and Manners upon Physical Development, & etc., and upon Morals," he makes his most explicit case for the existence of a new race among the poorer classes. Drawing upon the work of researchers in the South Seas and Africa, he demonstrates that high temperatures and the promiscuous intermingling of children in factories act to stimulate the early onset of puberty. This in turn leads to unnatural sexual activity at an early age, which destroys the health and moral constitution of the mill children. Later in the book, commenting upon the physical condition of adult factory workers, he notes that they are developing the physical characteristics of African natives, e.g. broad noses, thick lips, overall ugliness, and short stature. In women, he remarks, early sexual activity stimulates the breasts to swell to large size and great sensitivity, but later at childbearing age makes them flaccid, insensitive and poor in milk.[25]

Gaskell's speculations may seem extreme, but others suspected that the degeneration might reduce workers even below the state of the savage races to that of animals. Southwood Smith told Parliamentary investigators in 1844 that they need not visit the slums to see how the poor lived:

> They have only to visit the Zoological Gardens, and to observe the state of society in that large room which is appropriate to a particular class of animals, where every want is relieved, and every appetite and passion gratified in full view of the community. In the filthy and crowded streets in our large towns and cities you see human faces retrograding, sinking down to the level of these brute tribes, and you find manners appropriate to the degradation.[26]

Gaskell, for one, did not think such changes necessarily irreversible: former mill workers who had risen to the ranks of wealthy mill owners did not regain their physical stature, but sometimes their children did. But since Gaskell doubted whether the factory system would ever be reformed, such speculations were somewhat beside the point. Others took the permanent degeneration of the poor into another race as an established fact. Lord Ashley quoted a Manchester manufacturer who did not support factory legislation, but admitted that if the factory system continued in its present form the "county of Lancaster will speedily become a province of pigmies."[27]

Needless to say, such observations could have a double edge, and furnished ammunition for reformers as well as alarmists. Richard Oastler's campaign for factory legislation stressed the similar condition of black slaves in the West Indies and factory operatives in England. In fact, often it was claimed that slaves were in a superior condition because owners had strong economic incentives to keep their bodies in working condition by feeding and clothing them adequately, while wage slaves might starve and freeze. Yet, despite attempts to rouse those who were against slavery to sympathy for the manufacturing population at home, comparisons between the labouring classes and other races more often tended to stress only their mutual degeneration.

So prevalent were racist attitudes by mid-century that even sensitive and sympathetic observers endorsed them. For example, when Henry Mayhew was issuing his *Morning Chronicle* letters on the London poor in book form, he paid at least token obeisance to the prevailing wisdom by quoting an anthropological authority on race in his opening pages, who commented on the two races of mankind, the animalistic wanderers and the civilized settlers. (The poor, of course, belonged to the wandering tribes.) It is interesting that reviewers of the book generally failed to notice this addition to Mayhew's reports; even when they did it was not to take objection but to pick up the theme and elaborate it. So, according to one favourable report,

He has travelled through the unknown regions of our metropolis, and returned with full reports concerning the strange tribes of men which he may be said to have discovered. For, until his researches had taken place, who knew of the nomad races which daily carries on its predatory operations in the streets, and nightly disappears in quarters wholly unvisited by the portly citizens of the East as by perfumed whiskerandoes of the West End?[28]

Elsewhere in his writing, Mayhew tends to fall into the same language, as, for example, when he writes of moving from the world of the skilled artisans in the West End to that of unskilled in the East: "it seems as if we were in a new land, and among another race."[29]

Mayhew, in these beliefs, is only typical of his generation's growing conviction that the poor were distant not only morally, economically and spiritually, but in their very physical nature. Theories that associated race and poverty were to remain an important feature of social thought and inquiry in England for the rest of the nineteenth century, a lasting if unfortunate testament to the power of the image of *terra incognita* to represent the city and its inhabitants.

IV

It will be obvious from the above discussion that the use of the image of *terra incognita* in writing about the city involved the assumption by authors that their audience was ignorant of the facts which they claimed to be revealing. Perhaps it may strike the modern reader that this "ignorance" is not all that unusual: we have become accustomed to a constant stream of journalistic exposés of horrifying and previously unknown social conditions, and we are familiar with the fact of public ignorance about them. But in the early decades of the nineteenth century this fact was considered noteworthy, and writers usually remarked upon it with shock and dismay.

At the outset, it should be admitted that the ignorance of Londoners about their own city was nothing short of legendary. A pocket guidebook published early in the century claimed that

> its utility will be much felt by natives and perpetual residents, whose want of correct information relative to the wonderful city in which they reside, is proverbial. The inhabitants of London are, in general, so completely involved in the vortex of their own particular circle or business, that they remain in a state of total ignorance of all surrounding ... objects.[30]

A century earlier, Addison in a *Spectator* (No. 403, 12 June, 1712) went so far as to compare the different neighbourhoods of the city to so many distinct foreign nations:

> When I consider this great City in its several Quarters and

Divisions, I look upon it as an Aggregate of various Nations. .... The
Courts of two Countries do not so much differ from one another, as
the Court and City in their peculiar ways of Life and Conversation.
In short, the Inhabitants of St. JAMES's, notwithstanding they
live under the same Laws, and speak the same Language, are a
distinct People from those of CHEAPSIDE, who are likewise removed from those of the TEMPLE on the one side, and those of
SMITHFIELD on the other, by several Climates and Degrees in
their ways of Thinking and Conversing together.[31]

There is here a certain similarity to writing about the city in the nineteenth century, but it is only superficial. No doubt it is inevitable that in
any city above a certain size, e.g. metropolitan London from the sixteenth
century on, the very largeness of the place and the great numbers of its
inhabitants will ensure that there is a degree of social isolation among its
many districts and social and occupational groups. But when observers
before 1800 commented upon this, generally they did so with little
urgency; their tone almost invariably is one of moderate curiosity, and
little more. Addison, for instance, makes his comment at the beginning of
a paper, evidently thinking it a striking, eye-catching opening, but quickly
moves on to the essay's main and unrelated topic. By contrast, after 1800,
the tone of these observations becomes far more serious, typically betray-
ing shock, horror and bewilderment. If the old clichés about city life are
still used, they are given new intensity. The ancient maxim, that in
London one half of the city knows nothing of how the other half lives,
furnishes a good example: hackneyed though it was, it became near
mid-century a central metaphor for dozens of works about the city,
including Disraeli's *Sybil, or the Two Nations* (1845), Douglas Jerrold's
St. Giles and St. James (1851.), and the Rev. John Garwood's *The Million-
People City: or One Half of London Made Known to the Other Half*
(1853).

The massive social ignorance of readers was itself a frequent topic of
discussion in works of social exploration. Commenting upon readers' lack
of knowledge was a conventional gambit with which to open an essay, as
Henry Mayhew did in a brief survey of urban slum housing, "Home is
Home, Be It Never So Homely":

'But are there really such places?' the innocent and·sceptical
Well-to-do will ask.
... [T]o convince you, Reader, of the fact, you shall, if you will,
while you sit beside your snug sea-coal fire, in your cosy easy chair,
make a short tour with me.[32]

Other writers took the distress of the poor as proof in itself that their
readers could not know how the poor lived. Hector Gavin explained, in
his exhaustive sanitary survey of Bethnal Green, that this was one of the
reasons he began his work:

I was actuated by the conviction that it was impossible to account for the profound indifference which prevails amongst a great part of the people generally ... but by believing that they were ignorant as to the amount and extent of the ills which they endured. To believe that the middle and upper classes were fully cognisant that multitudes of their fellow-beings have their health injured, their lives sacrificed, their property squandered, their morals depraved, and the efforts to christianise them set at nought by the existence of certain well-defined agents, and yet to find them either making no effort to alleviate, or to remove these misfortunes, or with a stern heart denying their existence, would be to charge these classes with the most atrocious depravity, and the most cruel heartlessness and selfish abandonment.[33]

One senses here both the sincerity and intensity of emotion: it is clear that Gavin, and many other writers, simply could not believe that, if what they were revealing in their works were widely known, the reading public would not have acted already to ameliorate these awful conditions.

Perhaps more persuasive evidence of the genuineness of widespread ignorance of the urban *terra incognita* are the many accounts of reactions by various readers to the revelations about it. In 1831, Charles Greville, as Secretary of the Privy Council, had access to reports from medical men about the cholera epidemic, a matter of increasing concern to the government. But it was not the disease so much as accounts of life among the urban poor that made Greville start:

Dr. Barry's first letter from Sunderland came yesterday. ... He describes some cases he had visited, exhibiting scenes of misery and poverty far exceeding what one could have believed it possible to find in this country; but we who float on the surface of society know but little of the privations and suffering which pervade the mass.[34]

At various times, certain documents seem to have had especially powerful effects on readers, and one finds in letters, diaries and memoirs scores of references to the revelations they contain. Dickens' *Oliver Twist* (though a work of fiction) was one such in the late 1830s; so too was Chadwick's *Sanitary Report* in the early '40s; and Mayhew's *Morning Chronicle* letters in the early '50s. Thackeray (himself often praised for similar work) wrote enthusiastically of Mayhew's work:

What a confession it is that we have almost all of us been obliged to make! ... [T]hese wonders and terrors have been lying by your door and mine ever since we had a door of our own. We had but to go a hundred yards off and see for ourselves, but we never did ... until some poet like HOOD wakes and sings that dreadful '*Song of the Shirt*;' some prophet like CARLYLE rises up and denounces woe; some clear-sighted, energetic man like the writer of the *Chronicle* travels into the poor man's country for us, and comes back with his tale of terror and wonder.[35]

Still more convincing evidence of the discovery of "the poor man's country" comes from accounts of actual visits to it, and the reactions of the visitors. In 1841 Lord Ashley, who already had acquired some fair knowledge of the social condition of the poor from his work in the 1830s on factory legislation, was taken on a tour of the East End of London. Despite his experience, he was astonished by what he saw. He wrote in his journal:

> What a perambulation have I taken today with Dr. Southwood Smith! What scenes of filth, discomfort, disease! What scenes of moral and mental ill. Perambulated many parts of Whitechapel and Bethnal Green, to see, with my own eyes, the suffering and degradation which unwholesome residences inflict on the poorer classes. No pen nor paint-brush could describe the thing as it is. One whiff of Cowyard, Blue-Anchor, or Baker's Court, outweighs ten pages of letterpress.[36]

The smell of places like Cowyard overpowered many: apparently, nausea and vomiting were common reactions. Even experienced urban explorers could find things to cause them to become ill. In 1843 Edwin Chadwick wrote to an associate about field-work in connection with the report on the Health of Towns:

> My vacation had been absorbed in visiting with Mr. Smith and Dr. Playfair the worst of some of the worst towns. Dr. Playfair has been knocked up by it and has been seriously ill. ... Sir Henry de la Beche was obliged at Bristol to stand up at the end of alleys and vomit while Dr. Playfair was investigating overflowing privies. Sir Henry was obliged to give it up.[37]

Evidently, even long experience of such sights often was no proof against their power to shock.

Time and time again, in both private and public writing, one finds the heartfelt cry, "I could not have believed that such misery existed."[38] How was it that the middle and upper classes had become so ignorant about the life and world of the urban poor? The answer is that by the middle decades of the century, social segregation in the cities had proceeded to the point where rich and poor literally did inhabit separate worlds: divisions between classes – economic, political, moral, linguistic and even topographical – were by this time deeply embedded in the very warp and woof of the social fabric. To borrow the phrase popularized by Disraeli, there were in England not one but "Two Nations."

The causes of this great separation are, of course, quite familiar in their broad outline, and it will not be necessary to do more than mention them: in the economic sphere, industrialization and the associated transformation of society, what Carlyle dubbed the "cash nexus"; in the political, the ever-present fear of revolution after the events in France in 1789, and the domestic repression which followed; and in the social, the rise of modern classes and class relations. Less widely appreciated, however, are the particular ways in which these general developments affected the quotidian texture of urban life.

There was, in the first instance, a growing gap in the standard of living between the middle classes and the poor in London and other large towns. This period was one in which the middle classes were benefitting fully from the revolutionary expansion in production that accompanied technological and economic progress. Their houses became larger and more commodious; servants were cheap and plentiful; and many basic consumer goods fell in price as their quality improved. More important, dramatic improvements were made in health care, and for the middle classes maternal and infant mortality were falling while life expectancy was rising. But if this social group enjoyed the fruits of the industrial revolution, the urban poor were largely untouched by material prosperity. Indeed, many were affected adversely. The average urban working man or woman lived in a harsh, dangerous and violently insecure environment: even for those in steady employment (a small minority) the basic necessities of life – clean and salubrious housing, decent sanitation, medical care, adequate and unadulterated food, unpolluted water – could not be had at any price. This gap in itself was an important factor in middle-class ignorance about the life the poor led, as it became increasingly difficult for the privileged even to imagine a mode of existence so very different from their own: such conditions literally were inconceivable. For this reason, when revelations about the *terra incognita* did come, many felt they must be lies or exaggerations.

The moral life of the poor was also inconceivable. In the late eighteenth and early nineteenth centuries middle-class life had become centred on certain values and modes of conduct which stressed order, propriety, domestic fidelity, economic prudence and moral duty – the way of life which for us has become synonymous with the adjective "Victorian." The keystone of this world view was the belief that the home was the seat of all social and personal values, and the family the fundamental social unit. But the urban poor, by and large, had no homes, no family life, and often no families in the legal sense. Sexual impropriety, overcrowding in single-room dwellings, proximity to sickness and death, drunkenness, irreligion, financial improvidence, casual violence – these were the features of everyday life in the slums. To the middle-class citizen this was profoundly disturbing: in every area of moral life the poor were deficient; their very moral existence seemed a violent negation of all the sacred tenets of ordinary social intercourse. It is hardly surprising that the urban poor should seem like inhabitants of another world.

Moreover, the separation between the classes increasingly was *physical*. This was a new and unprecedented development in urban society, for until the end of the eighteenth century London was barely socially segregated at all. Most neighbourhoods, indeed many individual houses, were mixed both economically and socially, combining workplace and domicile for residents of all classes, occupations and trades. By 1800, this integration had begun decisively to break down: as Donald

J. Olsen writes, "The nineteenth century saw the systematic sorting-out of London into single-purpose, homogeneous, specialized neighbourhoods."[39] For the first time, single-class residential developments were being built in the metropolis for groups other than the aristocracy, and in those built for the middle classes, no provision at all was made for working-class residents (excepting always servants who lived in). At the same time, the middle classes deserted the City proper and other central districts, which became predominantly commercial and/or industrial in character. The East End by mid-century was virtually a working-class city in its own right, a vast tract of slums and factories with half a million residents, almost all of them poor.

This residential and economic segregation proceeded simultaneously with the redevelopment of central London. All over the city broad new streets were cut, both to speed traffic into and out of the new middle-class suburbs, and to improve the character of the immediate area. One of the earliest and most important of these ventures was the creation of Regent Street immediately after the end of the French wars. It was built through some of the worst slums in the West End, but once completed one could ride along its wide expanse on an omnibus (introduced to London in 1828), or stroll under its colonnade without a hint of the awful poverty behind. This was intentional: while planning the project, the architect John Nash noted that "the whole Communication from Charing Cross to Oxford Street will be a boundary and complete separation between the Streets and Squares occupied by the Nobility and Gentry, and the narrow Streets and meaner Houses occupied by mechanics and the trading part of the community."[40] This set a pattern for other street works, including, before 1855, Victoria Street, Cannon Street, Commercial Street, New Oxford Street and Farringdon Road. (Later, railway lines were sited similarly to create barriers between neighbourhoods, or to open arteries of communication through slums.)

These new streets and the fine buildings that lined them served to create safe, insulated corridors of transit between the suburbs and the central city: they effectively hid what lay just behind, the poor man's world of the dark, congested courts and lanes of London's slums. It was as if the very spatial stuff of the city had formed itself into a material correlative of the great barriers dividing the known urban world from the unknown – the *terra incognita*.[41]

V

Recently, several critics, Raymond Williams, Frank Kermode and J.G.A. Pocock chief among them, have written of the psychosocial dimension of literary activity, and the key role played in it by what they term (respectively) "structures of feeling," "fictions," and "paradigms."[42] They have stressed that among the most important functions of writing is the attempt to describe and make sense of experience, and the more important and problematic the nature of the experience, the more urgent becomes the effort to control it in and through language. Bearing this in mind, and bearing in mind also the rapid transformation of urban society in the early nineteenth century, it is easier to see why the image of the city as *terra incognita* gained such wide currency. The image, and all of the related and cognate images and motifs it suggested, were used so often because the image – in all of its complexity – described and helped to make sense of the perplexing and disturbing "discovery" of the inner city – in all of *its* complexity. The image helped control the experience, and then, in turn, modified the experience and attitudes toward it; this, in turn, modified the image and the way it was used; and so on, in a constantly changing, never still process which probably can never be fully analyzed.

Before considering further the significances of this image, however, a brief digression is necessary. In writing of the image of the city as *terra incognita* I have discussed and quoted from a number of texts written over approximately a thirty-year span of time. Doing so has afforded the advantage of suggesting how common the image was, but at the same time it has had the disadvantage of suggesting that this image was the only one used during this period. Of course, this is not so: in the first instance, the image of *terra incognita* persisted for a considerable period of time; and, throughout the first half of the nineteenth century, other ways of seeing the city, other modes of apprehension and expression, coexisted with that which lay behind the *terra incognita*. Some of these images of the city were positive, too, including traditional ones, like those of the city as a grand emporium or a great epitome (both exceedingly popular throughout the eighteenth century), and new coinages, like that of London as the world's capital, born of pride in the nation's, and of course London's, increasing dominance in world trade and international finance. But while such views of the city can be found throughout this period, it was the image of the city as unknown land which predominated. By the 1840s, a decade of profound social, economic and political crisis throughout England, this image surfaced everywhere in writing about the city; for the nation was gripped by fear and uncertainty about the condition of England, which was virtually the same problem as the condition of England's cities. Seen in this light, the image reflects more than is immediately apparent: it offers us insight into the way in which the articulate classes of early Victorian England looked at, experienced, thought about and conceived the larger social world they inhabited.

Now for the image itself. To begin, it is important to recall the central pre-condition for its use – the assumption that the audience is in a state of total ignorance about life in the inner city slums. If the general lines of the hypothesis I have advanced above are correct, then it is evident that what I have been calling middle class "ignorance" about the urban *terra incognita* really was a much more complicated phenomenon – or, more accurately, a spectrum of phenomena. Clearly, at one end of this spectrum was genuine ignorance. But it was ignorance born of increasingly widespread social segregation, which itself reflected the ideology of the powerful classes in early Victorian society, and which was, in so far as that ideology was expressed in social and political action, a necessary result of intentional activity. However genuinely unconscious and innocent that ignorance *per se* may have been, nevertheless it was structurally related to the fundamental assumptions and institutions of Victorian society as a whole. At the opposite end of the spectrum was surely something less than ignorance; here was wilful avoidance of the consequences of the knowledge of the inner city. There were those who knew or learned about the *terra incognita* but responded like Dickens' Mr Podsnap, waving it away with a sweep of the hand, thus erasing it from consciousness. Others blamed the poor themselves for the conditions of slum life: they were morally delinquent and so deserved what they got. Others, again, explained the slums in the Malthusian terms of political economy: they were necessary checks on the growth of population, and without them the poor would only breed faster, making life harder for their class in the long run.

Even so, these positions probably do not represent the responses of more than a small fraction of the upper and middle classes. The responses of most fell somewhere between, involving some actual ignorance, some self-deception, and some intentional avoidance – but also a deep-seated uncertainty about the political and social revolutionary potential of the urban masses. Moreover, these responses were reinforced by certain various widely held basic social assumptions about the moral depravity of the poor, the necessity of social segregation for its own sake, and the evils of any state intervention at the expense of what were seen as the all-important rights of property.

What is so remarkable about the image of *terra incognita* is that it could express and sustain *all* of these attitudes at once, conveying a different meaning to different readers, and to different needs of the same reader, without excluding any of the others. In the first instance, in so far as the image of *terra incognita* pictured the inner city as an unknown country, the image was an accurate reflection of the social ignorance of much of its audience. And in so far as the image pictured the urban masses as savage, uncivilized inhabitants of another country – even of another race – it also reflected accurately the material and social condition of a substantial portion of the city's inhabitants. At the same time, the image embodied an effort of distancing and avoidance: it suggested that these areas *needed* to be discovered, because heretofore no one had known of them, an assertion which at times was true, but also at times was nothing more than wish fulfilment to avoid admitting guilt at not having acted to ameliorate them. The image also tended to de-emphasize the *social* nature of the problems of the inner city: stressing analogies with geographical discoveries allowed the urban slums to appear as wholly natural rather than man-made phenomena. Furthermore, by concentrating upon the vast differences between middle-class readers and urban slum residents, the image could be used to point out the extremity of the social injustices under which they suffered, and so serve as a call for reform; but also it could serve to defuse collective guilt and underplay collective responsibility by saying, in effect, that the poor were not really fully human, and so did not need one's concern or assistance. In this manner, the image could be used to justify both social reform and social repression. And, lastly, it could give voice to many varieties of emotional response to these revelations: shock; outrage; disbelief; bewilderment; guilt; and fear – a fear which I think we can detect just below the surface in the oddly incongruous tone of flippant irony and nervous humour that appears so often in descriptions of the *terra incognita*.

In short, the image of the city as *terra incognita* was so pervasive and so powerful in early and mid-nineteenth-century writing about London and the other great towns of England because it so fully represented the social actualities of the early and mid-nineteenth-century city, and the strong yet often contradictory responses of middle-class writers and readers to those actualities. If the image today should seem extraordinarily complex and ambiguous, then that only testifies to the fullness with which it expressed the complex and ambivalent beliefs, fears, desires and reactions of a society to one of its most basic and urgent problems.

F.S. SCHWARZBACH
Washington University in St. Louis

NOTES

1. Boswell's *Life of Johnson*, ed. G.B. Hill and L.F. Powell (Oxford: Clarendon P., 1934), VI, 201.
2. *Life of Johnson*, VI, p. 201. The word "uniformity," according to the *O.E.D.*, did not in the eighteenth century have pejorative connotations; Boswell evidently anticipates its modern sense.
3. From "Letters to a Friend," in *Meliora*, ed. Viscount Ingestre (London, 1852; reprinted Cass, 1971), pp. 160, 164.
4. Anonymous, "Memoirs of a Working Man", in *Meliora*, p. 244.
5. Thomas Beames, *The Rookeries of London* (London, 1852, reprinted Cass, 1970), pp. 14, 18.
6. The *O.E.D.* cites a first usage in 1616 and another in 1630.
7. Park, *Travels into the Interior Districts of Africa* (London, 1799), p. 2.
8. Park, *Travels*, Appendix by Major Rennell, p. iv; original italics.
9. "African Discoveries," *Quarterly Review*, 33 (1825), 518.
10. *Confessions of an English Opium-Eater*, ed. Althea Hayter (Harmondsworth, Middx.: Penguin, 1971), p. 81.
11. It is interesting that a number of crucial episodes in De Quincey's life all occurred in or near Oxford Street: keeping company with Ann; losing her; discovering opium; and wandering among the poor on Saturday nights. At this time, c. 1800, rapid commercial development in Oxford Street had just begun, and until the 1830s the streets immediately adjacent remained shabby and overcrowded slums.
12. *New Monthly Magazine and Literary Journal*, 38 (1833), 188-9; *Stray Papers of William Makepeace Thackeray*, ed. Lewis Melville (Philadelphia: Jacobs, 1901), pp. 306-7; review attributed to Richard Ford (a writer on travel and foreign affairs), *Quarterly Review*, 64 (1839), 88-9.
13. Dr John Roberton wrote to Mrs Edwin Chadwick in 1845 of the work of dedicated medical men: "Often the family doctor mingles in the crowd of mill-people as they

leave at night and greets them again in the early morning as they congregate to their toils. ... [It] is a curious sight – the swarming streets at a quarter past five of a stormy winter morning. Who but this poor drudge sees it?" Quoted by R.A. Lewis, *Edwin Chadwick and the Public Health Movement* (London: Longmans, Green, 1952), p.77n.

14. *The Rookeries of London*, pp.30-1.
15. Quoted from *Journal of Civilization,* in *Parliamentary Gazetteer of England and Wales* (London, 1843), III, 213-4.
16. Dr R. Baron Howard, in Joseph Adshead, *Distress in Manchester* (London, 1842), p.50.
17. Letter to D.S. Bovett, quoted by H.P. Liddon, *Life of Edward Bouverie Pusey,* (London: Longmans, Green, 1898), III, 32.
18. *The Speeches of the Earl of Shaftesbury, K.G.* (London, 1868), p.191.
19. Peter Gaskell, *The Manufacturing Population of England* (London, 1833), p.283.
20. *Manchester and Salford Town Missions, Third Annual Report, 1840,* quoted by Edward Toyle, ed., *The Infidel Tradition from Paine to Bradlaugh* (London and Toronto: Macmillan, 1976), p.94.
21. Viscount Ingestre, Preface to *Meliora*, p.ix.
22. "Memorandum on police", n.d., c.1836, quoted by A.P. Donajgrodski, " 'Social Police' and the Bureaucratic Elite," in Donajgrodski, ed., *Social Control in Nineteenth Century Britain* (London: Croom Helm, 1977), p.70.
23. *Moral and Physical Condition of the Working Classes in England* (London, 1832; reprinted Cass, 1970), p.81.
24. *The Poor Law Report of 1834*, ed. S.G. and E.O.A. Checkland (Harmondsworth, Mddx.: Penguin, 1974), p.219.
25. *The Manufacturing Population of England*, pp.68-86, and *passim*.
26. *P.P. 1844, First Report of the Commissioners for Inquiring into the State of Large Towns and Populous Districts*, pp.82-3.
27. *The Speeches of the Earl of Shaftesbury, K.G.*, p.113.
28. *Eclectic Review*, 94 (1851), 424-5.
29. *London Labour and the London Poor* (London, 1861; reprinted Cass, 1967), III, 233. For a thorough discussion of Mayhew and the question of race, see Gertrude Himmelfarb, "The Culture of Poverty," in *The Victorian City*, ed. H.J. Dyos and Michael Wolff (London: Routledge and Kegan Paul, 1973), II, 707-36; but see also Anne Humpherys, *Travels in the Poor Man's Country* (Athens, Ga.: U. of Georgia Press, 1979), pp.71ff.
30. *The Picture of London for 1802* (London, n.d.), pp.3-4.
31. *Spectator*, ed. Donald F. Bond (Oxford: Clarendon P., 1964), II, 506.
32. *Meliora*, p.264.
33. *Sanitary Ramblings* (London, 1848; reprinted Cass, 1971), p.3.
34. *The Greville Memoirs*, ed. Henry Reeve (New York, 1875), p.26.
35. "Waiting at the Station," *Punch*, 18 (9 March, 1850), 93.
36. Edwin Hodder, *Life of the Seventh Earl of Shaftesbury* (London, 1886), I, 361.
37. S.E. Finer, *The Life and Times of Sir Edwin Chadwick* (London: Methuen, 1952), p.234; Chadwick to Major Graham, n.d., 1843.
38. *The Factory System Illustrated* (London: Frank Cass, 1967; rpt. of 1842, 2nd ed.) p.3.
39. *The Growth of Victorian London* (Harmondsworth, Mddx.: Penguin, 1979), p.18; see also pp.232-44.
40. Quoted by H.J. Dyos, "Urban Transformation: A Note on the Objects of Street Improvement in Regency and Early Victorian London," *International Review of Social History*, 2 (1957), 261.
41. Engels noted this about Manchester in 1854: see *The Condition of the Working Class in England* (London: Panther, 1969), pp.78-81, and also Steven Marcus, *Engels, Manchester and the Working Class* (New York: Random House, 1974), pp.168-78.
42. For relevant discussions, see Raymond Williams, *Marxism and Literature* (Oxford: Oxford U.P., 1977); Frank Kermode, *The Sense of an Ending* (New York; Oxford U.P., 1967); and J.G.A. Pocock, *Politics, Language and Time* (New York: Atheneum, 1973), pp.3-41.

The Spectacle of Reality
in Sea and Sardinia

Lawrence's tour de force of style in *Sea and Sardinia* carries him beyond the twin extremes of naive rapture and disillusioned rage which erupt uncontrollably in much else that he wrote in the 1920s. In *Sea and Sardinia*, these potentialities loom only just large enough to add interest to the scene, like the volcanoes, Etna and Eryx, which are among the menacing influences he leaves Sicily to escape. The motive of escape attaches the travel memoir to Romantic conventions, but *Sea and Sardinia* renews by radically revising the motif of a voyage "Any where out of the world" (in Baudelaire's phrase).[1] By the end of the book, Lawrence's holiday trip represents a distinctive form of imaginative freedom as striking within the larger body of Romantic and modern travel literature as among other writings by Lawrence himself.

In *Kangaroo* (1923), the main character, Somers, has gone all the way to Australia to get away from "the lava fire of rage and hate" which he perceives in himself and in all European men since the Great War. There are many places in the novel (especially in a chapter called "Bits"), where details of "sheer momentaneous life" on the new Continent succeed in soothing or at least diverting the hero in his state of violent upset. But Somers' hope of relief through travel is overwhelmed (as is the writing in the novel itself) by tirades of rage, by wild political fantasies, and by the confused pain of ambiguously intimate and disappointing male friendship. At the end, Somers and his wife set out from Australia for India (Lawrence and Frieda had gone in reverse from Ceylon to Australia in 1922); the final departure in the novel has an air of desperate aimlessness, for the volcanic eruptions of feeling earlier have devastated the promise of travel as recuperation for body or spirit: "He cared for nothing now, but to let loose the hell-rage that was in him. Get rid of it by letting it out. For there was no digesting it. He had been ... trying to soothe himself with the sops of travel and new experience and scenery. He knew now the worth of all sops. – Once that disruption has taken place in a man's soul ... something has broken in his tissue and the liquid fire has run out loose into his blood, then no sops will be of any avail."[2]

Sea and Sardinia antedates Somers' eruptions of hell-rage in *Kangaroo*, while coming after the vague urgencies of Birkin in *Women in Love*: "That's the place to get to – nowhere. One wants to wander away from the world's somewheres, into our own nowhere."[3] Skirting the conventional

Romantic sequence of yearning departure followed by disappointed arrival, the slim travel record of Lawrence's week in Sardinia in 1921 tantalizes by the apparent ease of its happiness – in a sense, the book resembles the island of Sardinia itself: a "somewhere" just beyond reach of Europe, much closer than Australia, yet unaccountably more different in the experience it offers than its proximity would suggest.

Yet Sardinia is not a place where Lawrence would choose to live, nor were holiday trips a mode of life that he could, on a large scale, approve (or afford).[4] His delight as a traveller in Sardinia, as a tourist really, is so special, so unstable, and perhaps necessarily so transitory, that it ends by narrowly demarcating as well as exemplifying the ideal of freedom longed for as a permanent condition by every wandering Laurentian hero, from Birkin to Lou Witt, in *St. Mawr*, determined to settle on her "nowhere" New Mexican ranch.

Finally, of course, it is the writing in *Sea and Sardinia* which makes the high spirits of the trip impressive, specifically as the achievement of a man who is remarkable as much for his power of language as for his energy in travel. While the figure of Lawrence in Sardinia may, from one point of view, seem that of a man on holiday from any or no occupation, Lawrence's style in the book, his evident delight in language and his absorption in the aesthetic as a distinct mode of experience, indirectly identifies the travel memoir as the work of a writer, of an artist whose imaginative and expressive resources differentiate him from other tourists, even from his adventurous wife. The achievement of style in *Sea and Sardinia* implicitly connects Lawrence's exhilaration in travel with the spirit of a certain kind of art, and this connection supports, however precariously, an equilibrium which Lawrence elsewhere denies fictional characters who are mere travellers or would-be settlers. Birkin remains restless and frustrated at the end of *Women in Love* because he has no audience but Ursula, and no occupation other than that of husband; Lou Witt boldly leaves her dilettante painter husband, but the possibilities of greater freedom and intensity of experience for her in the inhospitable mountains of New Mexico are uncertain at best. Somers, though a writer of sorts, is not presented in *Kangaroo* as having in his art a source of power against either the seductions of public or the disappointments of private experience. Although it is well-known that the distinction between the artist and other men discomfited Lawrence in an era of snobbish and smug aestheticism, one of the interests of Lawrence's non-fictional prose (the letters, as well as the essays and travel writing) is the crucial effect of Lawrence's felt identity as an artist on desires and choices which he leaves his main fictional characters to handle only through direct experience. In the travel memoir, it is true, no explicit allusions to literary ambitions or projects evoke Lawrence's artistic career, yet as in the best of the letters, too, such clues matter less than the pervasive impression of a sensibility which makes, and remakes, experience through brilliant forms of language. Neither Birkin nor Lou Witt, nor even the writer, Somers, has this capacity to redeem his experience through artistic expression, a capacity which appears so effortless in Lawrence's non-fictional prose that perhaps only the comparison of Lawrence to his less gifted fictional characters makes his difference from them vivid.

The artistic identity asserted by Lawrence's language at the start of *Sea and Sardinia* sounds positively defiant in its unregenerate Romanticism, especially set against the very different exertions of his most famous world-wandering contemporaries. The tone of the travel memoir at the start is impulsive: a colloquial prose version of the inspired spontaneity at the start of a Romantic lyric. "Andiamo," "Let us go then," he announces boldly, inviting the reader into the excitement of an immediate adventure. It seems uncanny that, in 1921, Lawrence can still strike sparks out of the old Romantic call to departure, as if "Prufrock" had not dampened that heroic phrasing for generations to come: "Let us go then, you and I, / When the evening is spread out against the sky / Like a patient etherised upon a table." Although already mortally ill in 1921 (perhaps for that very reason), Lawrence wants nothing to do with being "like a patient" of any sort. He shows himself full of energy, up and ready to go at dawn, equipped with his little "kitchenino," his knapsack, his canteens of hot tea, and Frieda ("q-b" for queen bee).

Nor does it matter to him that parts of Joyce's *Ulysses* have appeared, and that the boat to Sardinia stops first at Trapani, the port which Samuel Butler had pronounced to be the true location of all the original Odyssean wanderings. Hugh Kenner makes of Trapani a rich emblem of what the new map of the ancient literary world made available to the modernist imagination during "the Pound era." Kenner likes to guess that Joyce related the Homeric world to one city after Butler's model, "for what had been built out of the town of Trapani could be concentrated once more into the town of Dublin: like Trapani, a seaport on an island."[5]

Lawrence, however, was not seeking to build new relationships to the Homeric world, nor was he after any of the dense, intricate, ironic connections between modernity and the past so absorbing to such contemporary literary travellers as Eliot, Pound, or Joyce. On the contrary, Lawrence chose Sardinia in 1921 precisely because it seemed to promise freedom from all offerings of past as well as present connections: "Where then? ... Sardinia, which is like nowhere. Sardinia, which has no history, no date, no race, no offering. Let it be Sardinia. ... It lies outside, outside the circuit of civilization" (11).[6]

The literary associations of Lawrence's primitivism are to Romantic rather than to ancient or modernist images of travel. Like Rousseau more than a century before, Lawrence presents himself with an "innermost soul" rubbed raw by the tensions of society and yearning for ease and freedom. And in accord with Romantic convention from Rousseau to Rimbaud, the joy of escape is first and most fully achieved in the experience of motion itself – especially through the "nowhere" of sky and water. Rousseau had needed no more than a rowboat on a Swiss lake to release him into a state of almost unearthly bliss.[7] Lawrence is still in search of the same "elemental" liberty, and still able to achieve it on an unprepossessing boat, the fortnightly steamer from Palermo:

> It is the motion of freedom. To feel her come up – then slide slowly forward, with the sound of the smashing of waters, is like ... the magic gallop of elemental space. That long, slow, waveringly rhythmic rise and fall of the ship, with waters snorting as it were from her nostrils, oh, God, what a joy it is to the wild innermost soul. One is free at last – and lilting in a slow flight of the elements, winging outwards. Oh, God, to be free of all the hemmed-in life – the horror of human tension, the absolute insanity of machine persistence. ... And the long-drawn-out agony of a life among tense, resistant people on land. And then to feel the long, slow lift and drop of this almost empty ship, as she took the waters. Ah, God, liberty, liberty, elemental liberty. (35)

Lawrence's joy on the boat is active and heroic as contrasted with the tranquil and trance-like "bonheur" of Rousseau's reverie, but the Laurentian image of elemental liberty still follows within the mainstream of Rousseauist Romantic aspiration – away from society, from history, from culture, away from even the resistant pressure of consciousness itself.

Yet along with the familiar excitement of Romantic departure at the start of *Sea and Sardinia*, there is also sharp acknowledgement that 1921 is a late date for Romantic escape, and that the world is, or has become, quite small, as Ursula had already pointed out to Birkin: "After all, there *is* only the world, and none of it is very distant."[8] Lawrence's own capacity for recognizing the limit as well as the extent of free space in the universe (and in himself) affiliates him with the wary scepticism of an Ursula as well as with Birkin's yearnings; perhaps more accurately, he belongs to that least naïve of Romantic types, what Baudelaire called "les vrais voyageurs": irremediably restless but also precisely observant temperaments whose very capacity for acute measurements of reality impels them to ever more radical departures.[9] Italy, for example, the goal of so many earlier Romantic voyages (including those of Lawrence himself), looks now like just another outpost of European gloom and corruption: "Romantic, poetic, cypress-and-orange-tree Italy is gone. Remains an Italy smothered in the filthy smother of innumerable lira notes: ragged, unsavoury paper money so thick upon the air that one breathes it like some greasy fog"(37).

There is a recklessness to Lawrence's discarding of ruined Romantic symbols that gives the precedent of a belated Romantic voyager like Baudelaire ominous significance at the start of *Sea and Sardinia*. Baudelaire makes such an interesting bridge between Romantic and modern states of mind because he shows the monotonous intensities of disillusion which await the Romantic voyager who has a sharp eye for squalor. In the universe of his famous poem, "Le Voyage," there are finally no places "outside the circuit of civilization." Yet the poet will not relinquish the

Romantic ambition to escape, as later modern ironists do. At the end, he announces instead his readiness to set sail for Death, the only destination that is still untouched, "l'Inconnu."

Given the penetrating capacities of the Laurentian eye, *Sea and Sardinia* seems prepared in advance to present yet again the predictable *échec* of the Baudelairean traveller, high as a balloon over the sea, deflated by every close look into what seems so beautiful in imagination, or from the outside, from the sea. The conventional pattern indeed does appear at Trapani, for while unredeemed by Homeric reverberations, that Sicilian port is "civilized" enough to resemble the seamier parts of any town: "One should never enter into these southern towns that look so nice, so lovely, from the outside … we crossed the avenue which looks so beautiful from the sea, and which when you get into it, is a cross between an outside place where you throw rubbish and a humpy unmade road in a raw suburb, with a few iron seats, and litter of old straw and rag" (45). If this irascible observer is not going to control squalor within a Joycean structure of irony, it seems hard to envision how he shall do other than lapse into a futile repetition of the predictable Romantic collapse of illusion into despair.

The details of Lawrence's narration call out quite loudly for either irony or open disgust even before the boat has fully cleared the harbour of Palermo, for the loathed civilization turns out to be on the boat itself, fully in evidence when the surly crew produces the first wretched meal:

> Bash comes a huge plate of thick oily cabbage soup, very full, swilkering over the sides. We do what we can with it. … In the doorway hovers a little cloud of alpaca jackets grinning faintly with malignant anticipation of food, hoping, like blowflies, we shall be too ill to eat. Away goes the soup and appears a massive yellow omelette, like some log of bilious wood. It is hard and heavy, and cooked in the usual rank-tasting olive oil. The young woman doesn't have much truck with it: neither do we. To the triumph of the blowflies, who see the yellow monster borne to their altar. After which a long slab of the inevitable meat cut into innumerable slices, tasting of dead nothingness and having a thick sauce of brown neutrality: sufficient for twelve people at least. This, with masses of strong-tasting greenish cauliflower liberally weighted with oil, on a ship that was already heaving its heart out, made up the dinner. Accumulating malevolent triumph among the blowflies in the passage. So on to a dessert of oranges, pears with wooden hearts and thick yellowish wash-leather flesh, and apples. Then coffee.
>
> And we had sat through it, which is something. The alpaca bluebottles buzzed over the masses of food that went back on the dishes to the tin altar. Surely it had been made deliberately so that we should not eat it! (39-40)

So much, it might seem, for the "magic gallop of elemental space" celebrated only four pages earlier. Instead of "winging outwards" to liberty, the dingy steamer altogether replicates the hemmed-in, oily, corrupt (and expensive) civilization supposedly left behind. One waits for Lawrence's hell-rage to erupt.

But there is, amazingly, no hell-rage in *Sea and Sardinia*. It is not that Lawrence strains to hold his temper in check, any more than he orders sordid detail through irony. More remarkably, his imaginative gusto simply breaks right through the logic and the conventional patterns of Romantic and post-Romantic disillusion. For the Lawrence of *Sea and Sardinia*, even the squalid crew of "alpaca bluebottles" is enlivening to watch in action. His spirit, at least the spirit of his writing after the event, positively thrives on every oily detail of cabbage and crew. Lawrence is full of curiosity on the boat. Peeping around passages, into the kitchen, through cabin windows, he does not miss a single malevolent gesture of the crew or any sign of folly and pretension in the other passengers. And it is all registered in the same entertaining style of exact detail transformed and animated by joyfully insolent response.

The clear impossibility of performing any role other than that of passenger and spectator seems to release Lawrence to enjoy the wretched society of the boat, almost as a comically melodramatic stage performance. Or perhaps it is his own stamina which delights him as he sees the other passengers collapse, felled one after another by the heaving sea, the bad wine, or simply by deficiencies of imagination. While other passengers are shown to succumb to "faint wails" and general misery, Lawrence presents himself as undauntable: "The most downtrodden, frayed, ancient rag of a man goes discreetly with basins, trying not to let out glimpses of the awful within. I climb up to look at the vivid, drenching stars, to breathe the cold wind, to see the dark sea sliding. Then I too go to the cabin, and watch the sea run past the porthole for a minute, and insert myself like the meat in a sandwich into the tight lower bunk" (53). In Lawrence's strong voice, discomfort and even indignation are carried aloft by the comic and celebratory verve of the language. Delight is the dominant tone, a delight which can include squalid detail because it depends not on the beauty of objects, but on Lawrence's own indefatigable alertness to every ragged bit of life as it goes momentaneously by.

Before Lawrence ever gets to Sardinia, his description of the boat-trip prepares for a more elusive relationship between the imagination and reality than anticipated by the Romantic desire for escape at the start. The squalid reality of the boat, for example, exerts peculiarly little power over his initial heroic vision of the sea-voyage. Oppressive, even sickening details co-exist with Romantic symbols of joy and freedom, however incongruously, even within the same paragraph. Though it is true that he has to sleep in a "match box" cabin, he can easily climb up to the open space of the deck. And anyway, for all his claustrophobia in "hemmed-in" Europe, on the boat Lawrence does not mind sleeping like "meat in a sandwich." The boat-trip to Sardinia thus creates a new, enormously attractive image of a "vrai voyageur": as long as the motion of travel continues, as long as the spirit is cut loose from the tense entanglements of "home," hardly any actual awfulness along the way is so bad as to spoil the fun! On the contrary, the frayed and downtrodden details of the scene may be more engaging to the imagination than the blank emptiness of the sea.

It needs to be noticed, however, that (at first glance, at least) many details of Sardinia do fit Romantic expectation – almost too neatly. Lawrence is not quite accurate in saying that Sardinia appealed because it was "like nowhere," for he did have an elaborated vision of a place that conformed to symbols both familiar from other Romantic literature and developed further by himself in reaction against the bloodless and bloody Europe he knew. "Indomitable" Sardinia obviously belongs with the many other wild and primitive images through which Lawrence had already tried to envision alternatives to a society enfeebled, as he saw it, by money, mind, and will. In his writing before 1921, only the Cornwall of some of the stories offered geographical location for his visionary images of phallic beauty and blood-consciousness. In the major novels, these ideals appear primarily as either nostalgic or prophetic imaginings: in the myth of pre-history at the start of *The Rainbow*, for example, or in the theories of Birkin, whose fantasies are relatively poor in geographical specification. Sardinia, like the Australian bush or Mexico or the New Mexican mountains, is one of those actual, reachable places which Lawrence sought after the war for their anticipated correspondence to long-standing imaginative desires. And Sardinia does offer in plenty at least visual embodiments of key Laurentian social and psychological ideals.

The Sardinian peasants in beautiful costume, for example, seem dressed up as if to illustrate a Laurentian diatribe against the "proletarian homogeneity and khaki all-alikeness" (103) of post-war Europe. The very first costume encountered appears like an image in a Laurentian dream come true: "I seem to have known it before: to have worn it even; to have dreamed it" (72):

> On his head he has the long black stocking-cap, hanging down behind. How handsome he is, and so beautifully male! He walks with his hands loose behind his back, slowly, upright, and aloof. The lovely unapproachableness, indomitable. And the flash of the black and white, the slow stride of the full white drawers, the black gaiters and black cuirass with the bolero, then the great white sleeves and white breast again, and once more the black cap – what marvellous massing of the contrast, marvellous, and superb, as on a magpie. – How beautiful maleness is, if it finds its right expression. – And how perfectly ridiculous it is made in modern clothes. (71)

With the same exactitude that he elsewhere brings to the description of flowers or birds, Lawrence gives the cut and texture and design of Sardinian costume in such loving detail that it becomes an interesting, beautiful object, and also an inspiriting natural symbol.

Yet Lawrence's rapid leap from description to social, political, and sexual reverie also threatens to land him in the kind of shallow contempt for "ridiculous" modern reality that even sympathetic critics find disturbing as well as naïve in other of his writings in the 1920s.[10] There is only a short step for Lawrence between enthusiasm for Sardinian stocking-caps and revulsion against the whole modern "tide of enlightenment," what he too blithely disdains as "cosmopolitanism and internationalism" (102). The description of Sardinian costume soon does all but erupt into the notorious Laurentian mixture of rapture and vituperation, as Lawrence rushes with characteristic zeal into making a "sign" out of the picturesque. The costume is "a sign of obstinate and powerful tenacity. ... Coarse, vigorous, determined, they will stick to their own coarse dark stupidity and let the big world find its way to its own enlightened hell. Their hell is their own hell, they prefer it unenlightened. ... I love my indomitable coarse men from mountain Sardinia, for their stocking-caps and their splendid, animal-bright stupidity. If only the last wave of all-alikeness won't wash those superb crests, those caps, away" (102-3).

In 1921, facile celebration of "stupidity" cannot be taken as harmless imaginative play, especially in writing as explicitly engaged with social and political judgment as *Sea and Sardinia* is from the start. Imaginative exuberance, here, has its least attractive face: a blotchy mixture of sexual and political fantasy covered over by excessive trust in the picturesque. It is some version of this mixture that lures Somers into proto-fascist political involvement in Australia and that makes the Mexico of *The Plumed Serpent* the least convincing of Lawrence's favoured locations.

Sea and Sardinia, however, is saved from the crass symbolic equivalences of *The Plumed Serpent* and even from the confused impulse toward political action in *Kangaroo* by the very modesty of its lighthearted tone and anecdotal design. On this holiday occasion, Lawrence was relatively content to stay in his spectator's role and, more important, he was able to dramatize the impediments to political judgment and even to imaginative love consequent upon his circumstances as traveller. The emphatically visual character of the descriptive language for the costumes, for example, makes clear that Lawrence, as tourist, could hardly know more of these peasants than of exotic birds – with their superb crests and marvellous designs of colour. In the travel memoir, Lawrence never blurs the fact that he has only the tourist's minimal experiences to go on and a spectator's glimpse, mainly through windows, of a foreign life passing by as in a parade.

The diary-like simplicity of the travel memoir allows Lawrence to show how the special conditions of tourism not only free the imagination but also check its symbol-making propensities. In contrast to Wordsworth, the poet-traveller who leaves his picturesque leech-gatherer or solitary reaper before any prosaic needs interfere with his imaginative love, Lawrence has just enough further involvement with Sardinians to break apart his dream-like visions. The splendid peasant, for example, does not sustain his heroic aura for very long in *Sea and Sardinia*. When even Lawrence's great resilience as a traveller is pressed past a certain point, imaginative love gives way to thorough bad temper. Lawrence is not reluctant to display the sudden unravelling of the Romantic voyager into a tired, hungry English tourist, marooned among dirty and indifferent strangers.

One crisis occurs on the same day, and only a few pages after the hymn to the stocking-caps. In the "magic little town of Sorgono," there is only one squalid inn and only one available room, with "a large bed, thin and flat with a grey-white counterpane, like a large, poor, marble-slabbed tomb in the room's sordid emptiness" (106). Worse yet, no milk, no food, no fire, perhaps not for hours, perhaps never. Lawrence and Frieda take a walk and land in a stinking lane, the thick of the outdoor public lavatory. By the time they get back to the inn, Lawrence has reached a towering rage, not to be soothed by "q-b's" more philosophic equanimity: "Why don't you take it as it comes? It's all life." "But no, my rage is black, black, black. ... I cursed the degenerate aborigines, the dirty-breasted host who *dared* to keep such an inn, the sordid villagers who had the baseness to squat their beastly human nastiness in this upland valley. All my praise of the long-stocking-cap – you remember? – vanished from my mouth. I cursed them all, and the q-b for an interfering female" (110).

Lawrence's eruption of temper in Sorgono, however, becomes more comic than despairing through the deliberately melodramatic emphases of the style. In this writing, black rage becomes itself colourful, partly because Lawrence presents his own cursing self as no less of a spectacle than the base reality that he curses. Moreover, black rage yields, in hardly more than a page, to new wonder at a "brilliant flamy, rich fire" of oak-root that suddenly does manifest itself in a deserted room of the hotel where an old bearded man appears to roast a kid with elaborate ritual. Lawrence's symbol-making imagination can revive instantly in the warmth of such a fire: "It was evident he was the born roaster. He held the candle and looked for a long time at the sizzling side of the meat, as if he would read portents. Then he held his spit to the fire again. And it was as if time immemorial were toasting itself another meal" (113). But the lyric potentialities of this new symbol are held within the tone of witty touristic anecdote. Lawrence goes on to describe how the roasted kid disappears. More hours go by. All they ever see of the kid again are five pieces of cold roast: "Mine was a sort of large comb of ribs with a thin web of meat: perhaps an ounce" (125). The kid of Sorgono then turns into a different symbol, this time (with a tourist's version of almost Miltonic severity) an emblem of modern hunger: "Simply one is not *fed* now-adays. In the good hotels and in the bad, one is given paltry portions of unnourishing food, and one goes unfed." The ounce of cold roast kid expands into a general instance of the disappointment awaiting those who wander the world in search of who knows what kind of nourishment. As on the boat, the paltriness of food, as measured by Lawrence's exact eye, represents the discrepancy between social reality and the hunger of the stomach as well as the imagination. Yet this disillusion, in turn, is also soon diverted by the animated sound of a bus-driver's sarcastic analysis of the Sardinian labour situation. Although Lawrence scorns the man's smug socialism, he also catches with amused precision the lively intonations of his political invective.

To accompany Lawrence through Sardinia is to experience through his rapidly shifting tones the sometimes irate, mainly humorous, always intense activity of his extraordinarily responsive sensibility. The visible doing and undoing of symbols recalls the performances of imaginative activity in certain English Romantic lyrics: Wordsworth's "To a Butterfly," for example, or Coleridge's conversation poems. Yet the mixture of the sublime and the tawdry in the detail, and the reckless acrobatics of Lawrence's responses give a new, less solemn edge to this modern version of creative imagination. The very intemperateness of his responses, and his capacity, his need even, to respond to *everything* with equal energy, all become part of the amusing travel story. Every object encountered makes its vivid mark and, at the same time, is caught up in tireless but finally lighthearted interpretation. The rapid pace and colloquial informality of the writing make the acts of interpretation seem remarkably spontaneous; to see signs and portents everywhere is for Lawrence only a slight extension of the act of observation itself. But he discards the symbols almost as quickly as he makes them, and then he revives and transforms them yet again. What remains constant are not the symbols themselves so much as the imagination that encounters the squalid as well as the glamorous items of an alien world with unflagging curiosity and zest.

Lawrence's response to the Sardinian landscape follows the same unstable pattern as his reactions to the people. Visually, Sardinia is "harder, barer, starker" than even Cornwall, and it appeals, as anticipated, for its very lack of those knowable depths finally tiresome in Italy, where: "It is all worked out. It is all known: *connu, connu!*" (133). Sardinia is the "Inconnu" of Romantic desire, thrilling for its very resistance to human penetration: "that strange feeling as if the *depths* were barren, which comes in the south and the east, sun-stricken. Sun-stricken, and the heart eaten out by the dryness" (96). Lawrence's descriptive language assimilates Sardinia to his long-standing imaginative love for the unhumanized and the impenetrable in nature as well as in people.

Yet the natural symbolism quickly reaches the same limit as the human symbols in *Sea and Sardinia*. Lawrence hardly relinquishes for a paragraph his own altogether "human" performance of a consciousness reacting against as well as yearning towards the inhumanly primitive. The figure of "q-b," taking nothing morally to heart is played off against Lawrence's probing intensity: "I like it! I like it! cries the q-b" about the barren, sun-stricken scene. " 'But could you live here?' She would like to say yes, but daren't" (96). Lawrence keeps visible a vivid sense of the limits of his own daring, and of the crucial difference between liking and living in symbolic landscapes. Such distinctions become urgent in the brilliant finale of *St. Mawr*, specifically in the interpolated story of the New England woman who has learned painfully the difference between loving a beautiful but inhuman landscape and enduring it through time: "And if it had been a question simply of living through the eyes, into the *distance*, then this would have been Paradise. ... But even a woman cannot live only into the distance, the beyond. Willy-nilly she finds herself juxtaposed to the near things, the thing in itself. And willy-nilly she is caught up into the fight with the immediate object."[11] In *Sea and Sardinia*, the reality of "near things" appears not through an extended narration, but more offhandedly, through the colloquial intonations, the tawdry details, the questions and self-corrections of Lawrence's voice, set scepti- cally against his own capacity to live through the eyes, into the distance.

The contrast between distant vision and immediate objects recedes as a problem in *Sea and Sardinia* primarily because Lawrence has the capacity to take delight in "the near things" of the Sardinian human scene as well as in the distant picture. On the bus-ride to Terranova, for example, while the "high humanless hills" roll by, Lawrence has at least one eager eye on the human spectacle within the bus. There is, first, the driver, "wrapped in his gloom like a young bus-driving Hamlet" (161). And the bus- driver's mate: "He smoked his cigarette bounderishly: but at the same time with peculiar gentleness, he handed one to the ginger Hamlet. Hamlet accepted it, and his mate held him a light as the bus swung on. They were like man and wife. The mate was the alert and wide-eyed Jane Eyre whom the ginger Mr. Rochester was not going to spoil in a hurry."

In the enclosed world of the bus, and from his passenger's seat close behind, Lawrence freely invents dramas out of the gestures of these unknown people, renaming them as he likes, enjoying the incongruity as much as the fit of his identifications and plots. Although the literary allusions in these perceptions bear some superficial resemblance to modernist mock-heroic devices, Lawrence's playfulness creates a really quite different effect from the ironic correspondences between the commonplace and the literary in T.S. Eliot or Joyce, for what amuses Lawrence is the perception of a genuinely theatrical, if not heroic, flair to the spectacle of Sardinian reality. The bus-driver, to Lawrence's eye, really does belong to that family of dramatic and self-dramatizing heroes, which includes but is not limited to the Hamlets and Rochesters in books. Lawrence's wit, in other words, takes the real bus-driver more dramatically, and the literary Hamlet or Rochester less seriously than comparable yokings of the actual and the literary in modernist irony. Reality, at least in Sardinia, offers to Lawrence genuine examples of theatrical "type," suited to the "plots" of novel or stage.

Trivial incidents in Sardinia assume the colour of high, or at least operatic drama. Sometimes a fully formed plot offers itself in the most mundane circumstances: for example, in the quarrel over the pigs, on the same bus-ride to Terranova:

> There is an altercation because a man wants to get into the bus

with two little black pigs, each of which is wrapped in a little sack, with its face and ears appearing like a flower from a wrapped bouquet. He is told that he must pay the fare for each pig as if it were a Christian. *Cristo del mondo!* A pig, a little pig, and paid for as if it were a Christian. He dangles the pig-bouquets, one from each hand, and the little pigs open their black mouths and squeal with self-conscious appreciation of the excitement they are causing. *Dio benedetto!* it is a chorus. But the bus-mate is inexorable. Every animal, even if it were a mouse, must be paid for and have a ticket as if it were a Christian. The pig-master recoils stupefied with indignation, a pig-bouquet under each arm. "How much do you charge for the fleas you carry?" asks a sarcastic youth. (163)

Lawrence's language intensifies the dramatic expressiveness of common-place exclamation and vulgar objects. Every emotion is pitched to extremity: the bus-mate "inexorable," the pig-master "stupefied with indignation," even the pigs joining with delight as a chorus. As on the boat, however, Lawrence's pleasure in such dramas seems proportionate to his non-participation, even as a chorus. Perhaps his slight but fixed distance as a foreigner, with even a different language, is what allows the bus-ride in Sardinia to remain so much less unnerving than its Australian counterpart in *Kangaroo*, where the temptation to jump from passenger seat to podium drives Somers to the edge of breakdown. Or perhaps the difference comes from the character of the Sardinians themselves. The "very, very nice" Australians infuriated Somers, while the cursing Sardinians soothe and relax Lawrence.

A sense of paradox remains, however, in the fact that the events most enthusiastically described by Lawrence in Sardinia conform exactly to the patterns of modern social life rather than embodying alternatives to them. Fruitless quarrel with the "conductors" of a ticketed, timetable world is the very image of being caught in that insane "machine persistence" which Lawrence hoped to escape. Yet as enacted on the bus to Terranova or on the boat, even bureaucratic struggles become inspiriting, like battles on the popular stage where everyone overacts and the audience delights in every new turn of the catastrophe. The fat man, whose wife gets left behind on the God-forsaken train station of Mandas suffers, and so does his wife, but they, and the righteous guard, too, seem positively transfigured into something more like gaiety by the sheer style with which they perform their emotions:

> Now behold her with hands thrown to heaven, and hear the wild shriek "Madonna!" through all the hubbub. ... The train inexorably pursues its course. Prancing, she reaches one end of the platform as we leave the other end. Then she realises it is not going to stop for her. And then, oh horror, her long arms thrown out in wild supplication after the retreating train: then flung aloft to God: then brought down in absolute despair on her head. And this is the last sight we

have of her, clutching her poor head in agony and doubling forward. She is left – she is abandoned ...

So, his face all bright, his eyes round and bright as two stars, absolutely transfigured by dismay, chagrin, anger and distress, he comes and sits in his seat, ablaze, stiff, speechless. His face is almost beautiful in its blaze of conflicting emotions. For some time he is as if unconscious in the midst of his feelings. Then anger and resentment crop out of his consternation. He turns with a flash to the long-nosed, insidious, Phoenician-looking guard. Why couldn't they stop the train for her! And immediately as if someone had set fire to him, off flares the guard. Heh! – the train can't stop for every person's convenience! The train is a train – the time-table is a time-table. What did the old woman want to take her trips down the line for. Heh! ...

So they bounced and jerked and argued at one another to their hearts' content. (84-5)

In Sardinia Lawrence sees ordinary human misadventure played out with flourishes that liberate the spirit rather than stifle it, as in the "tense, resistant" life of the mainland. Although a sentimental woman or two may, like the "q-b" at Mandas, "shed a few tears," for Lawrence (as for the majority of Sardinians) the very stylization of suffering brightens the human figures and lifts them beyond common, personal sorrows. Lawrence's writing catches hold of this stylization and underlines it. The fat man becomes "almost beautiful," his wife is transfigured into the very symbol of abandoned womanhood. The guard is a virtual allegory of Inexorable Officialdom.

Lawrence was not, of course, the first northern traveller to enjoy the theatricality of the Mediterranean character. Henry James, in *Italian Hours*, suggests that to travel anywhere is "as it were, to go to the play, to attend a spectacle," especially among the Italians who show, at least to the foreign spectator, such an "enviable ability not to be depressed by circumstances."[12] James's metaphors of theatre, however, like his mildly ironic reflective tone, set up a much greater distance between spectacle and spectator than does Lawrence's style. Lawrence's seat is right up front, if not actually on the side of the stage, while for James, the foreign scene preserves its theatrical aspect only from a middle row of the opera house, or through the long vista of a painterly landscape. Thus, when James describes a *contadini* who slowly comes towards him up the winding path of an ancient hill town, singing "like a cavalier in an opera," he quickly goes on to correct the fancy by reporting that brief conversation with the man revealed him to be "a brooding young radical and communist, raging with discontent and crude political passion." James gives up his operatic image with mild self-mockery: "This made it very absurd of me to have looked at him simply as a graceful ornament to the prospect, an harmonious little figure in the middle distance." To James, the theatrical charm of foreign life is an illusion of "the middle distance,"

8

while it is Lawrence's originality to see greater rather than less intensity of flourish the nearer and closer his attention moves. Lawrence is less conventionally bound than James to the established operatic cast of smiling and singing *contadine*, and less bound than is commonly realized, to even his own cast of indomitable stocking-capped peasants. He may dislike the politics of brooding young radicals as much as James did, but even from close-up he sees them (as well as bus-drivers and plain husbands and wives) performing the opera of everyday life with as many flourishes as any cavalier on the regular stage.

The most striking "official" pageant which Lawrence sees in Sardinia thus becomes the emblem rather than the exception to the everyday spectacle of reality. In this pageant, a masquerade carnival, young boys and men, dressed up in make-shift women's costumes, mimic every type of female behaviour, from the drooping grief of a widow to the officious humility of an old housewife, sweeping everything in sight, including the spectators. Lawrence hugely enjoys the insolent extravagance of the masqueraders. Yet there is oddly little difference between their wild improvisations and the "real" dramas of bus or train station. All of Sardinia has the quality of a masquerade carnival to Lawrence, not mainly because some Sardinians still wear the old stocking-caps, but because Lawrence perceives in all the Sardinians a love of performance perhaps even more congenial to him than their supposed indomitable tenacity.

James is nevertheless right to see that it is the privilege and presumption of the tourist to take in the human misadventures of a foreign scene with the indifferent frivolity of a play-goer. For all his closeness of observation, Lawrence may appear no better than the stereotyped American or English or German enthusiast of charming Southern emotionality. Although he allows his figures to come forward, out of the "middle distance," his impression of drama still depends on the slight reduction of objects to something less than full-size. The trains and buses are all "little;" fat husbands, Hamlet-like bus-drivers, and little pig-bouquets all have an almost toy-like animation, and their passion never quite surpasses the entertaining unreality of a stage show.

The redeeming consequence of this touristic condescension, at least as enacted by Lawrence, is that the traveller, too, may be liberated to reduce the dimensions of his own self and his own passions. Lawrence's black, black rage at Sorgono has the same stylized excess as the indignation of the fat husband or the pig-keeper. Sardinia is congenial to Lawrence – travel is finally congenial – not so much because flight effaces the fever and the fret of human society, as because that fret itself changes colour and scale in the holiday atmosphere of a trip. In travel, and then in the zestful written record of travel, Lawrence discovered the magically right distance from reality for his imagination to work most happily – near enough for exact observation of the human scene, but just far enough to keep the figures (including himself) slightly less than life-size. The freedom Lawrence finds in Sardinia is not a freedom from familiar human predicaments, only from the tight and tense spirit which ordinarily pervades those predicaments at "home."

The essentially aesthetic character of the traveller's freedom becomes most explicit when Lawrence chooses for the last episode of the book a marionette show which he and the "q-b" attend, on their return to Sicily. The show is a bewildering but splendid legend-cycle about the Paladins of France, performed on three successive nights before an audience mainly of rapt Sicilian urchins. Handsomely costumed puppet knights flourish weapons and pronounce brave words: "So then, the glittering knights are ready. Are they ready? Rinaldo flourishes his sword with the wonderful cry 'Andiamo!' Let us go – and the others respond: 'Andiamo.' Splendid word" (211).

With the splendid "Andiamo," Lawrence returns to the spirited cry of his own initial departure to Sardinia. Now it is an actual stage show that carries him, along with the rest of the audience, into a magical and heroic space. Lawrence enjoys the fearsome battles of the old legend-plays. But what he also relishes is the manifest make-believe of the marionette figures, examples of how the very artifice of aesthetic form can liberate human passion. He wishes that all drama in the theatre maintained the same aesthetic freedom: "For in fact drama is enacted by symbolic creatures formed out of human consciousness: puppets, if you like: but not human *individuals*. Our stage is all wrong, so boring in its personality" (211).

During the marionette show, the distinction between the drama on the stage and the consciousness of the spectator blurs, as Lawrence appropriates the marionettes for the favourite symbolic creatures of his own consciousness. The very word, "Andiamo," for example, becomes the most splendid emblem yet of "massive, brilliant, outflinging reckless-ness in the male soul." And there is a ghastly old witch, to Lawrence the perfect embodiment of female evil: "With just a touch, she would be a tall, benevolent old lady. But listen to her. Hear her horrible female voice with its scraping yells of evil lustfulness" (212). The witch is marvellously burnt to bits, though Lawrence notes that only little boys take the victory for real: "Men merely smile at the trick. They know well enough the white image endures" (213). The "trick" is not only the stage-burning of the puppet witch, but the thrilling special freedom of the entire show: so profoundly satisfying in its projections of elemental human desires and fears, so profoundly liberating in the obvious make-believe of its puppets and their actions.

Placed at the end of *Sea and Sardinia*, the marionette show offers an implicit commentary on the real and imaginative pleasures of the entire holiday, for even though not in Sardinia, the show is in the spirit of the whole Sardinian trip. In paradoxical reversal of the famous Laurentian demand that art be as earnest as real life, in *Sea and Sardinia* the drama of real life becomes exhilarating just at the point where it assumes some of the unreality of art – a certain edge of play, a pleasure in the bravura of style and in the almost ritualistic performance of elemental human type

and role.[13] For the boys costumed as women in the carnival, the boring-
ness of individual personality was transcended by exaggerated imitation
of conventional roles and parts. The same self-transcendence occurs
for the fat husband or the Hamlet bus-driver or, more important, for
Lawrence himself. As he sees the Sardinians enact, indeed overact, the
passions of their personalities and predicaments, he adds the bravura of
his own style to their performances, so that actors and writer alike play
"to their hearts' content" an imitation of passion which preserves their
essential spirit free, intact, almost untouched.

Yet there remains another side of Lawrence which detests aesthetic
play, whether in the rat-like form of Loerke, preying on the social corpse,
in *Women in Love*, or in the more frivolous guise of Rico, in *St. Mawr*,
wandering foreign scenes, "being an artist." A sardonic glimpse of the
ignoble company to which Lawrence's touristic aestheticism may lead
appears near the end of *Sea and Sardinia* through the sketch of brief
reunion with artistic English friends in the Rome station. Madly thrilled
by exotic adventures in the Sahara and elsewhere, they are ready now
for Sardinia. Only Lawrence's sardonic withdrawal (and the sudden
departure of the train) saves him from being absorbed into a mockable
troop of itinerant social parasites, protected from reality by each other
and by the "sop" of taking the world as only a sequence of scenic displays:

> In my ears murmurs he of the monocle about the Sahara – he is back
> from the Sahara a week ago: the winter sun in the Sahara! He with
> the smears of paint on his elegant trousers is giving the q-b a sketchy
> outline of his now *grande passion*. Click goes the exchange, and
> he of the monocle is detailing to the q-b his trip to Japan, on
> which he will start in six weeks' time, while he of the paint-smears is
> expatiating on the thrills of the etching needle, and concocting a
> plan for a month in Sardinia in May, with me doing the scribbles and
> he the pictures. What sort of pictures? Out flies the name of Goya.
> And well now, a general rush into oneness, and won't they come
> down to Sicily to us for the almond blossom: in about ten days' time.
> Yes, they will – wire when the almond blossom is just stepping on
> the stage and making its grand bow, and they will come next day.
> (191-2).

Although the capacity to perceive the world – landscape and character –
as on a kind of stage had effectively sustained Lawrence's own exuberance in Sardinia, the connection between this attitude and the communal
thrills of a trivial and idle social group fills Lawrence with distaste.
Dashing down to view the annual debut of the almond blossom becomes
emblematic of an effete aestheticism, though these artists are Lawrence's
friends and though the "scribbles" he has just produced declare no more
earnest relation to either human or natural spectacle than their proposal.

Lawrence's distaste for the "drifting artist" type has contributed to the
only secondary status of his own performance in the role of artistic
traveller and travelling artist. Lawrence himself often seems to urge us

past his informal "scribbles" about places and incidents so that we can engage with the perennial would-be settler, carrying the same rather heavy rhetorical baggage all over the world. *Sea and Sardinia* is unusual within Lawrence's work because, for almost the whole space of the memoir, he allows the pleasures of the traveller to exemplify a more than trivial conception of imaginative freedom, a conception which still adheres to Romantic belief in creative perception, while going forward to a sharper, tougher, more modern definition of the right aesthetic spirit in which to take reality: not the sublime spirit of high Romanticism, but the more playful, rude, indecorous spirit of carnival, parade, and melodrama.

That this aesthetic spirit seems so unstable in the travel memoir accurately reflects, however, Lawrence's own uncertain assessment of its worth, as can be seen more explicitly in his judgments of artist-travellers all through *Studies in Classic American Literature*. The writers of the "new" American continent were just close enough to the margin of civilization, even when they were at home, to make the tension between travel and settlement their almost inevitable theme, an especially congenial theme to Lawrence in his own preoccupations of the period.

Lawrence dislikes, for example, the Whitman committed to democratic love for his homeland, admiring only the poet of unending journey: "Exposed to full contact. ... Meeting whatever comes down the open road. ... Towards no goal. Always the open road."[14] Yet the analysis of Melville reveals more ambivalent values. In *Omoo*, Melville is "at his best, his happiest": "For once he is really reckless. For once he takes life as it comes. For once he is the gallant rascally epicurean, eating the world like a snipe, dirt and all, baked into one *bonne bouche*."[15] Lawrence relishes this character of Melville, but in a sense only because of the crucial qualification that Melville could not keep it up: "Good as an experience. But a man who will not abandon himself to despair or indifference cannot keep it up." To Lawrence, moral seriousness (and not just Coleridgean "dejection") makes the dirt of the world finally indigestible. Whether the capacity "to take life as it comes" (as the "q-b" had advised at Sorgono) signifies epicurean recklessness, or indifference, or despair, it is finally as impossible and unacceptable to Lawrence as a permanent stance in art as in life. The very vividness of the dirt *as* dirt, even within *Sea and Sardinia*, intimates how Lawrence himself will not keep up the exuberance of this adventure for more than the space of a holiday.

On the far side of the holiday delights of travel for Lawrence looms the sick rage of a Somers or, even worse, the cynical indifference of the sculptor, Loerke, for whom all motion has become mechanical and all living spectacle has hardened into a granite frieze to decorate a factory. The orgiastic fair represented on Loerke's frieze curiously caricatures in advance Lawrence's own picture of reality as spectacle and carnival in *Sea and Sardinia*. Loerke made an aesthetic form out of modern life, "with peasants and artisans in an orgy of enjoyment ... whirling ridiculously in roundabouts, gaping at shows, kissing and staggering, and rolling in knots, swinging in swingboats, and firing down shooting galleries, a frenzy of chaotic motion."[16] Wordsworth had used very similar language in *The Prelude* to describe "the anarchy and din" of St Bartholomew's Fair in London, for the poet the emblem of that "monstrous spectacle" of modern life which lays "The whole creative powers of man asleep!"[17] To the rootless modern artist, Loerke, by contrast, social chaos has become virtually the only artistic subject, and the perception of anarchic motion has become a stimulant to formal technique. In the frieze, the kind of animated gesture which Lawrence describes so zestfully in the travel memoir is exaggerated into mechanical frenzy, while Lawrence's spirit of amused observation is hardened into contempt. The human sterility of Loerke's aestheticism is exposed in his imagining no satisfactions beyond his stone representation of modern grotesquerie. Lou Witt's spiritual richness, in *St. Mawr*, by contrast, shows in her ultimate boredom with the "cardboard show" of post-war social life, a reaction endorsed in the novella by Lawrence's own straining beyond the reckless satire that he can and does so brilliantly perform in parts of the narrative.

Sea and Sardinia records a bright interlude for Lawrence when the "show" of reality seemed neither cardboard nor granite, but as full of colour and life as the vivid language so near to his hand for recreating it. In "Morality and the Novel," Lawrence uses Van Gogh's painting of the sunflower to exemplify the "living moment" of perception which he asserts to be the supreme value in both art and life: "It has the fourth-dimensional quality of eternity and perfection. Yet it is momentaneous."[18] *Sea and Sardinia* shows Lawrence giving himself to his own keenest capacity to transfigure the "momentaneous" through the imaginative power of his responses. But the achievement of the little book cannot be detached from the disruptive energies which smoulder under its attractive surface. The imaginative play of the book does not presume to touch "eternity," for it never loses the limited meaning of holiday, and permanent holiday never loses the connotations of reprehensible indifference or despair.

Lawrence would not relinquish the Romantic effort to enlarge rather than reduce the dimensions of experience, in both life and art. Earlier Romantics had identified that enlargement with the promise of travel beyond the limits of ordinary time and space. Lawrence, in part, follows their lead. Yet his perception of how in travel the size and seriousness of experience diminish also compelled him to denigrate the art that is literally and figuratively associated with travel. The most severe comment on the aesthetic and touristic pleasures of *Sea and Sardinia* comes from the essay, "The Spirit of Place" at the start of *Studies in Classic American Literature*: "Men are free when they belong to a living, organic *believing* community, active in fulfilling some unfulfilled, perhaps unrealized purpose. Not when they are escaping to some wild west."[19] Against that earnest rebuke, the art of *Sea and Sardinia* proposes imaginative play itself as purpose – not a simple escape from reality, but an escape nevertheless, for the language of the book temporarily leaves behind such enormously depressing realities of Lawrence's experience in 1921 as ruined health, permanent homelessness, public disapprobation of his work, and bitterly broken friendships. The dingy steamer from Palermo carries Lawrence for a week away from those realities, not into elemental liberty, and not into the sublime, but into an aesthetic gaiety where even inexorable officials and pig-bouquets become wonderfully engaging objects, as perfect in their own way as a sunflower or a black stocking-cap. In Sardinia, the spectacle of reality awakens Lawrence's "creative powers" to a performance of the freedom still available to his imagination, wherever he might be. Yet this freedom is so precarious, so contingent on just the right coming together of spirit and place that its gaiety seems less a matter of principle than of luck. Lawrence's "scribbles" about Sardinia have the enduring brightness of art, but of an irreverent, consciously playful art, without illusions about the "trick" of style which can only temporarily defeat the wicked witches of consciousness, as in the puppet show.

MARGERY SABIN
Wellesley College

NOTES

1. "Any where out of the world" : "N'importe où hors du monde," *Le Spleen de Paris, Oeuvres complètes de Baudelaire*, ed. Y.-G Le Dantec (Paris: Bibliothèque de la Pléiade, 1954), p. 355.
2. *Kangaroo* (New York: Thomas Seltzer, 1923), p. 308.
3. *Women in Love* (London, New York: Penguin, 1976), p. 308.
4. In a letter to Eleanor Farjeon, dated one week after the Sardinian trip, Lawrence wrote: "We made a dash to Sardinia – liked the island very much – but it isn't a place to live in. No point in living there. A stray corner of Italy, rather difficult materially to live in." Quoted in *D. H. Lawrence: A Composite Biography*, ed. Edward Nehls (Madison: U. of Wisconsin P., 1957-9), II, p. 55.
5. Hugh Kenner, *The Pound Era* (Berkeley: U. of California Press, 1971), p. 48.
6. Quotations refer by page number in the text to *Sea and Sardinia and Selections from Twilight in Italy* (New York: Doubleday, 1954).
7. "Cinquième promenade," *Les Rêveries du promeneur solitaire, Oeuvres complètes*, vol. I: *Les Confessions, autres textes autobiographiques*, ed. Bernard Gagnebin and Marcel Raymond (Paris: Bibliothèque de la Pléiade, 1962), pp. 1045-47.
8. *Women in Love*, p. 307.
9. "Le Voyage," *Les Fleurs du Mal, Oeuvres complètes*, p. 198.
10. See, for examples, F. R. Leavis, *D. H. Lawrence: Novelist* (New York: Knopf, 1955), pp. 64-70, and Julian Moynahan, *The Deed of Life* (Princeton: Princeton U.P., 1963), pp. 104-14.
11. *St. Mawr and The Man Who Died* (New York: Vintage, 1959), p. 148.
12. Henry James, *Italian Hours* (Boston: Houghton Mifflin, 1909), pp. 165-6.
13. Paul Fussell, although appreciating the comic exuberance of *Sea and Sardinia*, simplifies the character of its freedom when he describes the book as a celebration of "sheer kinesis." *Abroad: Literary Traveling Between the Wars* (New York: Oxford, 1980), p. 158.
14. From *Studies in Classic American Literature* (1924), rpt. in *D. H. Lawrence: Selected Literary Criticism*, ed. Anthony Beal (New York: Viking, 1966), p. 402.

15. From *Studies in Classic American Literature*, rpt. in Beal, p. 372.
16. *Women in Love*, p. 414.
17. *The Prelude*, ed. E. de Selincourt and H. Darbishire (London: Oxford, 1953), VII, 681, p. 259.
18. "Morality and the Novel" (1925), rpt. in Beal, p. 109.
19. From *Studies in Classic American Literature*, rpt. in Beal, p. 301.

Debunking the Jungle: The Context of Evelyn Waugh's Travel Books 1930-9

In the early years of the twentieth century a new breed of literary travellers emerged, eager for experience of other cultures to place in a wider context what they saw as the ferocious egotism, and chauvinism, of their forebears. D. H. Lawrence, Norman Douglas and Aldous Huxley all paid serious attention to "primitive" cultures and disavowed their allegiance to the "mechanist," Christian civilisation of their homeland. Evelyn Waugh, Graham Greene, Robert Byron and Peter Fleming represented the next generation, one which liked to see itself as more overtly aggressive, irreverent, cosmopolitan, and impatiently dismissive of the "old men" who had made the war. The writer-adventurer of the 'thirties tended to be young with a public school/Oxbridge background and he had to operate in a fiercely competitive literary market. Travel was cheap and borders easy to cross. Large tracts of the world were still relatively unknown to the European reader. Alternative cultures were explored with eyes no longer dimmed by concepts of patronage or "progress." While in the grey light of the 'thirties Europe floundered through the Depression towards yet another global disaster, these smart young men provided intelligent light reading which satisfied both political scepticism and a frustrated thirst for the exotic. Hollywood was the "cheap" answer; the new brand of travel writing represented another, more sophisticated, form of escapism which had the greater merit of ostensibly being an attack on escapism. The second war, however, its subsequent travel and currency restrictions, the power-bloc development into cold war factions, largely killed this literary form.

Evelyn Waugh's travel books neatly chart this area of literary history. He wrote six: *Labels. A Mediterranean Journal* (1930), *Remote People* (1931), *Ninety-Two Days* (1934), *Waugh In Abyssinia* (1936), *Robbery Under Law: The Mexican Object-Lesson* (1939) and *A Tourist In Africa* (1960).[1] Significantly, his last serious work in the *genre* appeared in 1939. *A Tourist* was, despite its many felicitous touches, a miserably jog-trot affair written to pay for a cruise and probably the only work he regretted having published.[2]

The reasons for the book's failure are, however, complex. It was not, as some contemporary reviewers suggested, simply a question of the loss of youth and energy and certainly not due to a decline in literary ability. In Waugh's view, even as a relatively young man at the height of his powers, the changes which had been wrought in Europe by 1945 heralded a new dark age and entirely altered the perspective of European travellers. Editing his pre-war travel books for the collection *When The Going Was Good* (1946) he added a preface, bemoaning time wasted exploring the frontiers of civilisation while his European cultural heritage was being destroyed:

> Had we [Waugh, Graham Greene, Byron and Fleming] known, we might have lingered with 'Palinurus';[3] had we known that all that seeming-solid, patiently built, gorgeously ornamented structure of Western life was to melt overnight like an ice-castle, leaving only a puddle of mud; had we known that man was even then leaving his post. Instead we set off on our various stern roads; I to the Tropics and the Arctic, with the belief that barbarism was a dodo to be stalked with a pinch of salt. ... We have most of us marched and made camp since then, gone hungry and thirsty, lived where pistols flourished and fired. At the time it seemed an ordeal, an initiation into manhood ...
>
> My own travelling days are over, and I do not expect to see many travel books in the future. When I was a reviewer, they used, I remember, to appear in batches of four or five a week cram-full of charm and wit and enlarged Leica snapshots. There is no room for tourists in a world of 'displaced persons'. Never again, I suppose, shall we land on foreign soil with a letter of credit and a passport (itself the first faint shadow of the great cloud that envelops us) and feel the world wide open before us. (10-11)

His remarks about travel writing in the 'thirties were perceptive. The *genre* declined, despite the fact that best-selling authors like Greene and Waugh continued to visit distant lands. After the war the experience of these wanderings is, for the most part, only used in "translated" fictional form. Why?

Certain implicit ideas in Waugh's statement demand careful examination. There is, for instance, the suggestion that difficult and dangerous journeys represented for his generation "an initiation into manhood." This clearly reflects, for example, the mental unrest Christopher Isherwood describes in *Lions and Shadows* (1938). Those too young to have fought in the Great War and yet old enough to have been subjected to its propaganda felt that somehow they had missed "the Test." The older generation seemed thus to have secured a permanent psychological advantage. There was a sense in which the sons and younger brothers could never "grow up." Paradoxically, many of those boys who had been as keen to become cannon fodder as the dead sixth forms of their schools, suddenly found themselves, after the Armistice, adopting, partly as a defensive posture, anti-militarist attitudes which developed into a form of protest against the image of the heroic, muscular Christian male.

Perhaps this apparent refusal by their elders to treat them as adults resulted in their becoming what *The New York Times* described as "professional children."[4] The phrase refers to the work of Waugh and Aldous Huxley and we can certainly see a curious, almost sinister immaturity in many of the fictional characters of the 'thirties: Basil Seal and Pinkie, for instance. Unlike Dickens, however, Waugh did not celebrate the purity and wisdom of youth. Indeed, Waugh's work, especially after his reception into the Roman Catholic Church in 1930, supported the notion that man was born corrupt and should persistently struggle against this innate depravity. In his view, barbarism was the "natural" condition of man and only eternal vigilance could prevent its rule.

The themes of the "child vision" and of the conflict of civilisation and barbarism are equally important to any consideration of Waugh's travel books as distinctive literary works. As the central *ingénus* of Waugh's fiction gradually changed from fantastically passive, and therefore exploited, figures to more self-consciously simple men, so the first person narrator of the travel books alters. In the fiction his sympathy for the nursery barbarians, and their ability to exploit, wane with the encroachment of the new "dark age"; in the travel writing the narrator comes to care less and less for the *panache* of the opportunist. The movement is from an agnostic, a-political and playfully subversive view to a distinctly "conservative" and theological one. It must be remembered that what remains of the original texts in *When The Going Was Good* (1946) is a product of the later attitude. Unfortunately, it is by this anthology alone that most readers judge Waugh's travel writing as it is the only one to be reprinted by Penguin Books. Much of the incidental commentary, which was, after all, what endeared the books to the public, has been cut and the transition of authorial viewpoint ingeniously disguised.

The complete text of *Labels* in fact represents a fascinating "period piece." (Much of the flavour of this has been lost in the edited version of *When The Going Was Good*, barely fifty pages remaining of the original two hundred.) *Labels* was the only complete work written after the desertion by his first wife and before his reception into the Church in September, 1930. He was taking "instruction" while correcting the proofs, but was clearly unable to alter at this late stage the expression of certain attitudes out of keeping with his new faith. In an attempt to forestall complaint on these grounds, an "Author's Note" was added: "So far as this book contains any serious opinions, they are those of the dates with which it deals, eighteen months ago. Since then my views on several subjects, and particularly on Roman Catholicism, have developed and changed in many ways."[5] Published in the same month as his reception, it was clearly something of an embarrassment, especially as it dealt with the events of his honeymoon cruise.

To disguise the fact he invented a honeymoon couple, Geoffrey and Juliet, and described himself as a bachelor; the American title was *A Bachelor Abroad*. Inevitably, a certain bitterness percolates through the device. Their "marked solicitude for one another's comfort" (29) is amusingly described and stresses his dissociation from such sentimentality. Waugh is attempting to rationalise, with the help of this fiction, a period of particular emotional strain and the result is a combination of his earlier facetiousness and a new severity. *Decline and Fall* (1928) and his undergraduate stories had displayed a marked delight in violence and the grotesque, but within the framework of fantasy. *Labels* reveals a search for similar sources of stimulation, related in humorous vein, but with an underlying seriousness of purpose.

It is, indeed, an excellent example of that "polite and highly attractive scepticism" which he was to describe as a characteristic of Protestant culture soon after his reception:

> It seems to me that in the present phase of European history the essential issue is no longer between Catholicism on the one hand and Protestantism on the other, but between Christianity and Chaos.

> It is very much the same situation as existed in the early Middle Ages. ... In the eighteenth and nineteenth centuries the choice before any educated European was between Christianity, in whatever form it was presented to him ... and ... a polite and highly attractive scepticism ...

> It is no longer possible, as it was in the time of Gibbon, to accept the benefits of civilization and at the same time deny the supernatural basis upon which it rests ... Christianity is in greater need of combative strength than it has been for centuries.[6]

Labels reveals the seeds of this more positive intellectual position but remains predominantly sceptical. Waugh casts himself in this semi-fictional travelogue as the *ingénu*, the innocent abroad, puzzled and amused at the intimacies of the honeymooners and the stampede of Middle-West school-teachers craving "uplift" from antiquity. He even devalues his own credentials as an author. A "beautiful and splendidly dressed Englishwoman," believing him to be his brother, praises his "genius." "I suppose that real novelists get used to this kind of thing. It was new to me and very nice. I had only written two very dim books and still regarded myself less as a writer than an out-of-work school-master" (26-7). The language is interesting here: "very nice" rather than "delightful," "out-of-work" rather than "unemployed." Waugh was already a master of the precise, well-modulated English sentence. Here, though, he poses as a naïf and it is the narrator's "innocent" view which allows him to write freshly about a well-beaten track. To base a travel book on the experience of a common tourist route was in itself something of an impertinent and pugnacious gesture, and one for which he refused to apologise. In his literary column for the *Graphic* in 1930 he even indulged in the cardinal literary sin and reviewed *Labels* favourably, albeit with his tongue firmly in his cheek.

Behind the mock-modesty, however, we are constantly aware of a mind ruthlessly accurate in its observations. As we progress, we discover that the book is developing into a comparison of the "Southern," Mediterranean cultures he visits with the "Northern" civilisation he has left behind in the grip of a paralysing winter. No religious preconceptions colour these observations. There are, in fact, flippant references to religious conversions resulting from aeroplanes "looping the loop," and to the Holy Family as troglodytes. But the author's avowed "Protestant aloofness" is an ironical device. We can see a clear discontent with Protestant culture and an affinity with the warm south. Describing the view from the aeroplane taking him from Croydon he remarks:

> There was one sight, however, which was unforgettable – that of Paris lying in a pool of stagnant smoke. ... This sombreness and squalor, called up (particularly to me, who had lately been sick) all the hatred and weariness which the modern megalopolitan sometimes feels towards his own civilization. (14-15)

This culture is epitomised by pictures in a Paris exhibition where:

> Picabia and Ernst hung cheek by jowl; these two abstract pictures, the one so defiant and chaotic, probing with such fierce intensity into every crevice and convolution of negation, the other so delicately poised, so impossibly tidy, discarding so austerely every accident, however agreeable that could tempt disorder, seemed between them to typify the conflict of modern society. (20)

The description could equally well apply to Waugh's own two styles of graphic art in, respectively, his book illustrations and woodcuts. Above all, *Labels* reveals Waugh battling through the complexities of aesthetic theory to clear a space for his own camp. But neither of the "megalopolitan" approaches described here is seen as satisfactory and Cocteau's wire sculpture is merely "bogus." We are drawn with the author to examine a Mediterranean alternative and to delight in the Baroque.

This alternative is not, however, one which Waugh at this stage has decided to accept. The prevalent mood of the book is one of scepticism; he derives, or pretends to derive, a certain *frisson* from uncertainty, from being connected to nothing and no one. Behind the pose of naïvety lies the implicit desire to impress us as a man of the world. At one stage he concentrates on a malicious taxi-driver in Haifa who "had no religious beliefs ... no home and no nationality ... an orphan brought up by the Near East Relief Fund":

> Did he like his present job? What else was there to do in a stinking place like the Holy Land? His immediate ambition was to get a job as steward in a ship; not a stinking little ship, but one full of rich people like the *Stella Polaris*. I liked this man. (63-4)

The final expression of relish at this perverse product of a sterile culture is, significantly, excised from *When The Going Was Good* as are similar references throughout.

The fascination of such strange characters is constantly reiterated in

Labels and it represents a deliberate evocation of a sceptical post-war consciousness. *Goodbye To All That* is mentioned with respect. As they pass the Dardanelles an "American lady" asks sentimentally if he cannot "just see the quin qué remes ... 'From distant Ophir ... with a cargo of sandalwood, cedarwood, and sweet white wine' ":

> I could not, but with a little more imagination I think I might easily have seen troopships, full of young Australians, going to their death with bare knees. (139)

Masefield and the heroics of the Georgians are irrevocably rejected but, as yet, there was nothing to replace them.

In an article written during the cruise and posted home Waugh stated that: "the restraint of a traditional culture tempers and directs creative impulses. Freedom produces sterility. There is nothing left for the younger generation to rebel against except the widest conceptions of mere decency."[7] Nevertheless, Waugh was still unsure which "traditional culture" should command his allegiance; indeed, whether such allegiance was any longer possible. *Labels* demonstrates his sampling of various civilisations: France, Italy, Greece, the Holy Land, Egypt, Crete, North Africa.

At this point in his career, most value judgements of "society" return to the question of aesthetics. He judges a civilisation by its art, not its politics. In Egypt he visited the antiquities recently unearthed from the tomb of Tutankhamen:

> Here we are in touch with a civilization of splendour and refinement; of very good sculpture, superb architecture, opulent and discreet ornament, and, so far as one can judge of cultured and temperate social life, comparable on equal terms with that of China and Byzantium or eighteenth-century Europe, and superior in every artistic form to Imperial Rome or the fashionable cultures of the Minoans or Aztecs. (107)

The emphasis on control, on temperance and discretion, is everywhere apparent. Imperial Rome, with its strident chauvinism, its glorification of wealth and power, seemed to Waugh to prostitute these principles and turn opulence to decadence, "discreet ornament" to flamboyant decoration. The distinction is comparable to one he made in a 1929 essay on Firbank:[8] Firbank is "baroque," Wilde rococo. In the former nothing is irrelevant, everything is structurally interrelated, and the author is untraceable; in the latter all is garish decoration, exhibitionism. It is the difference noted in the essay between wit and epigram, between aesthetic modesty and egotism.

This distinction between design and decoration caused him to reject the "barbarities of Minoan culture" (136), the "vulgarity of Persian workmanship" (141) and much Mohammedan art:

> The period of Arab supremacy in Egypt coincides almost exactly

with the dominion of Latin Christianity in England; during those centuries when the Christian artists were carving the stalls of our cathedrals and parish churches, these little jigsaw puzzles were being fitted together beyond the frontiers, by artificers whose artistic development seems to have been arrested at kindergarten stage, when design meant metrical symmetry and imagination the endless, alternative, repetition, and regrouping of the same invariable elements. (110)

In this, of course, he was suggesting an alternative, specifically English, approach to that of his contemporaries (Robert Byron in particular) whose travel writings offered the "re-discovery" of Eastern and South American cultures and a somewhat sentimental, "picturesque" view of Europe. *Labels* contains what can only be a parody of Byron's romantic description (in *Europe Through The Looking Glass* [1926]) of Stromboli:

I do not think I shall ever forget the sight of Etna at sunset; the mountain almost invisible in a blur of pastel grey, glowing on the top and then repeating its shape, as though reflected, in a whisp of grey smoke, with the whole horizon behind radiant with pink light, fading into a grey pastel sky. Nothing I have ever seen in Art or Nature was quite so revolting. (169)

This exercise in bathos relies entirely for its effect upon the final word, and its humorous scepticism is representative of the tone of the entire book. It was Waugh's irrepressible sense of humour, his ability to conduct a serious discussion and simultaneously to present an irreverent view of the most sacred subjects, that endeared him to readers and critics alike. Although his writings are recognisably the product of a "generation," his point of view is entirely individual, representing no group or cause. No subject or section of the community was safe from his wit. But behind his judgements, and the façade of *savoir-faire*, lies a certain conviction of racial superiority. He delights in the taxi driver but only as a curiosity, and the accumulation of such curiosities helps the author to define what he genuinely holds to be valuable. There is no question of any truly democratic spirit at work here. Waugh was beginning to find himself struggling with a consciousness divided between conservative/ Catholic/Mediterranean aesthetic tastes and an essentially anarchic view of religious and political convention.

Labels, then, is an extraordinary work. Lawrence, Huxley and Douglas all, in their different ways, documented in their travel writings that scoriated "post-war consciousness" mentioned earlier. But Waugh, surely, added something peculiar to the *genre* in that he never disowns what he calls "a certain uncontaminated glory in the fact of race" (205). The viewpoint of his persona is essentially English: quietly confident in aesthetic judgement, the *faux-naïf* in the *beau monde* or the underworld, reserved but not timid. "I began to sympathise with American visitors to

Europe," he ingenuously states at one point. "We, who have grown up in a mature culture, have to some extent, an instinctive discrimination of the genuine from the spurious in our own civilization" (111). And again: "I was moved by something of the Crusader's zeal for cross against crescent, as I reflected that these skilful, spiritless bits of [Arab] merchandise were contemporary with the Christian masterpieces of the Musée Cluny" (110).

Although, at the time he wrote this, Waugh was neither Christian nor fervent patriot he finds aesthetic assurance of his cultural superiority in his Christian heritage. While he can lampoon the fiasco of Gallipoli and the arbitrary reasons for conversion to Catholicism, he still values what he terms the Englishman's "sense of period" (40). In many places *Labels* is more of a treatise on aesthetics than a travelogue. Instead of offering the reader an escape from the "hatred and weariness which the modern megalopolitan sometimes feels towards his own civilization," the narrative voice constantly reminds us of a boredom and scepticism which finds relief only in great art or by reporting the inept or grotesque in humorous understatement.

One of the few sections of the book displaying overt enthusiasm is that in which he describes Gaudi's Catalan *art-nouveau* architecture in Barcelona. Once again we are reminded of the baroque/rococo distinction:

> Gaudi bears to these anonymous contractors and job-builders [of "neo-Catalan" villas near Bognor] something of the same relation as do the masters of Italian baroque to the rococo decorators of the Pompadour's boudoir, or Ronald Firbank to the author of *Frolic Wind* [Philip Oke]. What in them is frivolous, superficial and *chic*, is in him structural and essential; in his work is apotheosised all the writhing, bubbling, convoluting, convulsing soul of Art Nouveau. (175)

Yet Waugh cannot resist adding that the major work, the Church of the Holy Family, remained unfinished at Gaudi's death when "the aged and partially infirm master was run down and killed by an electric tram-car in the main boulevard of the town" (175). In 1939 Waugh caused a similar fate to befall John Plant's artist father in *Work Suspended*, and one senses that, even in *Labels*, he is writing not so much about the exciting possibilities of the future as the relentless decay of what has been valuable in the past.

The emphasis is ultimately more on cultural retrenchment than exploration. Where other writers travel to find new cultural perspectives to replace the old, Waugh's journey serves only to engender a sensation of relief at his return. Seville may be "one of the most lovely" cities he has seen (197); nevertheless

> It seems to me that there is this fatal deficiency about all those exiles, of infinitely admirable capabilities, who, through preference or by force of untoward circumstance, have made their home out-

side the country of their birth; it is the same deficiency one finds in those who indulge their consciences with sectarian religious beliefs, or adopt eccentrically hygienic habits of life, or practise curious, newly-classified vices; a deficiency in that whole cycle of rich experience which lies outside personal peculiarities and individual emotion. (205-6)

Thus a book which began as an escape from the crippling winter of a "Northern" "megalopolitan" culture ends with its narrator's expressing a mixture of gratitude and melancholy at his re-absorption by it; an idiosyncratic account concludes on the final irony of condemning introversion and isolation as essentially sterile.

The paradox that this represents was one only resolved by Waugh's adoption of Catholicism and, moreover, of Catholicism as a faith which could be regarded as continuously "English." (The theme is dealt with at length in his biography, *Edmund Campion* (1935).) This spiritual leap successfully assimilated his straining towards the mystical habit of mind, the exuberance of the Mediterranean, the aesthetic satisfaction of the structural coherence of the Baroque, and isolated the pinched and parsimonious culture of "Northern" life as something specifically "Protestant." The Protestants became in his view the ultimate introverts, fashioning a God to justify human behaviour. From the time he became a Catholic, Waugh no longer felt the intellectual burden of "humanism"; human behaviour was by definition absurd and any attempt to make sense of it futile. Life on earth was an unpleasant episode to be endured with the spiritual consolation of the Church and the temporal relief afforded by art. But it was no more than a speck of eternity; from this point, the supernatural was the "real" to him. Catholicism effectively broke down much of the chauvinism of Waugh's earlier views and suggested a different basis for his instinctive cultural prejudices.

Remote People (1931) was written from this new point of view. Waugh left for Africa immediately after his reception into the Church. He had been commissioned by *The Times* to cover the coronation of Haile Selassie, and Waugh later continued from Addis Ababa down through Rhodesia to Cape Town at his own expense. *Vile Bodies* had been published in September 1930, and its success had effectively removed any immediate financial insecurity. The journey was to initiate a series of expeditions in the 'thirties: three in all to Abyssinia (1930-1, 1935-6, 1936), one to British Guiana and Brazil (1932-3), one to Spitzbergen (1934), and one to Mexico (1938). As has been said, the subsequent travel writings reveal a gradually hardening conservatism and, alongside this, we can see a more overt Catholic apologetic than was apparent in his novels of the period. *Remote People*, however, is relatively mild in its approach. Much of the *angst*, the neurotic reaction to attacks on standards, drops away. Only the boredom is left from that darker side of his nature, and his faith released in him an ability to revel in what he saw as the *Alice in Wonderland* absurdities of Abyssinia. For a brief period, despite his professional commitments as a journalist, travel became an escape into fantasy. With the spiritual security of Catholicism, the dilettante pose became viable again, although it was subtly different from that of *Labels*.

Waugh was "constitutionally a martyr to boredom" (116), and the book explains how he travelled to escape "the boredom of civilised life":

> The blackest things in European social life – rich women talking about their wealth, week-end parties of Cambridge aesthetes or lecturers from the London School of Economics, rival Byzantinists at variance, actresses off the stage, psychologists explaining one's books to one. (115-16)

This new style of dilettantism is now confident and severe; it has an air of professionalism, intolerant, as in *Labels*, of pretension, sentiment and "uplift," but now with positive theological values to act as a counter-weight in the argument. The *faux-naïf* persona has largely disappeared as a result of the stabilising influence of Catholicism. Arrived in Addis Ababa, he records in his diary: "Got up 7, went to Catholic church, island sanity in raving town."[9] But he is very far from the (apparently) extreme political position of *Waugh In Abyssinia* (1936). It seems that the Bellocan attitudes espoused in the *Express* article of 1930 (see p. 108 above) represented an abstract intellectual position. Here he is sympathetic to Abyssinian display and disorganisation and acutely aware of the pretentions of Western civilisation:

> no catalogue of events can convey the real idea of these astounding days, of an atmosphere utterly unique, elusive, unforgettable. If the foregoing pages have tended to give undue emphasis to the irregularity of the proceedings, to their unpunctuality, and their occasional failure, it is because this was an endless part of their character and charm. In Addis Ababa everything was haphazard and incongruous … every evening fell cool, limpid, charged with hidden vitality, fragrant with the thin smoke of the *tukal* fires, pulsing, like a live body, with the beat of the tom-toms that drummed incessantly somewhere out of sight among the eucalyptus trees. (63)

This obscure and insistent drumming became in *Black Mischief* (1932) an image of menacing barbarism, but in 1931 it represented the attraction of a "life-force." The immediate effect of his adoption of Catholicism was to allow him once again to delight in the "haphazard and incongruous" without succumbing to the atheist's despair over "absurdity." "This is an amazing country," he wrote to Harold Acton: "I am too intoxicated with it at present to be able to describe anything."[10]

Inevitably, as a recent convert, theological questions fascinated him. He travelled up country to the Coptic monastery at Debra Lebanos, the centre of Abyssinian spiritual life, in the company of Professor Thomas Whittemore[11] who becomes, as "Professor W," the constant butt of the humour in the Abyssinian section of *Remote People*. Waugh chiefly objected to his religiosity, his desire sentimentally to submerge himself in his surroundings and to fabricate truth to conform with this sentimentality:

> 'Look,' he said, pointing to some columns of smoke that rose from the cliffs above us, 'the cells of the solitary anchorites.'
>
> 'Are you sure there are solitary anchorites here? I never heard of any.'
>
> 'It would be a good place for them,' he said wistfully. (75)

In contrast, Waugh saw "the classic basilica and open altar" of European Catholicism as a "triumph" of "light" over "darkness"; "theology" had become to him the "science of simplification by which nebulous and elusive ideas are formalized and made intelligible and exact" (88).

It was this refusal to obscure the "truth" of his observations that first led Waugh into the political discussion of the travel books. *Remote People* contains nearly twelve pages in defence of white settlement which, while strenuously denouncing all proven injustice, conclude with:

> It is just worth considering the possibility that there may be something valuable behind the indefensible and inexplicable assumption of superiority by the Anglo-Saxon race. (191)

Waugh's position regarding Africa is ambiguous and was confused in Kenya by the subjective appeal of the settlers as fellow-victims of the megalopolitan culture of Northern Europe. He regarded them as:

> perfectly normal, respectable Englishmen, out of sympathy with their own age, and for this reason linked to the artist in an unusual but very real way. One may regard them as Quixotic in their attempt to recreate Barsetshire on the equator, but one cannot represent them as pirates or land-grabbers. (183)

This attempt to defend them by relating their position to that of the alienated contemporary artist was, perhaps, wilfully naïve. He had even admitted earlier in the book that "it is futile to attempt to impose any kind of theological consistency on politics, which are not an exact science but, by their nature, a series of makeshift, rule-of-thumb, practical devices for getting out of scrapes" (180). Yet a recurring desire to make political judgements on aesthetic grounds led him increasingly into the contortions of an untenable political position. It was this which caused him to ally himself, four years later, with Italian Fascism.

Remote People, however, displays little sympathy for the influences of Protestant British Imperialism. "In the last two decades of the nineteenth century," he wrote, "zealous congregations all over the British Isles were organising bazaars and sewing-parties with the single object of stamping out Arabic culture in East Africa" (166). He laments the resultant domination by the Indians. "The Arabs," he says, "are by nature a hospitable and generous race and are 'gentlemen' in what seems to me the only definable sense, that they set a high value on leisure; deprived by the Pax Britannica of their traditional recreations, these qualities tend to degenerate into extravagance and laxness, as they do in any irresponsible aristocracy" (167). His preference for Arab, rather than Indian (Hindu) culture, clearly derives from the idea that the latter represents the usurpation of the established traditions of the landed gentry. The unbusinesslike dilettantism of the Arabs appeals to him where the Indians' devotion to commerce appals:

> We came to establish a Christian civilization and we have come very near to establishing a Hindu one. We found an existing culture which, in spite of its narrowness and inflexibility, was essentially decent and valuable; we have destroyed that – or at least attended at its destruction – and in its place fostered a mean and dirty culture. Perhaps it is not a matter for censure, but it is a matter of regret. (167-8)

In 1931, then, Waugh's concept of a "decent and valuable" culture was not restricted to either Catholic or European ways of life. Although his discussion is phrased in the hackneyed nineteenth-century terminology of "gentlemanliness" versus "trade," he uses this to attack the British colonial "caste of just, soap-loving young men in the public-school blazers" (165). There is, then, no specific political thesis. Indeed, Waugh's interest in politics was the unexpected product rather than the inspiration of his first visit to Abyssinia:

> It is very surprising to discover the importance which politics assume the moment one begins to travel. In England they have become a hobby for specialists – at best a technical question in economics, at worst a mere accumulation of gossip about thoroughly boring individuals. One can trip about France or Italy with the utmost delight without holding any views on *L'Action française* or Fascism. Outside Europe one cannot help being a politician if one is at all interested in what one sees; political issues are implicit in everything. (159)

Only later did he attempt to transpose his African and South American experience into a European context.

Even so, in 1930 his feelings about Abyssinia vacillated so wildly between elation and depression that within days of that jubilant epistle to Harold Acton (p. 114 above) he was able to write to Henry Yorke: "Life here is inconceivable – quite enough to cure anyone of that English feeling that there is something attractive and amusing about disorder."[12] It is precisely "that English feeling" which allows him to delight in remote peoples during the 'thirties, but which, as all the travel books document, soon collapses beneath the boredom and frustration resulting from ill-organisation. The crucial factor is that his aesthetic sense hungers for the comforts of civilisation. On his arrival at Elizabethville he noted in his diary:

> These stimulating re-encounters with luxury! How often in London, when satiety breeds scepticism, one has begun to wonder whether luxury is not a put-up job, whether one does not vulgarly confuse expense with excellence. Then, with one's palate refined by weeks of (comparative) privation ... one meets again the good things of life and knows certainly that taste, at least in these physical matters, is a genuine and integral thing. Reconciliation.[13]

Over the next three years, however, even this "reconciliation" began to pall.

It was a peculiarly shiftless and unhappy time for Waugh. As he noted in the "Preface" to *When The Going Was Good*: "From 1928 until 1937 I had no fixed home and no possessions which would not conveniently go on a porter's barrow" (9). Even in England he "travelled continuously" (9). The *Diaries* and letters of the period of the expedition to British Guiana reflect none of the enthusiasm generated by the fantastic appearance of Abyssinia two years earlier. He drove himself to extremities of physical discomfort he would earlier have avoided, trekking across poorly-mapped country and once nearly losing his life. The only consolation appears to have been that he had "added to his treasury of eccentrics Mr. Christie,"[14] the character who was to form the model for Mr Todd in *A Handful of Dust* (1934). On his return, Waugh went straight from London to Bath to recuperate among the civilised amenities of an unspoiled Regency town. From there he wrote to Henry Yorke:

> Just back after a journey of the greatest misery. So I came to Bath which is absolutely right and live in a suite of rooms overlooking the Colonnade with servants as it might be a club and a decanter of Crofts 1907 always on my sideboard and am getting rid of some of the horrors of life in the forest.[15]

Unwilling to face the task, he deferred writing *Ninety-Two Days* for five months. It is ill-structured, clearly ground out for money, extremely amusing for the first half in which his wry assessment of various companions reads more like a novel than a travelogue. The latter part, however, slavishly follows the diary, detailing the tedious stages of the return to Georgetown and making a few superficial comments on the insubstantial nature of anthropological generalisations popularised by "Outlines" of culture.[16] In *When The Going Was Good* he significantly dropped the whole of chapters 6–9 (146-238), being almost all of the second part of the book. Another excised section concerning expatriate Germans remarks:

> I have encountered them, wistful and denationalised as Jews, in

Abyssinia, Arabia and East Africa, and they make real to me some of the clap-trap of Nazi patriotism. (131)

We might note here his growing interest in Fascism as an alternative political system.

He is aware of his own propensity for facile generalisation and yet, when filling up paper in this kind of writing, his argument occasionally degenerates into extended and trite analysis. The overall effect is of Waugh wallowing in experience he does not quite understand, with his new seriousness refusing to allow the delight in disorder expressed by *Labels* and *Remote People*. He attempts, for instance, to distinguish between the Indian and the Negro. The Indian is a "savage" (rather than a "barbarian") whose nature is closer to that of a "European":

> The Indians ... are a solitary people and it takes many hours' heavy drinking to arouse any social interests in them. In fact the more I saw of the Indians the greater I was struck by their similarity to the English. They like living with their own families at great distances from their neighbours; they regard strangers with suspicion and despair; they are unprogressive and unambitious, fond of pets, hunting and fishing; they are undemonstrative in love, unwarlike, morbidly modest; their chief aim seems to be on all occasions to render themselves inconspicuous; in all points, except their love of strong drink and perhaps their improvidence, the direct opposite of the Negro. (48-9)

He prefers their child-like modesty to the Negro's "ostentation." But here his sympathies stop. Their ugliness and ignorance present an aesthetic block which cannot prevent the presumption that the last out-posts of "culture" have been left in Europe. The churchyard in Antigua, for instance, holds "the memorials of a lost culture – the rococo marble tombs of forgotten sugar planters, carved in England and imported by sailing ship in the golden days of West Indian prosperity" (11).

Near the beginning of *Ninety-Two Days* he remarks:

> Just as a carpenter ... seeing a piece of rough timber, feels an inclination to plane it and square it and put it into shape, so a writer is not really content to leave any experience in the amorphous, haphazard condition in which life presents it; and putting an experience into shape means, for a writer, putting it into communicable form ...

> for myself ... there is a fascination in distant and barbarous places, and particularly in the borderlands of conflicting cultures and states of development, where ideas, uprooted from their traditions, become oddly changed in transplantation. It is there that I find experience vivid enough to demand translation into literary form (13-14).

It was this approach, surely, which resulted in both the virtues and failings of the travel books after *Labels*. "Translation into literary form" did not simply mean "writing it up," but imaginative reconstruction. Impatient with mere *reportage*, his desire to reconstruct leads either to spirited semi-fictional accounts of absurdities and frustrations or to rather facile anthropological generalisation. When forced to settle for *reportage*, as he does for much of the second half of *Ninety-Two Days*, he is often dull. Joyce's and Orwell's gift for making the ordinary appear interesting was not part of Waugh's artistic talents. Instead, he prefers to reduce the exotic and extraordinary to the level of the mundane, to de-mystify the romance of the jungle.

This works so long as Waugh is using it as a literary device to suggest irony. But too frequently it results in unmitigated misanthropy. Throughout *Ninety-Two Days* he adopts the weary voice of the bored traveller, which, in the first half, is constantly subverted by the vivacity of his narrative. The second part is in three sections: "First …," "Second …" and "Third Nightmare." All are nightmares of boredom. The reason for the variable quality of the book seems to be directly related to the fact that he needs characters, "unusual people" who "in retrospect, become fabulous and fantastic" (115). It is through these eccentrics, as a background to them, that Waugh describes landscape and alien cultures. When in 1934 he travelled to Spitzbergen and the frozen, almost uninhabited, wastes above the Arctic Circle, this proved to be the only one of his expeditions to remote lands during the 'thirties from which no travel book resulted. Equally, in *Ninety-Two Days*, stuck in Mr Bollolakos's hotel or a river boat, faced by "empty streets," his imagination falters. No characters offer themselves as a medium for reconstruction and the "amorphous haphazard condition" of his South American experience is all too visible in *Ninety-Two Days*.

When Waugh re-visited Abyssinia in 1935 there was no shortage of eccentrics. He was there as a war correspondent for the pro-Mussolini *Daily Mail*, a member of the press corps whose task was to report the Italian invasion. His personal circumstances had, however, changed dramatically. He was in love with Laura Herbert and the prospects of having his first marriage annulled looked hopeful. In fact, he proposed to Laura by letter on his return, while writing up *Waugh In Abyssinia* (1936), and eventually married her in 1937. In 1935 she was his hope for the future, a delicate being to re-kindle his finer instincts, a Catholic, a girl with social position and dignity. The letters to her reveal a passionate and sentimental side of his nature which he had kept buried since 1929. For the first time he was to work on a travel book in an optimistic frame of mind.

One letter to Laura states:

> No-one is allowed to leave Addis so all those adventures I came for will not happen. Sad. Still this will make a funny novel so it isn't wasted. The only trouble is there is no chance of making a serious war book as I hoped.[17]

When he came at last to write his "serious war book" he was, then, subject to several new conditions. He had neither witnessed any military engagement nor travelled far from Addis Ababa; since the publication of *Edmund Campion* (1935) he had taken on the rôle of active Catholic propagandist; he was deeply attached to Laura and concerned with impressing her simultaneously as a "gentleman," a co-religionist and a man of the world. It would, of course, be foolish to suggest that these were the only influences, but they were new and pressing concerns which temporarily drove the steady development of his aesthetic and religious beliefs to extremes.

The period during which Waugh began to attract literary enemies was 1935-9, when Britain was divided over the Italian invasion of Abyssinia, the Spanish Civil War and the whole question of the viability of fascism as a political alternative to communism. It was a time when public figures were required to take sides, and it was obvious which side Waugh would prefer. The choice did not, however, represent blind political fanaticism. Political ideology was scarcely a consideration. He sided with those he considered more likely to protect the individual, the Church and European civilisation. He sided, or so he thought, with culture against the barbarians and, as such, clearly distinguished between Italian and German Fascism. His pro-Franco sympathies were based quite simply on the need to keep the Communists out, but his rather naïve adoption of Mussolini's cause in Abyssinia was the expression of a more positive commitment. Returning to England in January 1936 he took the trouble to stop over in Rome and interview Il Duce.

The first chapter of *Waugh In Abyssinia* is titled "The Intelligent Woman's Guide To The Abyssinian Question," parodying Shaw as a typical intellectual casualty of humanism. It represents a survey of the development of the contemporary crisis. The aesthetic assumptions upon which the analysis is based are similar to those already discussed in *Remote People*, but far more rigorously applied. The native Abyssinians are seen as lethargic, greedy and uncultured, rejecting "successive waves of aesthetic stimulus" (64) from Europe; the Indians are commercial usurpers; the Arabs have lost their aristocratic social structure. Working from this recapitulation, he attempts historical generalisation and modifies his earlier argument. The European partition of Africa represented "Imperialism devoid of a single redeeming element," but:

> However sordid the motives and however gross the means by which the white races established – and are still establishing – themselves in Africa, the result has been, in the main, beneficial, for there are more good men than bad in Europe and there is a predisposition towards justice and charity in European culture; a bias, so that it cannot for long run free without inclining to good; things which began wickedly have turned out well. (25)

The phrase: "and are still establishing" is significant. By May 1936 Haile Selassie had fled; the Italian offensive had begun in earnest and in defiance of the League of Nations. The Abyssinian rulers before Selassie, according to Waugh:

> had nothing to give their subject peoples, nothing to teach them. They brought no crafts or knowledge, no new system of agriculture, drainage or roadmaking, no medicine or hygiene, no higher political organisation. (25-6)

Under the old régime, a cheap attempt had been made to delude visiting Europeans into believing the country "progressive," but Waugh suspects deliberate deceit: "Tricking the European," he states, "was a national craft" (27). As such, he welcomed the Italians as a civilising force and felt that he could not complete his book until he had once again visited the country and seen this extension of the new Roman Empire. Returning to Rome, he requested both a visa and financial support. No British journalists were being allowed into Abyssinia but, after much haggling, the Italians agreed.

By this time (August 1936), much of *Waugh In Abyssinia* had been written. It was this visit which prompted the two final chapters of the book: "Addis Ababa During The First Days Of The Italian Empire" and "The Road." When the work appeared in October, these pieces in particular outraged some reviewers. David Garnett remarked: "He does not tell us how many of the natives that 'most amiable and sensible man', Graziani, is hanging and shooting every day."[18] Ten years later, Rose Macaulay dubbed his book "a Fascist tract."[19]

Certainly, it lauds the efficiency and fine workmanship of the invaders:

> A main road in England is a foul and destructive thing, carrying the ravages of barbarism into a civilised land – noise, smell, abominable architecture and inglorious dangers. Here in Africa it brings order and fertility. ... It is a tremendous work, broad, even, perdurable; a monument of organised labour. (243)

The road became a symbol to Waugh, neatly fitting the Bellocan view that no country could be considered "civilised" that had remained un-conquered by Rome. But it was a symbol which his imagination failed to control in the ambivalent argument for imperialism. The final paragraph is aggressively simplistic:

> along the roads will pass the eagles of ancient Rome, as they came to our savage ancestors in France and Britain and Germany, bringing some rubbish and some mischief ... but above all and beyond and entirely predominating, the inestimable gifts of fine workmanship and clear judgement – the two determining qualities of the human spirit, by which alone, under God, man grows and flourishes. (253)

In the MS[20] it is noticeable that the phrase "some rubbish and some mischief ... the inestimable gifts of" is part of a large insertion attempting to moderate the argument and justify it on aesthetic grounds. It is clear that the viewpoint expressed is not that of a committed "fascist" but of a politically naïve aesthete. He had always loathed the youth-cult and bullying of the Nazis. Italian fascism, however, seemed more "adult."[21] Waugh's 1937 review of two travel books perhaps helps us to understand why:

> there is an essential difference between them which must be noted ... Mr. Sykes is civilised and Mr. Byron is cultured. Mr. Sykes is at home in Europe. He sees England as any outlying province of a wide civilization; he is by education a member of Christendom. Mr. Byron suffers from insularity run amok; he sees his home as a narrowly circumscribed, blessed plot beyond which lie vast tracts of alien territory, full of things for which he has no responsibility, to which he acknowledges no traditional tie, things to be visited and confidently judged. So he admits no limits to his aesthetic curiosity and no standards of judgement but his personal reactions. It is a grave handicap.[22]

The description of Robert Byron's approach, of course, precisely denotes the authorial attitude of *Labels*. Catholicism, however, as has been suggested, broke down the chauvinism of Waugh's point of view, or at least he liked to believe so. After 1930, he sees himself as European rather than English in his tastes, morally responsible for, because tied to, the culture of Christendom, and acutely aware of the dangers of artistic egotism. His preference for Italian fascism, then, was essentially an expression of aesthetic and religious concerns. Mussolini quite simply represented the country at the heart of Christendom.

Waugh In Abyssinia reflects this directly. Waugh returned in 1936 specifically to "meet some of the people ... engaged in the practical work of government and think out for himself what Fascism" meant. In 1935 he had been impressed by Count Vinci whose easy manners had discountenanced all Abyssinian attempts to "render [his] position ignominious" (168). In 1936 Marshal Graziani, the Italian Commander-in-Chief, provided a similar contrast:

> Too often when talking to minor fascists one finds a fatal love of oratory. ... I had been present when the German Consul-General paid a visit to the fascist headquarters – the officer-in-charge, a blackshirt political boss from Milan – had straddled before us, thrown out his chin, flashed his gold teeth and addressed his audience of half a dozen upon the resurgence of Rome, the iniquity of sanctions and the spirit of civilization and the Caesars, in a manner carefully modelled on the Duce speaking from the balcony of the Palazzo Venezia. There was no nonsense of that kind about Graziani. He was like the traditional conception of an English admiral, frank, humorous and practical. ... if he had to refuse anything he did so directly and gave his reasons. He did not touch on general politics or the ethics of conquest. (228-9)

The final paragraphs of the book, then, would seem to convey entirely the wrong impression of Waugh's attitudes. He was as little interested in the oratory, gold teeth and bombast of the blackshirts, "general politics" and the "ethics of conquest," as was Graziani. What he admired in Italian fascism was its simplicity and honesty, its practical common-sense based on Catholic cultural values. The expression of "aesthetic feelings" (65), and the disciplined structure of that expression, were to Waugh the essence of civilization. *Waugh In Abyssinia* and the book on Mexico three years later are principally concerned with this debate. His description of both countries is structured on a literary symbolism suggesting a dark and confused cultural vacuum beyond the dominion of the Catholic Church.

The visit to Mexico in 1938 was effectively "commissioned." Clive Pearsons, representing the Cowdray Estate, had approached Waugh offering to pay all expenses. The Cowdrays had lost heavily from General Cardenas' socialist expropriation of foreign interests, and Pearsons hoped that a popular book might be the best advertisement for their cause. Waugh had by this time re-married and had begun to settle into his new and strange life as a West Country gentleman.

In the spring of 1938 Graham Greene had gone to Mexico to describe the Catholic persecution,[23] and Waugh clearly felt, if with some trepidation at literary competition from his friend, that he was also needed to support the cause. On his return, he reviewed *The Lawless Roads* (1939) for *The Spectator*. They had, he says, taken different routes, under different circumstances and with different objectives. Waugh had made his first major excursion abroad with Laura; "Mr. Greene's was an heroic journey, mine was definitely homely. ... [his] cinematographic shots ... are all the more damning because they are not linked by any political thesis."[24]

This was the main point of departure. Waugh leaves the reader of *Robbery Under Law* in no doubt that he intends to promote a "political thesis," although it is an odd one, debunking as it does any intrinsic value in political organization:

> Let me, then, warn the reader that I was a Conservative when I went to Mexico and that everything I saw there strengthened my opinions. I believe that man is, by nature, an exile and will never be self-sufficient or complete on this earth; that his chances of happiness and virtue, here, remain more or less constant through the centuries and, generally speaking, are not much affected by the political and economic conditions in which he lives. (16-17)

His calm statement, significantly echoing the Creed, is not outrageously conservative. By advocating "conservatism" he does not mean to advance a system of political suppression or, in real terms, any specific movement. The quotation was prefaced in the "Introduction" by: "Politics, everywhere destructive, have here [Mexico] dried up the place, frozen it, cracked and powdered it to dust. Is civilization, like a leper, beginning to rot at its extremities?" (3). Yet he insists that his is "a political book. ... The succeeding pages are notes on anarchy" (3).

The idiosyncratic fashion in which Waugh employs the word "political" is perhaps revealed by his main complaint about the "Left." "Nowadays," he states, "Law is merely a formulation of the whims of the party in power" (83). Politics, to Waugh, were only useful in so far as they maintained laws to protect traditional moral and aesthetic standards. His horror of experimentation he saw as justified by the Mexican experiment in which, as he saw it, theft, murder and religious persecution had been legalised. The nightmare of this leprous decay is seen, as it was in *Campion*, in aesthetic terms:

> So the great steal began and with it, inevitably, the campaign of justification, of slander; and with the guilt and the hate, the wanton destruction; the libraries thrown out into the gutters, the carcasses slit up, the statues piled up and burned in the plaza. (213-14)

No account is taken of the Spanish exploitation of the Mexican peasantry. He relies for his argument upon the rather naïve determinism outlined in the "conservative" manifesto, the beginning of which is quoted above. The universality of Catholicism had, in his view, bound the country together and made it a culturally important and politically powerful nation. With the persecution of the priesthood all the benefits of civilization were disappearing, leaving the poor worse off than before, subject to the irrational greed of ignorant men. It was as simple as that. The "object-lesson" of the sub-title was that: "There is no distress of theirs to which we may not be equally subject" (277).

"We were educated," he says, "in the assumption that things would not only remain satisfactory without our effort but with a very minimum of exertion on our part become unrecognisably better ... progress is still regarded as normal, decay as abnormal. The history of Mexico runs clean against these assumptions" (276-7). The Victorian alignment of material and spiritual "progress" was, to Waugh, an absurdity. In any case, "spiritual" progress he considered unacceptable as a philosophical proposition outside the framework of Christianity. "Altruism," he states, "does not flourish long without religion":

> A conservative is not merely an obstructionist. ... He has positive work to do. Civilization has no force of its own beyond what is given it from within. It is under constant assault and it takes most of the energies of civilized man to keep it going at all. ... Barbarism is never finally defeated; given propitious circumstances, men and women who seem quite orderly, will commit every conceivable atrocity. (278-9)

Waugh's travel books thus act as a useful barometer of the shift in his opinions between 1930 and 1939. Having begun with *Labels* in the rôle of the anarchic wit, a representative of a post-war generation which had lost all faith in Church and State, he ends as Catholic conservative. Where *Labels* and *Remote People* delight in absurdity, eccentricity, ill-organisation, *Waugh In Abyssinia* and *Mexico* reflect a mildly hysterical thesis emphasising tradition and conquest. In 1939 the barbarians seemed to be thundering upon the gates of the citadel. The time for "polite and highly attractive scepticism" had long since passed. He craved active service in the Second World War, to be part of the battle in defence of civilisation. *Brideshead Revisited* (1945) fundamentally altered his fictional style, presenting a fuller, more committed Catholic vision than had been attempted earlier.

But he never wrote another "serious" travel book. Responding to the enormous success of *Brideshead* he said:

> When I gadded among savages and people of fashion and politicians and crazy generals, it was because I enjoyed them. I have settled down now because I ceased to enjoy them and because I found a much more abiding interest in the English Language.[25]

This remained his view till the end of his life. Looking back from premature old age he remarked rather sadly in his diary:

> It was fun thirty-five years ago to travel far and in great discomfort to meet people whose entire conception of life and manner of expression were alien. Now one has only to leave one's gates.

All fates are worse than death.[26]

MARTIN STANNARD
University of Leicester

NOTES

1. *Labels, Remote People, Ninety-Two Days* and *When The Going Was Good* (an anthology, 1946) were all published by Duckworth, *Waugh In Abyssinia* by Longmans Green, *Mexico* and *A Tourist* by Chapman and Hall. All appeared first in London and then in New York.
2. Cf. *The Letters of Evelyn Waugh*, ed. Mark Amory (London: Weidenfeld and Nicolson, 1981), p. 549. In a letter to Ann Fleming (22 September 1960) Waugh said: "I am not sending you or any of my honoured friends a copy of my African pot boiler because I despise it."
3. Probably a reference to Cyril Connolly's pseudonym for his book of *pensées*, *The Unquiet Grave* which, incidentally, Waugh found intellectually inept.
4. Gerald Sykes, *New York Times Book Review*, 13 April, 1958, p. 5.
5. *Labels*, p. 8.
6. "Converted to Rome: Why It Has Happened To Me," *Daily Express*, 20 Oct., 1930, p. 10.
7. "The War And The Younger Generation," *Spectator*, 13 April, 1929, p. 571; reprinted in Evelyn Waugh, *A Little Order*, ed. Donat Gallagher (London: Eyre Methuen, 1977), pp. 11-12.
8. "Ronald Firbank," *Life and Letters*, March 1929, pp. 191-6; reprinted in *A Little Order*, pp. 77-80.
9. *The Diaries of Evelyn Waugh*, ed. Michael Davie (London: Weidenfeld and Nicolson, 1976), p. 332 [3 Nov., 1930].

10. Unpublished letter, undated, to Harold Acton from "Hotel de France, Addis Ababa"; property of Sir Harold Acton.
11. A leading contemporary authority on Byzantine art and friend of Gertrude Stein, largely responsible for the restoration of the mosaics in St Sophia. Christopher Sykes describes him in his biography of Waugh as "an eccentric American professor, of great learning and imagination" (110); Berenson and many scholars apparently considered him a "pious fraud." Cf. Harold Acton, *More Memoirs Of An Aesthete* (London: Methuen, 1970), pp. 174-5.
12. *Letters*, p. 51.
13. *Diaries*, 9 Feb., 1931, pp. 352-3. The passage is expanded in *Remote People*, p. 233.
14. *Ninety-Two Days*, (London: Duckworth, 1934), p. 245.
15. *Letters*, p. 71.
16. Cf. *Ninety-Two Days*, pp. 174, 183 and 185.
17. *Letters*, p. 100.
18. *New Statesman*, 7 Nov., 1936, p. 735.
19. "The Best And The Worst II. Evelyn Waugh," *Horizon*, Dec. 1946, pp. 360-76.
20. The MS does not exist whole. It was split up and pasted in as endpapers to a limited edition of the book. This section is in Waugh's own copy, a "scrapbook" edition containing various documents and photographs, now in the Humanities Research Center, University of Texas at Austin.
21. Cf. his reviews of Cyril Connolly's *Enemies of Promise*, "Present Disconents," *Tablet*, 3 Dec., 1938, p. 744, and of Beverley Nichols' *News of England*, "The New Patriotism," *Spectator*, 22 April, 1938, pp. 714-15. The Connolly review has been reprinted in *A Little Order*, pp. 123-7.
22. "Civilization and Culture," *Spectator*, 2 July, 1937, pp. 27-8 – a review of Christopher Sykes' *Strange Wonders* and Robert Byron's *The Road to Oxiana*.
23. This resulted in *The Lawless Roads* (London: Heinemann, 1939), and *The Power And The Glory* (London: Heinemann, 1940).
24. "The Waste Land," *The Spectator*, 10 March, 1939, pp. 413-14.
25. "Fan-Fare," *Life*, 8 April, 1946, pp. 53, 54, 56, 58, 60; reprinted in *A Little Order*, pp. 29-34.
26. *Diaries*, 3 Sept., 1963, p. 791.

The Views of Travellers:
Travel Writing in the 1930s

"A reader may ask: What is the writer's
relationship with the place and the people he
writes about?"

"My anger that afternoon joined me to the
field, the slope, the hay. At other times my
relationship to the place and the people who
live here is less simple. I am not a peasant.
I am a writer: my writing is both link and
barrier."

John Berger, *Pig Earth*[1]

John Berger's remarks identify the substance of travel writing, the stance
of the traveller towards place and reader. Of course, this is not to imply, as
Berger's remarks may, that the traveller's stance is simply a matter of
authorial choice. Comparison of the travel writing of different periods
about the same place suggests that an individual's stance – which one
would presume to be unique – can be as much determined by cultural
factors as by personal preference. For instance, a great number of late
eighteenth-century travellers as well as Edwardian travellers journeyed
to Italy, but each traveller seems to have "chosen" to view what his
culture sanctioned. Rome is the goal of the late eighteenth-century
traveller to Italy, and his stance towards that city appears shaped by a
cultural conviction that London provided the criterion against which
Rome was to be judged, and by a body of public knowledge which
dictated what was to be seen and what were the appropriate responses.
When Edwardians travelled to Italy, they centred their attention on the
Alps – Lawrence's *Twilight in Italy* is framed by chapters on Alpine
life – or on Southern Italy, for instance Douglas' *Old Calabria*, in
which appears the following description: "A landscape so luminous, so
resolutely scornful of accessories, hints at brave and simple forms of
expression; it brings us to the ground where we belong."[2] The Edwardian
traveller tended to search out, as Douglas' statement suggests, unculti-
vated terrain, and to draw from the landscape values against which the
place he had left, and to which he wrote, was to be judged.

Of course, such generalisations may mask the variety of stances available in a period, especially one in which cultural norms would not
command immediate assent. Literary historians of the 1930s have always
stressed that it was such a period, one in which abrupt and important

changes in outlook and affiliation took place.[3] The alteration in title of a polemical work by Stephen Spender, from *Approach to Communism* in October 1936 to *Forward from Liberalism* on its publication in January 1937, exemplifies both those sudden changes of standpoint and the tendency to formulate them in terms of travelling. The travel book, whose claim to be the most important literary form of the 1930s has been consolidated by recent criticism, would appear to be the most appropriate form for writers restless with inherited beliefs, and eager to "explore" and "discover" new allegiances.

The stance of the 1930s traveller suggests that he enjoyed neither the culturally bestowed conviction of superiority of the late eighteenth-century traveller, nor the Edwardian traveller's confident exploitation of place as a source of renewal for himself and his reader. Indeed what distinguishes 1930s travel books is not any particular stance but the variety and complexity of stance. It was the mid-thirties, 1934-7, that produced the substantial crop of travel books, including Evelyn Waugh's *Ninety-Two Days*, J. B. Priestley's *English Journey*, Edwin Muir's *Scottish Journey*, Graham Greene's *Journey without Maps*, George Orwell's *The Road to Wigan Pier*, Robert Byron's *The Road to Oxiana*, and W. H. Auden and Louis MacNeice's *Letters from Iceland*. I have chosen to examine the stances of four of these works, all concerned in different ways with what Charles Madge,[4] an instigator of *Mass Observation*, called "the anthropological study of our civilisation": *English Journey* (1934) assumes the narrator's intimacy with place and reader; *Scottish Journey* (1935) denies such intimacy; *Journey without Maps* (1936) identifies the reader with place; *The Road to Wigan Pier* (1937) enquires into the grounds for their distinctness. What these stances permit and condition and what they signify is the subject of this essay.

J. B. Priestley's *English Journey* (1934) and Edwin Muir's *Scottish Journey* (1935) were companion volumes in a series commissioned by Heinemann, and are unusual among travel books of the period in two ways: they involve journeys "home" – both return to the places in which the writers were brought up – and are attempts to move across and grasp the social and cultural landscape of a whole nation. Almost without exception, when other travel writers refer to a country, most often to England, they mean an ideological formation, often seen in terms of a landscape associated with childhood. The England of the end of *Homage to Catalonia* (1938) is, Orwell makes clear, not the England of the "smudge of smoke and misery" of industrial towns. It is the "England I had known in my childhood," his understanding of which can be seen in his description which begins with a comforting pastoral landscape and ends with equivocal images of money and power: "the deep meadows where the great shining horses browse and meditate ... the huge peaceful wilderness of outer London ... the men in bowler hats ... the blue police-men – all sleeping the deep, deep sleep of England."[5] The acknowledgement is that there are Englands rather than England.

J. B. Priestley begins his travels through England at Southampton, "where a man might well first land."[6] An expectation that he will adopt the not uncommon stance of the foreign visitor – consider Lockhart's adoption of a Welsh persona to comment on Scottish life in *Peter's Letters to His Kinsfolk* – is soon undermined by his rapid alignment of himself with various groups. At one moment, he colludes with his educated readership, for "Let us have our laugh" at the vulgarity of the luxury liners. At another moment, he identifies himself as a West Riding man with his "rough and ready" standards, at another speaks to and with the whole nation – "We are an island people" – and at yet another distances himself from that very people who may suffer the fate assigned to them by a number of 1930s writers: "Monotonous but easy work and a liberal supply of cheap luxuries might between them create a set of people entirely without ambition to think and act for themselves."[7] This mobility of Priestley is an expression of his inability to find a stable way of seeing the people he meets. Analysis of England in terms of class conflict and the tensions between financial and industrial capitalism – "What had the City done for its old ally, the Industrial North?" – co-exists with an account in terms of a "real enduring England" – "of ministers and manors and inns, of Parson and Squire."[8] Priestley's England contains "peasants," "proletarians," "rural folk," northerners and southerners, "working folk," and various classes. Working class communists jostle an "amiable and slow peasantry" who are continuous with the "stout, and hale and jolly" peasants of Smollett's *A Six Months Tour of the North of England.*[9] It appears that Priestley, the traveller, could *observe* only division and conflict in England in 1934, but that Priestley, the citizen, wished to see unity. Certainly his stance – its mobility and assumption of intimacy with a number of groups – seems a simultaneous expression of contradictory beliefs: of a confidence in a "traditional" England of shared valuations – with "sturdy" labouring men and colourful "eccentrics" – and of his despair that a single standpoint can accommodate the various class experiences of England in the 1930s.[10]

Unlike Priestley's, Muir's stance is one of detachment from place and reader. This "in-between person ... of indefinable class position,"[11] as the historian T. C. Smout describes Muir, adopts the stance in lowland Scotland of an exile who returns to a place in which he has lived but to which he does not belong: "The Scots have always been an unhappy people. ... they are now, at least the better of them, almost contentedly so." Even in the Highlands, "my own country," Muir ventures only once a suggestion that he shares a view with those whom he meets: "I have described my own inability to cope with [English middle-class manners] because I feel sure that this is shared by the majority of Highlanders, who have never been to public schools and do not know whether they are saying the right thing or not."[12] Muir's detachment from his readers is no less firm. Although published in London, *Scottish Journey* is neither seriously addressed to English readers nor does it adopt their standpoint; although centrally concerned with Scottish life, it does not sustainedly speak to or with a Scottish readership. There are, of course, declarations of political conviction: "If Capitalism manages finally to smash these unions, it will be a loss of civilisation greater than the loss that would be brought about by another world war."[13] But Muir's inability on his journey to find any identity between himself and his countrymen – except in the Highlands which, according to a recent historian, "could not hope to become a centre of radical protest"[14] – ensures that his comments on the Scottish class struggle appear those of an observer rather than a participant, that his politics are marginal to the text: in *Scottish Journey*, the "I" rarely becomes "we." Muir's detachment seems the expression of genuine isolation, not the ironical pose of Lockhart's Peter.

However different the stances of Priestley and Muir, both have at their disposal, as "domestic travellers," kinds of knowledge which are unavailable to the traveller abroad, however well-informed. A certain kind of traveller abroad exploits his ignorance, showing interest in the cultural identity of the place he visits only in so far as that identity can be made to serve the interests he brings to the place, or as a correlative of his psychological condition. What recent praise of such travel books ignores is that places and people are the sites of various established meanings – cultural, literary and political – or, as Evelyn Waugh phrases it, "are already fully labelled," and that an attempt by the traveller to make of the place what he needs may simply sanction and confirm some of those established meanings.[15] Graham Greene's *Journey Without Maps* is an example of this kind of travel book, collapsing the tripartite distinction of traveller/place/reader, merging traveller with place, and making the reader someone who "overhears" rather than "hears," to make J. S. Mill's distinction. In *Journey Without Maps*, the record of a trek he made into Liberia, Greene uses Liberian life as a way of measuring his own pattern of life and English culture; his book is an "anthropological study of our civilisation" in a special sense.

The structure of the work, the move into the unmapped and uncolonised Liberia from colonised Sierra Leone, suggests movement into the unknown, into what Greene calls, with awareness of its literary weight, "darkness." "The tall black door in the narrow city street remained closed," the opening sentence of the book, signals the importance of barriers and the desire to penetrate inwards and, as one soon realises, backwards.[16] Even the animal life of Liberia's forests becomes an agent in Greene's quest: for instance, he writes of a "bird with wings creaking like unoiled doors." The cultural practices of Liberia are rapidly appropriated by the traveller. The Buzie devils become a means by which he can make contact with his "personal and racial childhood," the goal of his search: they remind him of a Jack-in-the-Green which he remembers from his childhood and which he knows was important in English religious life "as late as the ninth century."[17] Liberia, then, is used by Greene as a site on which he can recover contact with his own childhood and can experience a more primitive stage of his own culture. For Greene, Africa continues "the past from which one has emerged."[18] The consequence of using Liberia as a mask behind which he can explore his own distinctive concerns is that Greene ratifies that late nineteenth-century view of Africa as a place in which man might return to a more instinctual life. Greene's Africa is Rider Haggard's whom, twenty-five years later, Greene would acknowledge as a mentor – "without a knowledge of Rider Haggard would I have been drawn ... to Liberia?"[19] Passages from Haggard and Henty gloss perfectly Greene's lament about "what man had made of the primitive, what he had made of childhood."

> in all essentials the savage and the child of civilisation are identical ... we must look to the nineteen savage portions of our nature if we would really understand ourselves, and not to the twentieth, which, though so insignificant in reality, is spread all over the other nineteen, making them appear quite different from what they really are, as the blacking does a foot; or the veneer a table. It is on the nineteen rough serviceable portions that we fall back in emergencies.

> [Africans] are just like children. ... Left alone to their own devices they retrograde into a state little above their native savagery.[20]

Greene is, perhaps, the most "literary" traveller of the thirties, aware that some places have not so much cultural, social and economic histories as literary histories. Even Liberia, without a literary pedigree, is, for Greene, primarily a literary trope. It is revealing that Greene can at one point write (and the emphasis is his own) that "other writers more often complain in *their* parts of Africa of the noise and savagery of the jungle";[21] Africa is less the property of those who live there than of the European writers who have made it theirs.

I intend to give more space to George Orwell's *The Road to Wigan Pier*, my fourth and last example, because it offers an excellent opportunity to show that stance is not simply a matter of authorial choice, but is in part the consequence of the author's transformation of the stance that the mode of travel book he has chosen makes available to him. *The Road to Wigan Pier* is clearly a variant on what has come to be known as the "Into Unknown England" travel book: "It is a tradition that is best defined in terms of the language which the writers used to describe their activities. Acting as representatives of upper- or middle-class life, they cast themselves as 'explorers,' entering, for the good of society as a whole, a world inhabited by the poor and destitute."[22]

When one is aware of the tradition in which *The Road* is written, Samuel Hynes's judgement that it opens "not like a report but like a first-person proletarian novel" seems wrong.[23] During the opening pages, Orwell is intent on insisting that he is *not* a proletarian: "The first sound in the mornings was the clumping of the mill girls' clogs down the cobbled streets. Earlier than that, I suppose, there were factory whistles which I was never awake to hear."[24] Orwell only *hears* the women go to work and is always asleep when the factory whistles, of which he has no knowledge, sound. This early admission of ignorance ("I suppose") is an important sign of the stance he will later adopt. Orwell is not content, though, to identify himself as different from those whom he meets. At the Brookers', the first lodging house which Orwell mentions, is a "traveller for a cigarette firm," who recognises Orwell as an ally: he "caught my eye and suddenly divined that I was a fellow-Southerner." (16) Within the first few pages, then, Orwell has clarified in a preliminary way his identity, a visitor from the South. But if he wishes to acknowledge his affinity with the "traveller," he is also intent on distinguishing his stance from that of fellow southerners. After one night's stay at the Brookers', the "traveller" is so appalled by the conditions that he indignantly denounces the home to its owners and departs. Denunciation of the feckless poor and their disorder has a long tradition, and is clearly available to Orwell as a response.[25] It is one he scrutinises but rejects. Equally, later in the book, he considers and criticises what he sees as the "condemnation" of the middle class by the "highbrow of proletarian origin" (198). Indignation and denunciation, Orwell seems to say, are possible and even understandable but not adequate responses by a visitor to another way of life. The anecdote of the "traveller," which appears nowhere in the Diary, is Orwell's early acknowledgement that he must engage with the stances of other travellers to clarify and define his stance, that he situates himself among a plenitude of other visitors.

It is not only the righteous indignation of the "traveller" which is absent from Orwell's stance, but also any sense of the heroic character of his endeavour. Of course, this may merely reflect the unarduous character of a 1930s journey to the North compared with a journey into, say, the working-class districts of Victorian London. But it seems rather to articulate Orwell's recognition that the traveller's work is less strenuous than that of those among whom he moves. In one of the most celebrated parts of *The Road*, the account of a visit to a mine, Orwell formulates a number of the activities in terms of travel. For instance, he gives substantial attention to what is called "travelling," the exhausting unpaid journey of a miner to and from the coalface, and to his own experience of such a journey, his response to which he humorously displaces into a description – in terms of travel – of the "air [which] if left to itself ... will take the shortest way round, leaving the deeper workings unventilated" (28, 26). Even the way Orwell describes the coal-cutter which relieves the miners' labour and mocks his own exhaustion – it "travels along the coalface" – suggests that he is eager to remind himself and his readers that his own activity must be seen and judged in the context of the labour of others (30). In *The Road*, the objects of scrutiny are not passive before the observer's gaze but have a life which can challenge and chasten that gaze. Orwell makes the traveller, as much as the perceived, the object of scrutiny.

The incident which evidences most clearly Orwell's stance is his encounter with the young woman. Two versions of this meeting exist, one in *The Road*, the other in the "Diary." (Bernard Crick has recently made it plain that we should not assume that the diary is a simple transcription of a given reality, the other the "fiction," but that they are two versions of an event, the meaning of which Orwell tries to clarify and define.)[26] The first quotation is from the "Diary":

> Passing up a horrible squalid side-alley, saw a woman, youngish but very pale and with the usual draggled exhausted look, kneeling by the gutter outside a house and poking a stick up the leaden waste-pipe, which was blocked. I thought how dreadful a destiny it was to be kneeling in the gutter in a back-alley in Wigan, in the bitter cold, prodding a stick up a blocked drain. At that moment she looked up and caught my eye, and her expression was as desolate as I have ever seen; it struck me that she was thinking just the same thing as I was.[27]

As we moved slowly through the outskirts of the town we passed row after row of little grey slum houses running at right angles to the embankment. At the back of one of the houses a young woman was kneeling on the stones, poking a stick up the leaden waste-pipe which ran from the sink inside and which I suppose was blocked. I had time to see everything about her – her sacking apron, her clumsy clogs, her arms reddened by the cold. She looked up as the train passed, and I was almost near enough to catch her eye. She had a round pale face, the usual exhausted face of the slum girl who is twenty-five and looks forty, thanks to miscarriages and drudgery; and it wore, for the second in which I saw it, the most desolate, hopeless expression I have ever seen. It struck me then that we are mistaken when we say that 'It isn't the same for them as it would be for us,' and that people bred in the slums can imagine nothing but the slums. For what I saw in her face was not the ignorant suffering of an animal. She knew well enough what was happening to her – understood as well as I did how dreadful a destiny it was to be kneeling there in the bitter cold, on the slimy stones of a slum backyard, poking a stick up a foul drain-pipe. (18)

The "Diary" says that "she looked up and caught my eye"; the travel book that "I was almost near enough to catch her eye." The brief encounter of the "Diary" in which Orwell and the woman looked at one another, becomes in *The Road* less substantial and direct. Clearly, this particular encounter has important similarities with others which punctuate Orwell's travel writing, but it also differs in one crucial way. The important meetings in Orwell usually entail direct engagement: for instance, *Homage to Catalonia* is framed by two crucial encounters, the first with an Italian militia man, the second with an enemy officer. These meetings which signal Orwell's entrance into Catalonia and his departure from it both entail the shaking of hands: "As we went out he stepped across the room and gripped my hand very hard. Queer, the affection you can feel for a stranger!". "The little officer hesitated a little, then stepped across, and shook hands with me. I do not know if I can bring home to you how deeply that action touched me."[28] Even less significant encounters are usually characterised by a related directness: for instance, the traveller from the South in *The Road* "caught my eye and divined that I was a fellow-Southerner."

The "Diary" version of the incident with the young woman formulates it in the dominant manner – "caught my eye"; *The Road* version offers a variation on that manner – "almost near enough to catch her eye." The use of a related phrase to describe his meeting with the "traveller" and the young woman – the incidents are a few pages apart – invites us to recognise how much more problematic for Orwell is the encounter with the working-class woman. He refuses to pretend that he, a southern traveller, has access to what this young northern woman, from a different class from his own, believes, thinks and feels. His stress on his perception of her ("I had time to see everything about her – her sacking apron, her clumsy clogs, her arms reddened by the cold") is his confession that he can only *see* her. Even when he does venture an account of her thoughts, he makes it clear that he does so on the basis of minimal evidence – her face "wore, *for the second I saw it*, the most desolate, hopeless expression" – and on a "reading" of her face: "For what I saw in her face was not the ignorant suffering of an animal. She knew well enough what was happening to her – understood as well as I did how dreadful a destiny it was to be kneeling there in the bitter cold." This is a powerful revision of the "Into Unknown England" habit of viewing the poor as savages or animals determined by their environment. Jack London's *People of the Abyss*, to which Orwell refers in *The Road*, shows how the "Into Unknown England" tradition can shape even the view of someone who proclaims himself a Socialist: "Some were poor, wretched beasts, inarticulate and callous, but for all that, in many ways very human."[29] Orwell raises this way of viewing the young woman ("animal," "destiny") only to reject it, and replace it with the view that her knowledge of her own condition is equal to that of the observer. (It is a measure of Orwell's regression in *Animal Farm* that he should return to the working class-as-exploited-animals tradition.) In *The Road*, the traveller is not an observer privileged with kinds of knowledge denied to the participants. What he can see and know, Orwell seems to say, is determined by the place from which he sees.

The "Diary" has several descriptions of Orwell's journeys by foot ("Had a long and exhausting day ... being shown every quarter of Sheffield on foot and by tram");[30] *The Road* has no such accounts, and stresses Orwell's journeys by train, of which the one under scrutiny is an example (it is significant that in the "Diary" version of this incident Orwell is on foot). Orwell's trains are, of course, among the many that fill 1930s writing. As Paul Fussell says: "it would be hard to designate another time when it was so conventional to conceive of life specifically as a journey by *rails*."[31] In Part Two of *The Road*, Orwell compares the travel of the "nomad who walks or rides" with that of the passenger of "an express train or a luxury liner," and admits that since no one ever wants to do anything in a more cumbrous way than is necessary, a traveller will choose the more comfortable form of transport (232). "Nomad" and "passenger" signify not only different kinds of traveller, but also past and present Orwells. The Orwell of *Down and Out in Paris and London* (1933) "becomes" a nomad by the simple act of a change of clothes: "My new clothes had put me instantly into a new world. Everyone's demeanour seemed to have changed abruptly. ... No one had called me mate before in my life – it was the clothes that had done it."[32] Orwell's decision to situate himself on a train in *The Road* is at once a rejection of the stance of identification of *Down and Out* and an expression of his conviction that identification of the middle-class individual with the working class is not possible, and that he is irremediably a "passenger," – "a passer by or through," according to the OED – in his relation to that class. The possibility of relationships *within* a class is very differently understood by Orwell, as his encounter on a train to Mandalay with a man in the Educational service shows. Orwell and this "stranger," "whose name I never discovered," confess to each other "forbidden things," their hatred of the British Empire, leaving each other the following morning "as guiltily as any adulterous couple" (177). The sexual analogue merely confirms the easy intimacy of people within a class.

Within such a general context, Part II of *The Road*, Orwell's substantial account of his history, and especially of his class position, makes sense not as an instance of "confessional literature"[33] (Samuel Hynes' verdict) but as a discursive version of the stance enacted in Part I, and as an explanation of that stance. Orwell's subject in both parts is class relations. In the first part, as in the passage about the young woman in which he assumes an identity of belief between himself and his reader ("we are mistaken when we say"), Orwell aligns himself sustainedly with the reader; in the second part, he makes explicit what is implicit earlier, his membership of the middle class: "I would not do it [write about himself] if I did not think that I am sufficiently typical of my class, or rather sub-caste, to have a certain symptomatic importance" (153). How can and should such an individual relate to the working class? Galsworthy's "perpetual quiver of indignation" over the plight of the oppressed, the misguided belief that one can become a member of the working class, the tendency of certain socialists to deny the working-class consciousness of their own conditions and to try to impose "a set of reforms" on "them" – these and other stances are examined and rejected (190, 213). The stance Orwell promotes is that imaged throughout Part I: one that acknowledges both the position from which the observer "sees" the working class and the knowledge and understanding of that class of its own conditions. The middle-class person is for Orwell a traveller in his dealings with the working class. Not primarily in the sense that he has to travel to meet them in their places of work or at home, but in the sense that he should not pretend more knowledge of or intimacy with that class than a traveller can have of a place he visits but to which he does not belong.

The germ of Orwell's stance, or at least of that part of it which admits ignorance rather than pretends intimacy, may be discovered in a writer such as Elizabeth Gaskell, who acknowledges at the opening of *Mary Barton* her uncertainty about the reason for the walk in the fields: "I do not know whether it was a holiday . . ."[34] But to make the comparison is to realise its limited usefulness. Orwell is aware, unlike Elizabeth Gaskell, that it is necessary for the middle-class observer to discuss and define his own position within the text as well as admit his inevitable ignorances. What he wishes to and can know is to a large extent the function of his class position. In *The Road*, epistemological questions are not sociologically inert. Of course, our judgement of the adequacy of such a stance will be different from Orwell's. For him, its adequacy seems not so much a question of its absolute value as a matter of its superiority to other available stances. I recognise that this account of *The Road to Wigan Pier* ignores Orwell's omission of the numerous meetings he had with trades union officials and working-class socialists. The reasons for Orwell's suppression of his knowledge of the organised political life of the working class are difficult to understand and have often been discussed. What is important in the context of his argument is the way in which Orwell revised the meanings available in the form he had chosen. But forms do not only permit, they also *condition* meaning. To have shown the working class active in its own making, Orwell would need to have chosen some literary form other than the travel book.

This survey of stance in four mid-1930s travel books makes possible a couple of general points about travel writing and its conventions and their significance. In his recent critical book *Pleasurable Instruction: Form and Convention in Eighteenth-Century Travel Literature*, Charles L. Batten Jr writes that "For over a century we have tended to think of travel literature as a miscellaneous form of writing primarily governed by the subjective whim of its authors."[35] Although such a judgement does not do justice to the limited number of useful accounts of travel literature, it does imply what is accurate about most critical readings of travel writing: the concentration on social content and the neglect of the conventions through which meaning is produced. While travel writing, like all forms, does contain useful information, a comparison of, say, the two related but different versions of Orwell's travels in the North – the "Diary" and *The Road* – suggests how complex is the relation between the actual experience of the traveller and its transcription into forms of writing.

I have tried to identify one important convention of travel writing in one particular period and to show how the variations in this one convention permit and condition various meanings. A convention in this context is not merely an aesthetic expression, but the bearer of social meaning. Certainly, this survey of four travel writings in the mid-1930s – *the* moment of commitment according to most literary histories – at once confirms that judgement which speaks of the social and political mobility of the writers of the 1930s and challenges that other account which stresses that they found stability and comfort in new commitments. It is not necessary to go elsewhere – for instance, to biography – to discover the social position of travellers in the mid-1930s or the social relations in which they were involved: these positions and complex relations are inscribed in the stances of the various writers, and these stances are more certain evidence than their places of residence or declared commitments.

PHILIP DODD
University of Leicester

NOTES

1. John Berger, *Pig Earth* (London: Writers and Readers Cooperative, 1979), pp. 5, 6.
2. Norman Douglas, *Old Calabria* quoted in John Alcorn, *The Nature Novel from Hardy to Lawrence* (London: Macmillan, 1977), p. 47. For my account of Edwardian travel I am indebted to Professor Alcorn's book; for my judgements on late eighteenth-century travel to the essay by Patricia Spacks, "Splendid Falsehoods: English Accounts of Rome, 1760-1798," *Prose Studies* 3 (1980), pp. 103-16.
3. Two relevant recent accounts are Bernard Bergonzi's *Reading the Thirties: Texts and Contexts* (London: Macmillan, 1978) and Samuel Hynes' *The Auden Generation: Literature and Politics in the 1930s* (London, Sydney, Toronto: Bodley Head, 1970).
4. In a letter to the *New Statesman* 30 January, 1937. The phrase is quoted in Hynes' *The Auden Generation*, p. 280.
5. George Orwell, *Homage to Catalonia* (Harmondsworth: Penguin, 1966), p. 221. From the standpoint of an outsider, D.H. Lawrence confirmed Orwell's judgement, recognising his separation from what Orwell saw as "my" England: "So much beauty and pathos of old things passing away and no new things coming: this house of the Ottolines – it is England – my God, it breaks my soul – *their* England, their shafted windows, the elm trees, the blue distance." A letter to Lady Cynthia Asquith, November 1915, *The Collected Letters of D.H. Lawrence* ed. H.T. Moore (London: Heinemann, 1962), I, 378 (my emphasis).
6. J.B. Priestley, *English Journey* (London: Heinemann in association with Gollancz, 1934), p. 3.
7. *English Journey*, pp. 14, 110, 244, 405.
8. *English Journey*, pp. 411, 400, 397.
9. *English Journey*, pp. 20, 4, 253, 254, 360; the passage from Smollett is quoted in James Sambrook's *William Cobbett* (London and Boston: Routledge & Kegan Paul), p. 18.
10. *English Journey*, pp. 29, 62.
11. *Scottish Journey*, intro. by T.C. Smout (Edinburgh, Mainstream, 1979), p. x.
12. *Scottish Journey*, pp. 30-1, 206, 207.
13. *Scottish Journey*, p. 149.
14. "From Client to Supplicant: Capital and Labour in Scotland, 1870-1945," *Scottish Capitalism: Class, State and Nation from before the Union to the Present* ed. Tony Dickson (London: Lawrence & Wishart, 1980), p. 259.
15. Evelyn Waugh, *Labels: A Mediterranean Journal* intro. by Kingsley Amis (London: Duckworth, 1974), p. 16. *Labels* was first published in 1930.
16. Graham Greene, *Journey Without Maps, The Collected Edition of Graham Greene*, 18 (London: Heinemann & Bodley Head, 1978), pp. 8, 1. First published by Heinemann.
17. *Journey Without Maps*, pp. 134, 99.
18. *Journey Without Maps*, p. 7.
19. *A Sort of Life* (New York: Simon and Schuster, 1971), p. 55.
20. *Journey Without Maps*, p. 265. H. Rider Haggard, *Allan Quatermaine* (London, Calcutta, Sydney: Harrap, 1925), pp. 12, 14. G.A. Henty, *By Sheer Pluck* quoted in G.D. Killam, *Africa in English Fiction 1874-1939* (Ibadan: Ibadan, U.P., 1968), p. 21.
21. *Journey Without Maps*, p. 181.

22. "Preface," *Into Unknown England 1866-1913; Selections from the Social Explorers* ed. Peter Keating (London: Fontana, 1976), p.[9].

23. *The Auden Generation*, p.273.

24. George Orwell, *The Road to Wigan Pier* with a Foreword by Victor Gollancz (London: Gollancz, 1937), p.5. Subsequent references will be inserted parenthetically in the text.

25. Thomas Hardy attacks such denunciation in "The Dorsetshire Labourer": "Nothing, for instance, is more common than for some philanthropic lady to burst in upon a family, be struck by the apparent squalor of the scene and to straightway mark down that household in her note-book as a frightful example of the misery of the labouring classes." *Thomas Hardy's Personal Writings*, ed. Harold Orel (London, Melbourne: Macmillan, 1967), p.172.

26. Bernard Crick, *George Orwell: A Life* (London: Secker & Warburg, 1980), p.182.

27. *An Age like This 1920-1940: The Collected Essays, Journalism and Letters of George Orwell* ed. Sonia Orwell and Ian Angus (Harmondsworth: Penguin, 1970), I, 203.

28. *Homage to Catalonia*, pp.7, 212.

29. Quoted in *Into Unknown England*, p.234. In rejecting the vocabulary of this tradition, Orwell also rejects a naturalistic stance which would see "man as an animal whose course is determined by his heredity, by the effect of his environment and by the pressures of the moment." See Lillian R. Furst and Peter N. Skrine, *Naturalism* (London: Methuen, 1971), p.18.

30. *CEJL*, I, 218.

31. Paul Fussell, *Abroad: British Literary Travelling Between the Wars* (New York, Oxford: Oxford U.P., 1980), p.63.

32. George Orwell, *Down and Out in Paris and London* (Harmondsworth: Penguin, 1975), p.115.

33. *The Auden Generation*, p.276.

34. Elizabeth Gaskell, *Mary Barton* (Harmondsworth: Penguin, 1970), p.40.

35. Charles L. Batten Jr, *Pleasurable Instruction: Form and Convention in Eighteenth-Century Travel Literature* (Berkeley, Los Angeles, London: U. of California Press, 1978), p.117.

Authorial Voice in
V.S. Naipaul's The Middle Passage

Since the publication of Wayne Booth's *The Rhetoric of Fiction* (1961) there has been widespread recognition that the voice which speaks to us in a work of fiction is not that of the writer himself – Fielding or Austen or Tolstoy – but rather that of an "implied author,"[1] a persona which the writer assumes, consciously or unconsciously. This is a point which can be extended to all areas of human discourse, including such non-fictional forms as historiography, autobiography and – travel writing. Just as the novelist dons a particular costume and acts a particular part in each of his fictions, so the writer who sets out to give an account of his travels inevitably has to invest himself with his own particular version of the role of the traveller, among the most popular being those of guide, social commentator, tourist and explorer. Such roles are not, of course, mutually exclusive and many travel-writers avail themselves of several in the course of a single work.

V. S. Naipaul's *The Middle Passage* (1962), an account of his travels in five Caribbean territories, provides an interesting case-study of the way in which persona is employed within the travel book. It is a work in which the writer shows himself to be well acquainted with earlier travel-writing about the region and, by alluding to his predecessors in the genre, implicitly places himself in a tradition of such writing. Indeed it is possible to read *The Middle Passage* as more metatravelogue than straightforward traveller's tale, since, in addition to this foregrounding of the tradition to which it belongs, the work also identifies the difficulty of finding an appropriate tone of voice in which to write about the West Indies:

> How can the history of this West Indian futility be written? What tone shall the historian adopt? Shall he be as academic as Sir Alan Burns, protesting from time to time at some brutality, and setting West Indian brutality in the context of European brutality? Shall he, like Salvador de Madariaga, weigh one set of brutalities against another, and conclude that one has not been described in all its foulness and that this is unfair to Spain? Shall he, like the West Indian historians, who can only now begin to face their history, be icily detached and tell the story of the slave trade as if it were just another aspect of mercantilism?[2]

Here the problem of finding the right tone is specifically that encountered by the historian, and when Naipaul himself attempted a West Indian history in *The Loss of El Dorado* (1969) he adopted the method of confining himself to an account of the "two moments when Trinidad was touched by 'history'."[3] In this work his analysis eschews both academic detachment and concerned indignation in favour of a meticulously detailed record which endeavours to illustrate the nature of colonial society and the extent of its dependence on the metropolis. The " 'history' " of Trinidad comes, in Naipaul's view, to consist only of a narrative of encounters with the metropolis. He is quite explicit about this in saying that "A place like Port of Spain, in the uncluttered New World, has no independent life; it alters with the people who come to it,"[4] and in regarding Trinidad as "exempt from history"[5] during the long interval between the two episodes on which he focuses. In short, Naipaul's one and only incursion into the realms of history writing to date is characterised by its novelistic accretion of circumstantial detail and an authorial stance which denies colonial society any autonomous life of its own. The tone is much less dispassionate than that of most historians and one is always aware of a voice which, without ever quite identifying itself with the coloniser, holds itself aloof from the society which is being discussed.

The Middle Passage is no history of the territories which Naipaul visits, but it is as much a social investigation as a traveller's journal and it demonstrates a concern with cultural identity in the Caribbean and Guianas. Consequently the problem of finding an appropriate voice is equally acute here, and it is fitting that Naipaul's remarks on the difficulties which face the West Indian historian occur in this work, since his own attempt to render his traveller's-eye view of the "West Indian futility" involves him in similar problems. As a result there is little distinction in this respect to be made between his travel-writing and his history writing.

In the Note to the Penguin edition of the work, which first appeared in 1969, Naipaul admits that *The Middle Passage* has less shape than he would have liked, and within the text this weakness manifests itself in a failure to bring together a number of recurrent themes, all loosely concerned with cultural identity. This, in turn, is mirrored by Naipaul's employment of a number of different personae. Yet, looked at from another point of view, the book's use of multiple personae is a strength rather than a weakness, for, although it is an index of Naipaul's inability to find a single suitable tone, it enables him to essay several different viewpoints more or less simultaneously. It is in this sense that *The Middle Passage* is as much a self-conscious investigation of the problems which beset the travel-writer who takes the Caribbean as his subject as an account of the places he visits, as much metatravelogue as straightforward traveller's tale. The text itself dramatises the very difficulty which Naipaul sees as facing those who write about the West Indies, even if it never arrives at a fully satisfactory solution.

The problem of finding the correct tone for a travel-book about the West Indies is especially acute for Naipaul. For, while his account follows a standard format employed by British and North American visitors – a chapter on each of the societies visited – his own situation is a curiously hybrid one, since he comes as an outsider to write about his own part of the world. The tension between the perspectives of foreigner and local is particularly to the fore when he writes about Trinidad, the island of his birth, but the same outsider-insider dichotomy informs the whole work. At times his aloofness and detachment approximate those of the foreign visitor, but ultimately, as in *The Loss of El Dorado*, the tone employed cannot be identified as the voice of an outsider. The tension between the two perspectives is further compounded by factors surrounding the composition of the work and the specific nature of Naipaul's West Indian background.

The circumstances surrounding the composition of the work are outlined by Naipaul in his Foreword to the first edition. The Trinidad and Tobago Government awarded him a three-month scholarship, which enabled him to return to Trinidad from England where he had been living for a decade. While he was back in Trinidad, the Prime Minister, Dr Eric Williams, suggested that he should write a book about the Caribbean, and his original scholarship was extended to enable him to visit other parts of the region.[6] After some initial hesitation caused by his uncertainty as to whether he would make the transition from fiction to non-fiction successfully – "The novelist works towards conclusions of which he is often unaware; and it is better than he should" (p.[6]) – he agreed to write the book, but did not allow the patronage he had received to compromise him in any way. In the Foreword he asserts that *The Middle Passage* is in no sense an " 'official' book" and this is borne out in the text itself, which is frequently scathing about Trinidad and the Caribbean more generally.[7] When the book was completed, it was, like all of Naipaul's other works, published by André Deutsch and so, arguably, Trinidadian sponsorship was supplanted by the constraint of metropolitan publication. Certainly there is ample evidence to suggest that Naipaul is writing with British readers in mind: refusing to play the part of the "innocent" travel writer, he frequently places his remarks in context by alluding to British travellers' accounts of the West Indies and provides basic information about the Caribbean situation, presumably for the benefit of such readers.

The specific nature of Naipaul's West Indian background also compounds the problem which he has in finding an appropriate tone. As he sees it, his origins as a third generation Caribbean East Indian set him apart from the black-white mainstream of West Indian society. Later, in *The Mimic Men* (1967), he has his Indian protagonist-narrator, Ralph Singh, envisage himself as an intruder standing between "the mutual and complete comprehension of master and slave,"[8] and in *The Middle Passage* such a view is anticipated by comments on the Indian's alienness:

> Everything which made the Indian alien in the society gave him strength. His alienness insulated him from the black-white struggle. ... His religion gave him values which were not the white values of

the rest of the community, and preserved him from self-contempt; he never lost pride in his origins. More important than religion was his family organization, an enclosing self-sufficient world absorbed with its quarrels and jealousies, as difficult for the outsider to penetrate as for one of its members to escape. It protected and imprisoned, a static world awaiting decay. (88)

Whether this view of the Caribbean East Indian's situation is, or was, accurate is a moot point. It is, however, the way in which Naipaul sees his predicament and hence another determinant of the authorial voice adopted in *The Middle Passage*. For him, his Indian background makes him someone who is both inside and outside Caribbean society and, though in his early novels he is at pains to repudiate his Hindu heritage through an ironic exposure of its rites and beliefs, he remains a product of his upbringing[9] in a way that the more Creolised type of Trinidadian Indian, such as his fellow-novelist Samuel Selvon, never is.

Naipaul's view of the Indian's alienness in the society is by no means the only aspect of his Hindu background contributing to the blend of detachment and involvement which characterises the authorial voice of *The Middle Passage*. His two subsequent travel books about India, *An Area of Darkness* (1964) and *India: A Wounded Civilization* (1977), both attack the quietism which lies at the heart of the Hindu psyche and prevents it from engaging with any real degree of commitment in activities which could bring about social amelioration. Such quietism is seen to stem from *karma*, "the Hindu killer, the Hindu calm, which tells us that we pay in this life for what we have done in past lives: so that everything we see is just and balanced, and the distress we see is to be relished as religious theatre, a reminder of our duty to ourselves, our future lives."[10]

Naipaul's attack on *karma* in his two Indian books is complemented at times, though by no means always, by a sense of concerned indignation about the lack of social progress which it occasions and, when he comments in *An Area of Darkness* on the mythic nature of the Indian novel it is clear that he is aligning himself with the Western novelist:

Indian attempts at the novel further reveal the Indian confusion. The novel is of the West. It is part of that Western concern with the condition of men, a response to the here and now. In India thoughtful men have preferred to turn their backs on the here and now and to satisfy what President Radhakrishnan calls 'the basic human hunger for the unseen'.[11]

Yet towards the end of *An Area of Darkness*, his account of his first traumatic journey back to his ancestral homeland, and the book in which he first mounts his attack on the psychological paralysis engendered by *karma*, he realises the extent to which he too has been a victim of such a psychology:

To preserve this conception of India as a country still whole, historical facts had not been suppressed. They had been acknowledged and ignored; and it was only in India that I was able to see this as part of the Indian ability to retreat, the ability genuinely not to see what was obvious: with others a foundation of neurosis, but with Indians only part of a greater philosophy of despair, leading to passivity, detachment, acceptance. It is only now, as the impatience of the observer is dissipated in the process of writing and self-inquiry, that I see how much this philosophy had also been mine. It had enabled me, through the stresses of a long residence in England, to withdraw completely from nationalities and loyalties except to persons ... and taught me to shield all that I knew to be good and pure within myself from the corruption of causes.[12]

Like the lapsed Catholic, Naipaul has, then, been irrevocably shaped by the religion of his upbringing, even though he consciously rejects it, and the legacy of the *karma*-psychology is at least as important a determinant of his authorial stance as the fact of East Indian alienness in the Caribbean. Along with the habitual pose of detachment of the English ironic tradition, to which Naipaul is also strongly indebted, that legacy provides the distinctive tone of aloofness and non-involvement that pervades much of *The Middle Passage*. Yet Naipaul is seldom simply detached, seldom simply aloof. Throughout the work the authorial voice seems to alternate between balanced non-involvement and a generally suppressed tone of hysteria, which occasionally breaks through the urbane surface, as when Naipaul describes his attempts to get a cup of coffee on an exasperating Georgetown morning.

So Naipaul's own complex relationship to his West Indian subject-matter adds an extra dimension to the problem of finding the right tone in which to write about the "West Indian futility." One of his ways of dealing with the problem is to interlace first-hand observation and commentary with references to earlier "authorities," most of them British. The opening pages have the effect of immediately imposing a foreign filter. Naipaul establishes the mood of the work by employing two epigraphs taken from the imperialist historian James Anthony Froude, whose travel-journal, *The English in the West Indies* (1888), has achieved notoriety in the Caribbean for its racism.[13] The first – the epigraph to the whole work – involves a total dismissal of West Indian society:

They were valued only for the wealth which they yielded, and society there has never assumed any particularly noble aspect. ... There are no people there in the true sense of the word, with a character and purpose of their own. (p.[7])[14]

The second – the epigraph to the first chapter – is much more specific. Naipaul quotes a passage in which Froude gives an account of the various "gentlemen" who are with him in his railway carriage as he embarks on the first leg of his West Indian journey, along exactly the same route – Waterloo to Southampton – as Naipaul will later take.[15] This has the effect of providing ironic counterpoint to Naipaul's comments on his own fellow-travellers, "a crowd of immigrant-type West Indians" (9), who he renders as caricatures:

> One man with a Nat King Cole hairstyle was dandling a fat bonneted baby that was gift-wrapped in ribbons and frills, with a rubber nipple stuck like a gag and a final flourish in its drooping, dripping mouth. Two ladies with felt hats and pink stockings sat slumped against the window. They wore gauze-like dresses over satin petticoats of a fiery pink. The powder on their faces had dissolved in patches, and they crumpled tiny embroidered handkerchiefs in large shining hands. (9)

Through the use of the two epigraphs, and the ironic portrayal of his black travelling-companions, which immediately establishes his own distance from such West Indians, Naipaul implicitly adopts the persona of a latter-day Froude,[16] a traveller sentenced to journey among those whom he regards as his inferiors. This identification with Froude is confirmed when, later in the first chapter, he endorses the view expressed in the Froude epigraph to the whole work by saying, at the end of his passage on the difficulties of West Indian historiography:

> The history of the islands can never be satisfactorily told. Brutality is not the only difficulty. History is built around achievement and creation; and nothing was created in the West Indies. (29)

Elsewhere in *The Middle Passage*, as for example when he writes with clear enthusiasm about the calypso (75-6), Naipaul shows himself quite capable of seeing the limitations of the essentially Eurocentric view of "creation" implied here. At this point in the opening chapter, however, he is so thoroughly immersed in the persona of Victorian outsider that he engages in a Froude-like generalisation which his own later evidence undermines.

In addition to modelling aspects of his authorial persona on Froude, Naipaul also frequently employs other British "authorities." Trollope's *The West Indies and the Spanish Main* (1859), referred to on no less than a dozen occasions, and Kingsley's *At Last: A Christmas in the West Indies* (1871) both figure prominently among Naipaul's allusions and are supplemented by numerous more recent British travel-books about the region, among them James Pope-Hennessy's *West Indian Summer* (1943), Patrick Leigh Fermor's *Traveller's Tree* (1950) and Michael Swan's *The Marches of El Dorado* (1958).

The effect of this barrage of references is complex. On the one hand, it prevents Naipaul from succumbing to a naive empiricism and simply recording his subjective impressions. On the other hand, it implies a Eurocentric point of departure. Far more serious is Naipaul's tendency to present the West Indies as a static, unchanging world, even though he is writing on the eve of Independence. It is not simply that he makes comments such as "This was not the landscape for the camera: the tropical forest cannot be better suggested than by the steel engravings in the travel books of the last century" (161-2). In addition he repeatedly insists that *Plus ça change, plus c'est la même chose*. "No attitude in the West Indies is new," he writes early in the work (26), and he subsequently affords numerous instances of a West Indies arrested in time, condemned to repeat the same experiences over and over again, without ever learning the lessons of history. In this context Trollope in particular has been everywhere before Naipaul: his remarks on the difficulty of getting West Indians to eat locally produced food are, in Naipaul's view, equally valid for the contemporary Caribbean (49-50);[17] his "tips" on spotting those with the slightest tincture of "coloured" blood are said to "hold good today" (216);[18] and his comments on "the attitudes ... of people who objected to regular work" are seen to be another timeless truism (246).[19]

So Naipaul both imposes an extraneous filter on his material and engages in a static ahistoricism which prevents him from ever asking whether the views of his nineteenth-century predecessors are applicable to the West Indies at the beginning of the 1960s. The evidence for viewing his chosen authorial voice as that of a latter-day Victorian does not stop here. He also resorts to employing a favourite Victorian analogy for Empire, the parallel with imperial Rome, in quoting Tacitus for one of the epigraphs of the Trinidad chapter (42), and referring to contemporary black protest in the Caribbean as "the last, delayed Spartacan revolt" (91). Moreover Naipaul's remarks on black West Indians are often redolent of Froude and have been viewed as exhibiting a similar negrophobia.[20] From the outset, as he leaves Waterloo on the train to Southampton, he displays a disdainful attitude to his black travelling-companions, and the title of the work suggests that he regards his journey as a form of bondage, since it relates it to the infamous second leg of the triangular trade, which took Africans from the Guinea Coast to slavery in the West Indian plantations. Returning to the Caribbean is a nightmare for Naipaul, as becomes clear in one of those passages where the persona of colonial outsider slips, and his own "fear" of his homeland is allowed to spill onto the page:

> I had never wanted to stay in Trinidad. When I was in the fourth form I wrote a vow on the endpaper of my Kennedy's *Revised Latin Primer* to leave within five years. I left after six; and for many years afterwards in England, falling asleep in bedsitters with the electric fire on, I had been awakened by the nightmare that I was back in tropical Trinidad. (43)

Though this fear of the Tropics may be seen to echo Froude's negrophobia, one also detects an intensely personal angst.

In *An Area of Darkness* Naipaul discusses the gradual deterioration of "the English national myth" in the nineteenth century and relates this specifically to the concerns which inform the travel writing of the century:

> we can observe a progressive deterioration from Darwin (1832) to

Trollope (1859) to Kingsley (1870) [sic] to Froude (1887) [sic].
More and more these writers are reporting not on themselves but on
their Englishness.[21]

The implications are interesting. First, Naipaul, rightly, automatically
assumes that travel writing is about far more than the places visited. It is,
as he sees it, a report either on the writer as an individual or on the writer
as a type, in this case a national type. It we take these assumptions and
apply them to the authorial voice employed in *The Middle Passage*, it
quickly becomes clear that, for all his indebtedness to nineteenth-century
English models, Naipaul is not following his authorities in providing a
version of "the English national myth." A passage like that in which
he describes his electric fire nightmare is – despite the larger cultural
contrast implied between the warmth of Trinidad and the coldness of
Europe, and the irony that each is seen to pervade the other, in the forms
of the electric fire and the Latin primer – very much a case of reporting on
himself. While one may relate it to his ambivalent East Indian West
Indianness, the overriding impression conveyed is nonetheless that of a
hypersensitive and ultimately highly individual sensibility.

Arguably the persona has set out from London with metropolitan
assumptions and culture strong in his mind, but gradually, as he travels
further, such assumptions are eroded and give way to a more personal
vision. After he leaves Trinidad, Naipaul's journey becomes more and
more of an ordeal and the hypersensitive aspects of the persona become
more prominent. The first two chapters contain the work's most hostile
observations on contemporary West Indians, including a racist reference
to Indians and blacks as being "like monkeys pleading for evolution" (87)
in their aspirations towards whiteness. However, once Naipaul leaves
Trinidad, the detached essayistic manner of the first part of the book
is increasingly supplanted by a record of his personal uneasiness in
unfamiliar surroundings, such as an Amerindian mission whose residents
are stricken with yellow fever and a Surinamese spirit-possession cere-
mony. With the account of his own island behind him, Naipaul seems to
gather fresh wind and begin to write in a more varied vein. He does
not altogether dispense with allusions to earlier travel writers – he
remains faithful to Trollope to the last and finds new "authorities,"
such as Michael Swan for British Guiana and Patrick Leigh Fermor for
Martinique – but from the third chapter onwards there is more emphasis
on first-hand observation.

During the remainder of the work it is Naipaul the hypersensitive
traveller who occupies the centre of the stage, and fresh attributes of
the persona begin to appear. In Georgetown – "most exquisite city in
the British Caribbean ... for the visitor the most exasperating" (126) – he
becomes a slightly comic figure, struggling manfully to get efficient
service in the city's hotels and restaurants and, as his exasperation grows,
inventing combinations of words to describe the Guianese character:

Inhospitable, reactionary and lethargic except when predatory:

these were the words. And thereafter, whenever my frustration neared breaking point, I played with them, changing an adjective, adding another, until I was able to 'look up and out to the cause of all mankind'. (127)

The irony begins to cut both ways, since the comic effect relies as much on the portrayal of his own fastidious sensibility as on the indifference of those whom he encounters. The persona which he is now adopting is placed more exactly when he introduces some excerpts from his diary by saying that they read like "extracts from the diary of an enfeebled explorer" (127).

The persona of "enfeebled explorer" dominates the British Guiana and Surinam chapters of the work, as the feigned assurance of Naipaul's Victorian Man of Letters pose gives way to a basically humorous portrayal of himself as a pathfinder beset by the hardships of travelling. A trip to the Rupununi, British Guiana's southern savannah country, further tests his composure and encounters with Amerindians undermine the enfeebled explorer's already low morale:

> Among more complex peoples there are certain individuals who have the power to transmit to you their sense of defeat and purposelessness: emotional parasites who flourish by draining you of the vitality you preserve with difficulty. The Amerindians had this effect on me. (111)

A brief foray across the Brazilian border offers no respite. The township of Boa Vista which Naipaul visits is rendered as pure Greeneland: its centre is "an immense featureless dustbowl" (116); the hotel where he stays, though new, "already felt like a ruin, like a relic of a retreating civilization" (116-7); and his room is sparsely furnished, has a bulbless reading lamp, a hot water tap that does not run, and a view of a patch of wasteland which has been used as a rubbish-dump. Increasingly the journey is becoming an assault-course for the enfeebled explorer.

A trip to Berbice with the Jagans is another enervating experience and it is followed by a second journey into the Guianese hinterland, this time to Kamarang in the south-west of the country. Here Naipaul encounters "pork-knockers" (prospectors) who, regarding him as an "informed tourist" (156), immediately set about living up to their reputation for his benefit. This persona, however, remains subordinate to that of the enfeebled explorer and by now the focus of attention is increasingly narrowing itself down to a dramatization of the traveller's psyche.

During the Kamarang episode Naipaul has a travelling-companion, Mr Winter, a laconic, elderly American whose prudence and preparedness initially make him seem something of a foil to the Naipaul persona. Gradually, however, as both begin to wilt under the threat of yellow fever contagion, their initially very uneasy relationship develops into a bond of kinship. Description of the area visited becomes considerably less important than a portrayal of its psychological impact on the traveller and, if this interior is not exactly a heart of darkness, it is nevertheless a testing-ground, which has a distinctly debilitating effect on the two visitors. In their common precautions against contagion, both emerge as enfeebled explorers.

Naipaul's relationship with Mr Winter has its parallel in the Surinam chapter, when he goes on an excursion to a hydro-electric project sixty miles south of Paramaribo. His account of this trip centres on the effect which it has on one of his fellow-travellers, a young Italian photographer named Angelo. Though he is satirically depicted, Alberto is clearly another variation on the type of the suffering traveller, and hence an appropriate focus for Naipaul, who is able to take a back seat for the time being, since he has a surrogate, another humorously conceived enfeebled explorer, to write about:

> Asphalt gave way to dirt, and soon we were on the red road through the forest. We didn't see the forest; we saw only red dust. It blew into our faces and we turned up the glass. ... We didn't look powdered; we looked dyed, and the dye was getting deeper. ... We stifled. Alberto lost his fresh, brushed look of the morning. Dust reddened his neglected hair. He ceased to talk of his travels (' 'Aiti was something disgusting') and sat hunched in his corner. 'I am suffering,' he said, his hoarse voice fruity with anguish. ... 'Goodness, I'm suffering!' (192)

The British Guiana and Surinam sections also employ another authorial voice, characterized by its succinct and evocative imagistic description:

> Georgetown is a white wooden city. One would like to sketch it on rough dark grey paper, using black ink and thick white paint, to suggest the lightness and fragility of the two-storeyed buildings, a fragility most apparent at night, when light comes through the verandas on the top floor, through windows, through open lattice-work, and the effect is of those Chinese ivory palace-miniatures lit up from within. (94)

> A derelict man in a derelict land; a man discovering himself with surprise and resignation, lost in a landscape which had never ceased to be unreal because the scene of an enforced and always temporary residence. (209)

This voice, which achieves its most powerful effects through blending first-hand observation with illuminating imagery, is far removed from both the manner of the Victorian traveller and the enfeebled explorer. It is a voice which is much closer to Naipaul the novelist, and it informs many of the most interesting passages in *The Middle Passage*.

In the latter part of the work, beginning in the Surinam section, yet another persona is employed as discussion centres more obviously on questions of cultural identity. Earlier such questions have been introduced, but a serious treatment has been obscured by the employment of the Victorian filter with its implication that nothing changes in the society. Now, although colonial "authorities" are employed – even to authenticate the preponderance of mosquitoes in Surinam[22] – there is the beginnings of a more concerted consideration of the cultural situation of a society moving towards Independence.

The movement beyond the Anglophone Caribbean, which affords Naipaul a broader opportunity to make comparative assessments, appears to act as a catalyst in propelling him into his new role of cultural analyst, a role which he fills most adequately in the Surinam and Martinique sections. In the Surinam chapter he adopts the method of employing single paragraph vignettes to give a picture of the country's cultural situation, and particularly the nationalist aspirations of certain segments of the society; in the Martinique chapter he provides a vivid account of the island's colonial dependence on the *métropole*, which is reinforced by comparison with Trinidad.

Despite this, there is a definite falling off in the latter stages of the work and this comes to a head in his account of Jamaica, his last port of call. Throughout the second half of the book he quotes liberally from an eclectic range of sources, some of which begin to seem little more than perfunctory space-fillers. Thus he includes three largely gratuitous quotations from the *1959 Yearbook of Jehovah's Witnesses* and when he eventually reveals that he picked this volume up during an idle moment in an Antiguan hotel, we begin to get the feeling that anything will do. This feeling is heightened in the Jamaica chapter by his extensive dependence on a well-known report[23] for his account of the Rastafari Movement in Kingston.

Naipaul has employed several personae in the work: he has written as Victorian traveller, enfeebled explorer, novelistic observer, cultural analyst and, lastly, as purveyor of second-hand information. His inability to adopt a unitary persona has proved both a strength and a weakness, for while it has made the work diverse and centrifugal, it has had the positive effect of dramatizing the problem of tone which Naipaul has identified early on. He avoids the trap of simply assuming a single conventional authorial voice, like Froude's, which would be inappropriate for the heterogeneous societies about which he is writing. However, he leaves himself open to the charge of being rather aimlessly eclectic, since his method fails to produce a genuine answer to the problem of tone, such as is offered by the innovatory techniques of such West Indian writers as Wilson Harris, George Lamming and Edward Brathwaite.

There remains the Epilogue to the work, "Finale at Frenchman's Cove." Naipaul is invited by the proprietor of a luxurious Jamaican North Coast resort to spend time there as his guest. At Frenchman's Cove Naipaul finds himself transported, as if magically, into the West Indies of the travel poster. The resort is a capitalist Eden which caters for its guests' every whim. At last he is delivered from the discomforts of his journey; it is as if the enfeebled explorer has come home. To his credit, however, Naipaul remains uneasy: "I couldn't be a tourist in the West Indies after the journey I had made" (253). Perverse and difficult to please to the last, he finally rejects one possible authorial role, that of affluent tourist.

JOHN THIEME
Polytechnic of North London

NOTES

1. See *The Rhetoric of Fiction* (Chicago: Chicago U.P., 1961), pp.67-77.
2. *The Middle Passage* (Harmondsworth: Penguin, 1969), p.29. Subsequent references are to this edition and are included in the text.
3. *The Loss of El Dorado* (Harmondsworth: Penguin, 1973), p.14.
4. *El Dorado*, p.18.
5. *El Dorado*, p.126.
6. See the Foreword, and *Trinidad Guardian*, 25 December 1960, p.3.
7. Naipaul's comment on "West Indian historians, who can only now begin to face their history, be icily detached and tell the story of the slave trade as if it were just another aspect of mercantilism" is particularly suggestive of Eric Williams' *Capitalism and Slavery* (Chapel Hill: U. of North Carolina Press, 1944).
8. *The Mimic Men* (Harmondsworth: Penguin, 1969), p.214.
9. His family were brahmins who observed Hindu practices to a greater extent than most Trinidadian Indians. His maternal grandfather was a pundit and his father, the writer Seepersad Naipaul, was also intended to become one.
10. *India: A Wounded Civilization* (Harmondsworth: Penguin, 1979), p.25. This theme is explored more fully in my article "V.S. Naipaul and the Hindu Killer," *Journal of Indian Writing in English*, 9 (1981), 70-86.
11. *An Area of Darkness* (Harmondsworth: Penguin, 1968), p.214.
12. *An Area of Darkness*, p.188.
13. For West Indian reactions against Froude see J.J. Thomas, *Froudacity* (London: T. Fisher Unwin, 1889; rpt. London and Port of Spain: New Beacon Books, 1969) and Eric Williams, *British Historians and the West Indies* (Port of Spain: P.N.M. Publishing Co., 1964), pp.137-46.
14. *The English in the West Indies* (London: Longmans Green & Co., 1888), pp.305-6.
15. *The English in the West Indies*, pp.14-15.
16. Cf. Ralph Singh's attitude to Froude in *The Mimic Men*, pp.77-8 and 213-4.
17. *The West Indies and the Spanish Main* 2nd ed. (rpt. London: Frank Cass, 1968), p.21.
18. *The West Indies*, see, for examples, pp.56-7, 188-91, 225.
19. *The West Indies*, p.80.
20. See particularly John Hearne, *Caribbean Quarterly*, 8 (Dec., 1962), 65-6.
21. *An Area of Darkness*, p.196.
22. Naipaul cites the fact that Stedman, author of the eighteenth-century work *Narrative of a Five Years' Expedition against the Revolted Negroes of Surinam*, once killed thirty-two mosquitoes at a single stroke.
23. M.G. Smith, Roy Augier and Rex Nettleford, *The Ras Tafari Movement in Kingston* (Mona, Jamaica: U. of the West Indies, 1960).

Travel Writing Victorian and Modern:
A Review of Recent Research

In a thoughtful article surveying approaches to seventeenth- and eighteenth-century travel literature (*TSLL* 1978), Percy Adams makes the point that this sub-genre has traditionally attracted the attention of historians and geographers rather than students of literature. It is only comparatively recently that travel literature has come to occupy a place in literary studies, fitting uneasily perhaps into a niche somewhere between fiction and autobiography. Paul Fussell, in a book on travel writing in the 1930s, *Abroad. British Literary Traveling Between the Wars* (Oxford: Oxford University Press, 1980), sees the travel book as a rich amalgam of many literary elements, having affinity with the moral or ethical essay, the comic novel, the romance, whether quest, picaresque or pastoral, and the war memoir. He quotes Norman Douglas' remark that "the reader of a good travel-book is entitled not only to an exterior voyage, to descriptions of scenery and so forth, but to an interior, a sentimental or temperamental voyage, which takes place side by side with the outer one." The ideal travel book invites the reader to undertake three tours, "abroad, into the author's brain, and into his own." Martin Day, in "Travel Literature and the Journey Theme" (*Forum* [Houston] 1974), pursues the question of definition and sees travel literature not as a genre, but rather as a metaphor or archetypal pattern, whose appeal and ultimate claim to artistic stature is its ancient and universal theme of the journey of life.

The most fruitful time for travel writing in the twentieth century was, by general consensus, the period between the wars. Samuel Hynes, in his *The Auden Generation: Literature and Politics in England in the 1930's* (London: The Bodley Head, 1976) notes the proliferation of travel books at the time: "What is striking about them is that none is a travel book in quite the same sense that *Eothen* or Stanley's *Journal* is. The difference is in the degree to which the 'thirties writers turned their travels into interior journeys and parables of their times, making landscape and incident – the factual materials of reportage – do the work of symbol and myth – the materials of fable." The 'thirties, as he observes, was an age of feature-journalism. Writing about exotic places was a popular form of escape art. More significantly, during the decade the English became increasingly aware of the importance of the outside world: "As abroad became a threat, it became a reality." The journey, too, was the most insistent of 'thirties metaphors – a journey over the frontier, out of the familiar and secure into the unknown, a frightening experience which had to be taken if one was to reach the new life. The travel books, in Hynes' words, "simply act out in the real world the basic trope of the generation."

The place of modern travel writing in literary studies is clearly no longer in question. Victorian travel writing is more problematical. Fussell, in justifying the omission of Dame Freya Stark from his survey, insists that to write a distinguished travel book one has to be equally interested in the travel and in the writing. Freya Stark, he claims, was not interested in the latter. By these standards the works of Livingstone, Speke, Mary Kingsley, Isabella Bird, to name only a few of the period's most committed traveller-explorers, might be judged wanting. But the problem about Victorian travel writing is not so much the degree of literary self-consciousness as the nature of the travel. Journeys into little-known continents, travels to the remote corners of the globe, and latter-day equivalents of the Grand Tour are obvious material for travel books. But much travelling by the Victorians took place within their own country. W.J. Keith in *The Rural Tradition* (Hassocks: Harvester, 1975) identifies a tradition of "rural writing" which embraces writers from Isaac Walton, Gilbert White and Cobbett through George Borrow, Richard Jefferies and George Sturt to W.H. Hudson. The work of these less adventurous travellers has much in common with that of their more exotic colleagues and can be said to constitute a form of travel writing.

Peter Keating, in *Into Unknown England 1866-1913. Selections from the Social Explorers* (Manchester: Manchester University Press, 1976), sees the work of the "social explorers" as a modern variant of an age-old literary device, the chronicle of a journey, during the course of which the range and variety of human life is explored. The distinctive feature of the nineteenth-century model was that it presented a rigorous exploration and analysis of one class by another. As Keating suggests, "social exploration" was more a frame of mind than a literary form, and its concerns permeate the literature of the period from fiction and non-fictional prose through to Royal Commission reports. Nevertheless, it deserves inclusion here.

Accepting this fluid concept of travel writing, I have attempted to survey research and critical approaches to it since 1970. My subject has been firmly that of travel literature and not the wider one of travel, so that a discussion of work on the history of exploration, the expansion of empire, technological developments in forms of travel and the rise of tourism will not be found here. But given the close relationship of these subjects to travel writing, particularly during the nineteenth century, the distinction has not always been an easy one.

There is, alas, no bibliography of travel writing. Edward G. Cox's three volume *A Reference Guide to the Literature of Travel* (Seattle: University of Washington, 1935-49) contains comparatively little material after 1800. The third and fourth volumes of the *New Cambridge Bibliography of English Literature* (Cambridge: Cambridge University Press, 1969 and

1972) provide working bibliographies of most of the major travellers and travel writers, with useful cross references to those authors whose major genre is not that of travel writing.

Background on the scope of nineteenth-century travel is usefully presented in J.N.L. Baker's *A History of Geographical Discovery and Exploration* (London: Harrap, 1931), H.R. Mill's *The Record of the Royal Geographical Society* (London: Royal Geographical Society, 1930), and Sir Clements Markham, *The Fifty Years' Work of the Royal Geographical Society* (London, 1880). Ian Cameron's recent *To the Farthest Ends of the Earth: The History of the Royal Geographical Society 1830-1980* (London: Macdonald and Jane's, 1980) is essentially a popular work, beautifully illustrated, but it does have a useful bibliography.

Recent specialized bibliographies include R.L. Hees and D.M. Coger, *Semper Ex Africa: A Bibliography of Primary Sources for Nineteenth Century Tropical Africa* (Hoover Bibliographical Series: 47, 1972), R.S. Pine-Coffin, *Bibliography of British and American Travel in Italy to 1860* (Florence: Leo S. Olschki, 1974), and Richard Bevis, *Bibliotheca Cisorientalia. An Annotated Checklist of Early English Travel Books on the Near and Middle East* (Boston: G.K. Hall, 1973). Pine-Coffin includes an appendix of relevant work after 1860, including secondary sources on the travel writing and travels. Bevis' book is a checklist of books in English on the Middle East, written by travellers and published before 1915.

Edmund Swinglehurst's *The Romantic Journey: The Story of Thomas Cook and Victorian Travel* (London: Pica Editions, 1974) and J.A.R. Pimlot's *The Englishman's Holiday* (1947, reprinted Hassocks: Harvester, 1976) provide background to the social changes which produced increased Victorian travel. J. Vaughan's *The English Guide Book c. 1780-1870* (Newton Abbot: David and Charles, 1974) is a useful study of a form of writing which became essential reading for all Victorian travellers, and one which has strong connections with the writing of travel books.

Many of the classic Victorian travel books have long been out of print. The attention given by historians to imperialism and exploration, and no doubt the intensification of interest in the Victorian period generally have prompted reprints and new editions. Francis Galton's *The Art of Travel: or Shifts and Contrivances Available in Wild Countries* has been edited by Dorothy Middleton (Newton Abbot: David and Charles, 1971). Mary Kingsley's *Travels in West Africa* has been abridged and introduced by R. Glynn Grylls (London: C. Knight, 1972). Her *West African Studies* was reprinted by Frank Cass in 1964. Both Galton and Mary Kingsley have been the subject of books: Derek W. Forrest's *Francis Galton: the Life and Work of a Victorian Genius* (London: Elek, 1974), and Jean G. Hughes, *Invincible Miss: The Adventures of Mary Kingsley* (London: Macmillan, 1968). Dickens' *American Notes* has been edited by J.S. Whitley and A. Goldman in the Penguin English Library

(Harmondsworth: Penguin, 1972). One important North American travel book, Barbara Bodichon's *An American Diary 1857-8*, was first published in 1972, edited by Joseph W. Reed (London: Routledge). Two of John Murray's famous *Handbooks*, indispensable to any intelligent nineteenth-century traveller, have been reprinted. *Murray's Handbook for Travellers in Switzerland*, edited by Jack Simmons, appeared in 1971 as part of the Victorian Library reprint series published by Leicester University Press, and *Murray's Handbook for Scotland* was reprinted by David and Charles, also in 1971. Robert Louis Stevenson's *The Cevennes Journal: Notes on a Journey through the French Highlands*, the manuscript notebook which Stevenson kept during his travels and from which he wrote *Travels with a Donkey*, has been edited by Gordon Golding (Edinburgh: Mainstream, 1978). David Duff has edited *Victoria Travels: Journeys of Queen Victoria between 1830 and 1900 with Extracts from her Journals* (London: Muller, 1970) and her *Highland Journals* (London: Webb, 1980).

In a period in which it is estimated that travel books came close second in popularity to the novel, many of the legendary best sellers were travel books on North America. Captain Basil Hall's *Travels in North America* (1829) and Mrs Frances Trollope's *Domestic Manners of the Americans* (1832) paved the way for *American Notes* and the glut of English travellers and travel books which followed. *Abroad in America: Visitors to the New Nation 1776-1914* (Washington: the Smithsonian Institution, 1976) is a collection of essays on some of the more notable travellers. The volume is edited by Marc Pachter. Walter Allen's *Transatlantic Crossing: American Visitors to Britain and British Visitors to America in the Nineteenth Century* (London: Heinemann, 1971) is a series of extracts from the travel books and letters of well-known travellers from both sides of the Atlantic. Peter Conrad, in *Imagining America* (London: Routledge and Kegan Paul, 1980), makes use of the travel books for a wide-ranging exploration of attitudes to America. In "discovering" America, he argues, the travellers were given the opportunity of discovering themselves. America provided the opportunity for each person to reimagine himself, to "invent a self better adapted to the individual [he had] become since outgrowing the imposition of birth." The Victorians felt threatened by America for this reason, according to Conrad, but more recent travellers have considered the freedom which America granted for this process to be the country's greatest virtue. Mrs Trollope, Dickens and Anthony Trollope are his chief Victorians, with Wilde, Rupert Brooke, Kipling and Stevenson their successors, followed by Wells, Lawrence, Auden, Huxley and Isherwood later in the twentieth century.

Mrs Trollope's *Domestic Manners* was probably the most notorious of the Victorian travel books on America. Certainly it established her literary reputation. Most books about her, including Johanna Johnston's *The Life, Manners and Travels of Fanny Trollope* (London: Constable, 1979), give it prominence for these reasons, but there are few attempts to analyse it further. Mrs Trollope is one of the three subjects of Frederick

John Bethke's *Three Victorian Travel Writers: an Annotated Bibliography of Criticism on Mrs. Frances Milton Trollope, Samuel Butler and Robert Louis Stevenson* (Boston: G.K. Hall, 1977). Bethke confines himself strictly to the travel writing of the three, noting contemporary responses to them as well as modern scholarly or critical work. The bibliography is an extension of an interest in Victorian travel writing developed in Bethke's doctoral dissertation on "Elements of Autobiography in Six Continental Travelogues by Victorian Novelists" (Columbia, 1972).

Isabella L. Bird, like Mrs Trollope, began her travels on the American circuit (*The Englishwoman in America*, 1856, *Aspects of Religion in the United States*, 1859, *A Lady's Life in the Rocky Mountains*, 1879) and later turned her attention to Hawaii, Persia, China, India, Korea and Morocco. Patricia Barr's *A Curious Life for a Lady: The Story of Isabella Bird* (London: Macmillan: Murray, 1970) is the only book-length treatment of this flamboyant lady traveller-cum-explorer, but her achievements were marked by a recent exhibition at the National Library of Scotland which took its title from the Barr biography.

Victorian travellers to the near and middle east have never suffered from lack of attention, due perhaps to the frequently exotic nature of both the travel and the travellers. In "Spiritual Geology: C.M. Doughty and the Land of the Arabs" (*VS* 1972), Richard Bevis sees a combination of religious piety and a passion for natural science as the main causes of Doughty's attraction to the near east, a combination which strongly informs *Arabia Deserta*. It is precisely because *Arabia Deserta* transcends Doughty's patriotic and religious prejudices that its greatness is assured, according to Stephen Ely Tabachnick in his book *Charles Doughty* (Boston: Twayne, 1981). Tabachnick devotes three chapters to a discussion of Doughty's best-known work, which he describes as "an oratorical autobiography of travel." Annette McCormick, in her Ph.D. thesis (Bedford College, London, 1952), examined the style of *Arabia Deserta* and pursued this further in "An Elizabethan-Victorian Travel Book: Doughty's Travels in Arabia Deserta" in *Essays in Honour of Esmond Linworth Marilla* edited by T. Kirby and W. Olive (Baton Rouge: Louisiana State University Press, 1970), and in "Hebrew Parallelism in Doughty's Travels in Arabia Deserta" in *Studies in Comparative Literature* edited by Waldo McNeir (Baton Rouge: Louisiana State University Press, 1962). Jonathan Bishop also discusses Doughty in "The Heroic Ideal in Doughty's *Arabia Deserta*" (*MLQ* 1960).

It is the actor in Sir Richard Burton which Jonathan Bishop sees as the most obvious element in his style, in "The Identities of Sir Richard Burton: the Explorer as Actor" (*VS* 1957). Burton's imperialist impulses attract the attention of J.F. Gournay in "Travel Narratives and British Imperialism in the Near East" in *Politics in Literature in the Nineteenth Century* (Lille: Centre d'Etudes Victoriennes, University of Lille, 1974). William Rogers' Ph.D. dissertation, "Arabian Involvement: a Study of Five Victorian Travel Narratives" (Berkeley, 1971) is relevant to

Victorian travel in the east, as is his "Romance, Science, and W.G. Palgrave's Central and Eastern Arabia" (*Exploration*, 1978).

The popularity of journals of travels to Iceland in the late nineteenth century is possibly one of the reasons William Morris chose not to publish his *Icelandic Journals*, written in 1871 and 1873, according to Frederick Kirchhoff in "Travel as Anti-Autobiography: William Morris's Icelandic Journals," in *Approaches to Victorian Autobiography* edited by George P. Landow (Athens, Ohio: Ohio University Press, 1979). The travels were undertaken as a result of serious crises in Morris' life, and his self-confrontation takes the form of an objective response to the Icelandic landscape. The journals are a quest for self-knowledge whose closest analogues are Romantic poems such as *The Prelude* and *The Fall of Hyperion*.

The difficulties of separating the study of Victorian travel books from the study of Victorian travel are particularly apparent in relation to Africa, where the centenaries of many significant events and the emergence generally of an interest in African history have combined to produce a daunting number of new books on exploration and the explorers. Few of them, it is fair to say, are directly concerned with travel writing as such, but many of them make use of the travel books. Two useful review articles in *Victorian Studies* discuss recent work up to 1970: Robert O. Collins, "Old Wine, Emu, and I.P.A." (*VS* 1969), and Alan R. Taylor, "Armchair Travels and Researches in Darkest Africa" (*VS* 1970). The annual "Victorian Bibliography" in each summer issue of *Victorian Studies* is the best source for later work on travel and exploration, and the book review section gives full coverage to the subject. A review article in *VS* (1974) by Roy Sieber, for example, gives an extensive assessment of several books on Livingstone published to mark the centenary of his death in 1873. A more recent bibliographical venture, the *Annual Bibliography of Victorian Studies*, edited by Brahma Chaudhuri (Edmonton, Alberta: Litir Database), of which only the volumes for 1977 and 1978 have as yet been published, contains a separate section on geography and travel.

The association of Italy with Victorian travellers is a fruitful area for study; one, disappointingly, which has had few takers. R.S. Pine-Coffin's bibliography (see p.153) should provide the bare bones of any survey up to 1860. The title of Olive Hamilton's *Paradise of Exiles. Tuscany and the British* (London: André Deutsch, 1974) does not fulfil its promise. Figures like Thomas Adolphus Trollope, Ruskin, Queen Victoria, Landor, Ouida, the Brownings, the Sitwells, and D.H. Lawrence are given substantial sections, and some travel books are alluded to, but the end product is a sentimental, naive and superficial survey, with a topographical slant.

Documentation of the sale and circulation of travel books is relatively easy to come by in nineteenth-century literary histories. Not so easy to pinpoint is the influence those thousands of volumes had on the popular consciousness or on the literary imagination. Chauncey C. Loomis, in

"The Arctic Sublime" in *Nature and the Victorian Imagination* edited by U.C. Knoepflmacher and G.B. Tennyson (Berkeley: University of California Press, 1977), describes the influence of Arctic exploration and the resulting travel books on both the popular and literary imagination. The Arctic, according to Loomis, aroused the same intense emotional response as mountains. It was a source of sublimity as well as a challenge to man's strength and courage. He traces the influence of travel books about the Arctic on writers such as the Brontës and Conrad, and sees it in works such as *The Frozen Deep* by Dickens and Wilkie Collins. David Robertson, in "Mid-Victorians amongst the Alps," also in Knoepflmacher and Tennyson, outlines the enthusiasm of the Victorians for mountaineering, particularly in the Alps, and describes the activities of the Alpine Club and the attendant literature by writers such as John Tyndall, Leslie Stephen, James D. Forbes and contributors to the *Alpine Journal*.

One of the most widely-read journals of exploration was, of course, Darwin's *The Voyage of the Beagle*. In his excellent article "From Chronicle to Quest: the Shaping of Darwin's 'Voyage of the Beagle' " (*VS* 1980), John Tallmadge examines the changing Victorian taste in travel literature from sources of factual information to accounts of travellers' personal responses to their experiences, and then outlines Darwin's conscious efforts to shape his *Journal of Researches* (the work's title until 1905) to accord with a well-established tradition and a clear set of literary conventions. The result, according to Tallmadge, is a natural history classic, which both exemplifies and transcends the conventions of early Victorian travel writing.

A new edition of Henry James's *English Hours* with an introduction by Leon Edel (Oxford: Oxford University Press, 1981) underlines a point made by Frederick Kirchhoff, in "City as Self: Henry James's Travel Sketches of Venice" (*Prose Studies* 1979), that the accepted subordination of James's travel writing to his fiction ignores their unique nature and importance. *Italian Hours*, Kirchhoff argues, combines the two traditions of travel writing, the travelogue and autobiography. They are about James and they are about Venice, or, more fancifully, they are the "locus" at which Venice and James merge into a single identity. Carl S. Smith takes the opposite position and prefers to see the travel writings as valuable for their illumination of James's intellectual development, the culmination of which is the fiction. In "James's Travels, Travel Writings and the Development of his Art" (*MLQ* 1977), he sees the larger part of James's concern in the travel books as epistemological, occupied with the nature of his apprehension of reality rather than with the precise facts of his travels. In an earlier article, "Henry James and the Travel Sketch: the Artistry of Italian Hours" (*Centennial Review* 1975), Thomas Pauly examines James's development of the travel "sketch" and the series of sketches written over a long period of time which resulted in *Italian Hours*.

One colourful late-Victorian figure to emerge recently from a critical neglect of nearly forty years' duration is the traveller, adventurer, and, later, radical politician Robert Bontine Cunninghame Graham, whose best-known travel book, *Mogreb-el-Aksa* (1898), records his adventures while trying to reach the forbidden city of Tarudant. The new interest in Graham centres mainly on his friendship with Conrad and Shaw and his involvement in the early years of the Labour Party and later the Scottish Nationalist Party, but there are sections on his travel books in Cedric Watts and Lawrence Davies' *Cunninghame Graham: a Critical Biography* (Cambridge: Cambridge University Press, 1979), Jeffrey Meyers, "The Genius of Failure: R. B. Cunninghame Graham" (*London Magazine* 1975) and John Walker, "R. B. Cunninghame Graham: An Annotated Bibliography of Writings about Him" (*ELT* 1979). Walker has also edited Graham's *South American Sketches* (Norman: University of Oklahoma Press, 1978), and Alexander Maitland has produced a selection of Graham's essays and tales under the title *Tales of Horsemen* (Edinburgh: Canongate Press, 1981). Watts and Davies' biography includes the substance of an article by Watts in *YES* 1977, "Conrad and Cunninghame Graham: A Discussion with Addenda to their Correspondence."

Edward Lear the traveller is usually overshadowed by Lear the poet and painter. A revised edition of Vivian Noakes's *Edward Lear: the Life of a Wanderer* (London: Fontana, 1979) pays some attention to his travel writings.

W. J. Keith's *The Rural Tradition* (see p. 152) deals with a number of writers who have maintained a modest but steady critical following over the years, figures such as Richard Jefferies, George Sturt, W. H. Hudson, Edward Thomas and Henry Williamson. Keith attempts to isolate the features and traditions of "rural writing" – he contrasts it, for example, with the pastoral tradition – but the subject is dealt with more challengingly and more comprehensively by Raymond Williams in *The Country and the City* (London: Chatto and Windus, 1973). The strength of Keith's book lies in individual chapters on Borrow, Jefferies, George Sturt, Hudson, Thomas, Williamson and H. J. Massingham, as well as the earlier practitioners of this "tradition," Walton, Gilbert White, Cobbett and Mary Russell Mitford.

Two books on the novel are relevant to this theme: Glen Cavaliero's *The Rural Tradition in the English Novel 1900-1939* (London: Macmillan, 1977) and John Alcorn's *The Nature Novel from Hardy to Lawrence* (London: Macmillan, 1977). Alcorn's chapter on "The Spirit of Place in the Travel Book" contains a discussion of Norman Douglas, D. H. Lawrence, W. H. Hudson, Samuel Butler and H. M. Tomlinson.

Jefferies' fiction has had a revival of late, which perhaps explains the reprinting of Edward Thomas' 1909 biography, *Richard Jefferies* (London: Faber, 1978). J. R. Ebbatson links Jefferies and William Morris in "Visions of Wild England" (*William Morris Society Journal* 1976).

W. H. Hudson is well served by John R. Payne's *W. H. Hudson: a Bibliography* (London; Dawson, 1977), and by John T. Frederick's volume in the Twayne English Authors series, *William Henry Hudson* (Boston: Twayne, 1972).

George Sturt's *A Small Boy in the Sixties* was reprinted by Harvester in 1977, and *The Bettesworth Book* and *William Smith, Potter and Farmer 1790-1858* by Caliban Books in 1978.

Henry Williamson's death in 1977 was the occasion of a collection of essays, *Henry Williamson. The Man. The Writings. A Symposium*, with an introduction by Brocard Sewell (Padstow: Tabb House, 1980), which includes "A Frequency of Phoenixes: Some Notes on the Nature Writings" by Sylvia Bruce, and "The Power of the Dead" by E.W. Martin, the latter including a discussion of the "nature" books and the "country" writings.

Peter Keating in his introduction to *Into Unknown England 1866-1913* sees "social exploration" as a way of looking at and describing society, which undergoes frequent changes of style and manner yet is continuous both in its attitudes and the nature of its concerns. His selected "explorers" are James Greenwood, George R. Sims, Andrew Mearns, Charles Booth, William Booth, Robert Sherard, B.S. Rowntree, Rider Haggard (for his *Rural England*, 1902), Jack London, C.F.G. Masterman, Stephen Reynolds, Mary Higgs, Lady Bell and Mrs Pember Reeves. To Keating they occupy a mid-way position in a tradition begun by Cobbett, Engels and Mayhew and continued by the author of *The Road to Wigan Pier*.

Carol L. Bernstein includes several of Keating's "explorers" in her discussion of "Nineteenth-Century Urban Sketches: Thresholds of Fiction" (*Prose Studies* 1980). Sala, Mearns, Greenwood, James Grant and Dickens are the major figures in her examination of prose writings about "the city" and London in particular.

The writings of the social observers who flocked to the northern industrial cities, especially Manchester, in the 1830s and 1840s have long attracted the attention of historians. But Stephen Marcus, in *Engels, Manchester and the Working Class* (London: Weidenfeld and Nicolson, 1974), examines these social documents as a literary critic in order "to ascertain how far literary criticism can help us understand history and society, to see how far the intellectual discipline that begins with the work of close textual analysis can help us understand certain social, historical or theoretical documents." Marcus' subject is Engels' *The Condition of the Working Class in England in 1844*, but in order to put it into context he discusses the observations made by visitors and travellers to Manchester, both English and foreign, and also the response by creative writers such as Dickens, Disraeli and Carlyle. Marcus' book is one of the few which crosses the boundary between literary criticism and history – an ambitious undertaking which deserves to be emulated.

Mayhew has long deserved similar treatment. The four volumes of *London Labour and the London Poor* were reprinted by Frank Cass in 1967. John D. Rosenberg edited a four-volume paperback of the same in 1968 (New York: Dover). Anne Humpherys has edited *Voices of the Poor. Selections from the Morning Chronicle 'Labour and the Poor' 1849-50* (London: Frank Cass, 1971). In *The Unknown Mayhew* (London: Merlin Press, 1971), E.P. Thompson and Eileen Yeo have a useful introduction to their selection of letters from the *Morning Chronicle*, mainly those not already published in *London Labour and the London Poor*. More recently, Caliban Books has issued *The Morning Chronicle Survey of Labour and the Poor: The Metropolitan Districts* (3 vols. 1980-1), with an introduction by Peter Razzell. The volumes sadly lack explanatory notes and are in need of more complete editing. The publishers claim that only a third of the *Morning Chronicle* material was used in *London Labour*, the chief factor in the initiation of this project.

Anne Humpherys' *Travels into the Poor Man's Country. The Work of Henry Mayhew* (Athens: University of Georgia Press, 1977) is the first full-length study which attempts to treat Mayhew from the perspectives of both social history and literary criticism. Professor Humpherys provides a section on the biographical and historical background to his work, an examination of his investigative techniques, and an analysis of his style in the major works. She also has a chapter on "Mayhew and the Literature of his Time" which places him in the context of Dickens, Kingsley, Jerrold and Thackeray, and gives a useful bibliography of works by Henry, by Henry and Augustus Mayhew and works about Henry Mayhew. Gertrude Himmelfarb's "Mayhew's Poor: a Problem of Identity" (*VS* 1971) discusses the publishing history and contemporary reception of *London Labour and the London Poor*, and also puts it into context with other works of its time.

J. Ginswick is editing an important seven volume project, *Labour and the Poor in England and Wales, 1849-1852* (London, Frank Cass, 1982—) which will bring together for the first time in book form the letters to *The Morning Chronicle* from the agricultural and manufacturing districts and the towns of Liverpool and Birmingham. The editor, who contributes introductions to volumes one, four and six, has collated, re-arranged and divided the material into sections so that the reports emerge as unified and continuous accounts. The first three volumes, which cover the industrial and manufacturing districts of England and Wales, are published this year.

Engels was undoubtedly the most famous foreign visitor of the mid-century, but the recent publication of *The London Journal of Flora Tristan*, translated, annotated and introduced by Jean Hawkes (London: Virago, 1982), the journal of one of his predecessors, is a reminder of the number of foreign travel books yet to be properly recognized. This is the first English translation of Flora Tristan's enthusiastic and impressionistic account of English, mainly London, life in 1840.

Although the stuff of many Victorian travel books provides the substance of Rider Haggard's fiction, it is for his very different *Rural England* that he is included here. Most material on Haggard links the fiction with imperial themes, as in Norman A. Hetherington's "Rider Haggard,

Imperialism and the Layered Personality" (*VS* 1978). Peter Berresford Ellis's new biography, *H. Rider Haggard. A Voice from the Infinite* (London: Routledge, 1978), does include a discussion of *Rural England* and also has a good bibliography. The fiction of writers such as Haggard, Conrad, and Kipling, and later Greene, Waugh, and Naipaul impinges on the themes of much of the travel literature under discussion here. Three books on that fiction, Martin Green's *Dreams of Adventure, Deeds of Empire* (London: Routledge, 1980), Jeffrey Meyers' *Fiction and the Colonial Experience* (Ipswich: Boydell Press, 1973) together with M.M. Mahood's *The Colonial Encounter: A Reading of Six Novels* (London: Rex Collings, 1977), are relevant to the study of many Victorian and later travel books. Professor Mahood includes a particularly helpful bibliography.

The single most significant contribution to the study of twentieth-century travel writing has been Paul Fussell's *Abroad. British Literary Traveling Between the Wars* (see p. 151). The preface declares the book to be about travel writing but also about travel. The first is its strength, and the second its decided weakness. Fussell is at his best in chapters which discuss a single writer or group of writers. The one on Robert Byron is outstanding, but those on Waugh, Greene, Lawrence and Norman Douglas are also important. He has an impressive grasp of his material, weaving into his introductory sections a discussion of figures such as Peter Fleming, Rebecca West, Peter Quennell, Alec Waugh, Osbert Sitwell, Lawrence Durrell, Isherwood, Auden, J.R. Ackerley, and Robert Graves. Fussell is less assured when he discusses the intellectual climate which produced the travellers, the permeation of what he calls the "travel spirit," the gradual change from "travel" to "tourism," and the significance of frontiers and passports. Here he is inclined to lurch from the obvious to the banal and to rely, curiously, on autobiographical material.

More reliable on the climate of the twenties and thirties is Samuel Hynes's *The Auden Generation: Literature and Politics in England in the 1930's* (see p. 151), a chronological account of authors and literary landmarks, which briefly discusses each of the major travel books of the period. Hynes is particularly good on the centrality of travel, both literal and metaphorical, to the intellectual fabric of the thirties, and to the revolution which occurred in the form of the traditional travel book.

Fussell's chapter on Lawrence presents a useful discussion of the four major travel books. Lawrence's travel books have not in fact suffered the critical eclipse which has beset those of some of his contemporaries. *Etruscan Places* has attracted more attention than the others. Del Ivan Janik, in "D.H. Lawrence's *Etruscan Places*: The Mystery of Touch," *Essays in Literature* (Western Illinois University, 1976), argues that in the Etruscan civilisation Lawrence found a model for a world view that dominated his writings in the last four years of his life. Donald Gutierrez, in a much less impressive essay, "D.H. Lawrence's Golden Age" (*D.H. Lawrence Review* 1976), similarly suggests that the dying Lawrence saw in the Etruscans a culture which confirmed his own beliefs and viewed death as a continuation of life. Billy T. Tracy's attempt, in "D.H. Lawrence and the Travel Book Tradition" (*D.H. Lawrence Review* 1978), to bring the travel books out from under the shadow of the fiction and to place them in the tradition of travel writing is less than convincing, alas, in that she seems to have little depth of understanding of that very tradition. David Ellis' "Reading Lawrence: The Case of *Sea and Sardinia*," in *D.H. Lawrence Review* 1977, completes that periodical's assiduous attention to the travel books in the past five years. Clive James has written of Lawrence's sense of place in the travel books and the letters in "D.H. Lawrence in Transit," in *D.H. Lawrence: Novelist, Poet, Prophet* edited by Stephen Spender (London: Weidenfeld and Nicolson, 1973). The title of James C. Cowan's *D.H. Lawrence's American Journey: A Study in Literature and Myth* (London: The Press of Case Western Reserve University, 1970) promises more than it delivers. Cowan makes use of the travel books, but his subject is the fiction written while in America and the symbols and myths Lawrence derived from that experience.

That the first British publication of Forster's *Alexandria: a History and Guide* (London: Michael Haag, 1982) only appeared recently, emphasizes the comparative neglect of Forster's travel books. John Beer and G.K. Das did something to rectify the situation in their centenary volume *E.M. Forster: a Human Exploration* (London: Macmillan, 1979). Mohammed Shaheen's "Forster's Alexandria: the Transitional Journey," John Drew's "A Passage via Alexandria," J. Birje-Patil's "Forster and Dewas," and Evelyn Hanquart's "E.M. Forster's Travelogue from the Hill of Devi to the Bayreuth Festival" collectively underline the significance of travel as an allegorical theme in Forster's fiction and individually emphasize the links of the travel books with the novels. G.K. Das's *E.M. Forster's India* (London: Macmillan, 1977) is also helpful. Two other articles on *The Hill of Devi* should be noted: Sinil Chand's "'Completeness, not re-construction': Forster's Use of Letters in *The Hill of Devi* for 'Part III' of *A Passage to India*" (*The International Fiction Review* 1977) and A.L. Weir's "Two Views of Eroticism: The Indias of E.M. Forster and Pierre Loti" (*Exploration* 1979).

Huxley's *Jesting Pilate* is a travel book with a difference, a book written to encourage the reader not to undertake the journey, an account of a Grand Tour turned on its head, according to Jerome Meckier in "Philip Quarles's Passage to India: *Jesting Pilate, Point Counter Point* and Bloomsbury" (*Studies in the Novel* 1977). Meckier links the travel book with chapter six of the novel and sees Huxley's travels as the necessary education for a satirical novelist. Without *Jesting Pilate*, he argues, Huxley's sceptical persona might not have matured so rapidly, and the negative philosophy of the first three novels might have been quite different.

It was a joke of the 'thirties, according to M.M. Mahood, to inquire if one was going to a psychoanalyst or going to Africa. Mungo Park, Livingstone, Stanley, Rimbaud and Conrad represented only "a more costly, less cosy" alternative to Freud. Similarly, Thomas R. Knipp, in "Gide and Greene: Africa and the Literary Imagination" (*Serif* 1969), confirms that Africa was "a state of mind," that between the wars imaginative westerners "imposed upon Africa a collection of values and characteristics dredged up from their own subconsciousnesses by their own psychological needs." Knipps compares Gide's *Travels in the Congo*, an account of African travels recorded in the journal form, with Greene's *Journey without Maps*, a work in which "travels are informed and infused with meaning by an imagination moved and engaged by a sought experience." Fussell has a useful chapter on *Journey without Maps*, a book in which Professor Mahood declares "so much of the worst of Greene is a pointer to his potential best." S.E. Ogude's "In Search of Misery: A study of Graham Greene's Travels in Africa" (*Odu* 1975) is solely concerned with the image of Africa which emerges from Greene's four works of non-fiction which deal with it, and not with the travel books as such. Joel Harris Rosencrantz links the novels with the travel books in his Ph.D. dissertation, "Graham Greene's Travel Writings. Sources of his Fiction" (New York University, 1978). *The Lawless Roads* and *Journey without Maps* form volumes 18 and 19 of *The Collected Edition of Graham Greene* (London: William Heinemann and the Bodley Head, 1978). Both volumes contain new introductions by the author.

Waugh's travel books have been better served by energetic enthusiasts than perceptive critics. Both Richard J. Voorhees in "Evelyn Waugh's Travel Books" (*Dalhousie Review* 1978) and J.R. MacSween in "The Labels of Evelyn Waugh" (*Antigonish Review* 1978) are concerned to re-establish the travel books, but apart from finding them entertaining, informative about Waugh himself and linked significantly with the fiction, they are not inclined to make a strong critical case for them. Margaret Morriss' "Critical Responses to *Labels* and *Remote People*" (*Evelyn Waugh Newsletter* 1979) is a study of their contemporary reception. Fussell's chapter on Waugh should be consulted, and Knipps, in his article on Gide and Greene, includes a discussion of Waugh's travel books.

Fussell's chapter on Robert Byron goes a long way to rescue his neglected works, particularly *The Road to Oxiana*, which according to Fussell is to the modern travel book what *Ulysses* is to the novel and *The Waste Land* to modern poetry. A tangible result of renewed interest in Byron is the new edition of *The Road to Oxiana* with an introduction by Bruce Chadwin (London: Picador, 1981).

In "Letters from Iceland: Going North" in *The 1930's: a Challenge to Orthodoxy* edited by John Lucas (Hassocks: Harvester, 1978), Tom Paulin stresses the political implications of Auden and MacNeice's work. They are not writing a travel book, but rather writing about European culture by focussing on a democratic community which works under the physical shadow of its landscape and the spiritual shadow of its heroic past.

The continuity of the tradition of social exploration is emphasized yet again by Gordon B. Beadle in "George Orwell's Literary Studies of Poverty in England" (*Twentieth Century Literature* 1978). He sees *Down and Out in Paris and London* as modelled on Jack London's *The People of the Abyss* (1902), and the first part of *The Road to Wigan Pier* as written in the tradition of Cobbett's *Rural Rides*. The tradition of social exploration is undeniable, but most critics have difficulty in classifying Orwell's work. Fussell sees the paternity of *Homage to Catalonia* in the travel book, but Donald Compton in "False Maps of the World – George Orwell's Autobiographical Writings and the Early Novels" (*Critical Quarterly* 1974) sees *Down and Out, Homage to Catalonia*, and *Such Such were the Joys* as straight autobiography, while according to him *The Road to Wigan Pier* has "the intimate and fragmentary quality of a personal notebook." Hynes has a pertinent discussion of *The Road to Wigan Pier* and its relevance to the travel theme.

V. S. Naipaul's continuing commitment to travel writing has been recently reaffirmed with the publication of his *Among the Believers: an Islamic Journey* (London: André Deutsch, 1981), a record of travels in Iran, Pakistan, Malaysia and Indonesia during the latter part of 1979. Critics have been reluctant to deal with Naipaul's travel books separately, although Paul Theroux's *V. S. Naipaul: an Introduction to his Work* (London: André Deutsch, 1972) is helpful in this respect. The work most discussed is *An Area of Darkness*. Ezekiel Nissim's "Naipaul's India and Mine," in *New Writing in India* edited by Adil Jussawalla (Harmondsworth: Penguin, 1974); Vijay Mishra's "Mythic Fabulation: Naipaul's India" (*New Literature Review* [Canberra] 1978); Margaret Nightingale's "V. S. Naipaul's Journalism: To Impose a Vision" (*New Literature Review* 1979); and Alastair Niven's "Crossing the Black Waters: Nirad C. Chaudhuri's *A Passage to England* and V. S. Naipaul's *An Area of Darkness*" (*Ariel* 1978) all address the travel books as a distinct genre.

From even this cursory survey it is clear that for literary studies the travel book, like autobiography, is here to stay. The reissue, after over forty years, of Edwin Muir's *Scottish Journey*, with an introduction by T. C. Smout (Edinburgh: Mainstream, 1979) is yet another mark of the prevailing climate. And lest we believe Paul Fussell's lament that the birth of tourism heralds the death of travel, the publication of Naomi Mitchison's *Mucking Around: Five Continents over Fifty Years* (London: Gollancz, 1981) along with that of Naipaul's latest volume, as well as of Paul Theroux's widely acclaimed *The Great Railway Bazaar: by train through Asia* (London: Hamish Hamilton, 1975) and *The Old Patagonian Express: by train through the Americas* (London: Hamish Hamilton, 1979), is a small but insistent reminder that the genre is by no means dead.

JOANNE SHATTOCK
University of Leicester

For Product Safety Concerns and Information please contact our EU
representative GPSR@taylorandfrancis.com
Taylor & Francis Verlag GmbH, Kaufingerstraße 24, 80331 München, Germany

* 9 7 8 1 1 3 8 9 6 3 8 6 3 *